LGBTQI Parented Families and Schools

Exploring the experiences of LGBTQI+ parents and their children and their relationship with schools, this book illuminates how these families work with schools, and how schools do, or do not, support children of LGBTQI+ parents. Based on empirical research and making space for the voices of both parents and children, the research extends beyond previous studies of gay and lesbian parenting to include bisexual, transgender, queer, non-binary, and intersex parents. The authors consider the influence of pressure groups, school inspection frameworks, legislation, and the media, and examine the ways in which some schools are working to become more inclusive.

Anna Carlile is Senior Lecturer in Inclusive Education at Goldsmiths, University of London, UK.

Carrie Paechter is Professor of Education and Director of the Nottingham Centre for Children, Young People and Families, Nottingham Trent University, UK.

Routledge Critical Studies in Gender and Sexuality in Education
Series Editors Wayne Martino, Emma Renold, Goli Rezai-Rashti, Jessica Ringrose and Nelson Rodriguez

Schooling Sexual Cultures
Visual Research in Sexuality Education
Louisa Allen

The Politics and Pedagogies of Liking
Adam Greteman and Kevin J. Burke

Queering Families, Schooling Publics
Keywords
Anne M. Harris, Stacy Holman Jones, Sandra L. Faulkner, and Eloise D. Brook

Boys, Masculinities and Reading
Gender Identity and Literacy as Social Practice
Laura Scholes

Young bisexual women's experiences in secondary schools
Mary-Anne McAllum

Hidden Sexualities of South African Teachers
Black Male Educators and Same-sex Desire
Thabo Msibi

Black Men Teaching in Urban Schools
Reassessing Masculinity
Ed Brockenbrough

LGBTQI Parented Families and Schools
Visibility, Representation, and Pride
Anna Carlile and Carrie Paechter

For a full list of titles in this series, please visit www.routledge.com

LGBTQI Parented Families and Schools
Visibility, Representation, and Pride

Anna Carlile and Carrie Paechter

NEW YORK AND LONDON

First published 2018
by Routledge
711 Third Avenue, New York, NY 10017

and by Routledge
2 Park Square, Milton Park, Abingdon, Oxon, OX14 4RN

Routledge is an imprint of the Taylor & Francis Group, an informa business

© 2018 Taylor & Francis

The right of Anna Carlile and Carrie Paechter to be identified as author of this work has been asserted by them in accordance with sections 77 and 78 of the Copyright, Designs and Patents Act 1988.

All rights reserved. No part of this book may be reprinted or reproduced or utilised in any form or by any electronic, mechanical, or other means, now known or hereafter invented, including photocopying and recording, or in any information storage or retrieval system, without permission in writing from the publishers.

Trademark notice: Product or corporate names may be trademarks or registered trademarks, and are used only for identification and explanation without intent to infringe.

Library of Congress Cataloguing-in-Publication Data
A catalog record for this book has been requested

ISBN: 978-1-138-94072-7 (hbk)
ISBN: 978-1-315-67414-8 (ebk)

Typeset in Sabon
by Apex CoVantage, LLC

Printed and bound in Great Britain by
TJ International Ltd, Padstow, Cornwall

This book is dedicated to the parents, teachers, children and young people who generously gave us their time, ideas and experiences.

Contents

1 Introduction 1

2 Ideologies of Parenting and Schooling: Visibility, Invisibility and Alternative Family Forms 12

3 Media Representations of LGBTQI+ Parented Families 35

4 LGBTQI+ Parented Families and Their Visibility/Invisibility in School Policies 55

5 LGBTQI+ Parents' Perspectives on Their Children's Schools 73

6 Experiences of Children of LGBTQI+ Parents at School 109

7 'Usualizing' LGBTQI+ People and Issues in Schools: The Educate & Celebrate Approach to Creating School Change 136

8 Conclusion: Ways Forward for LGBTQI+ Parented Families and Schools 163

Index 168

1 Introduction

It is January 2003. My eight year old daughter is showing me a book by Jacqueline Wilson, The Illustrated Mum (Wilson, 1999). On the front cover is a cartoon picture of a 30 something woman with curly hair and tattoos, like me. 'Look mummy', she says, 'it's just like you!' 'Is she a lesbian mum?' I ask, my heart pounding with grateful hope. I so desperately want visibility for my children's sake. 'No silly, she's got tattoos', said my daughter. Later on I flick through the book, rapidly picking up the narrative. It seems that the illustrated mother is not a very attentive or well-organized parent. But I am still grateful. Flawed as she is, and not even queer, I am still happy that my daughter can experience some semblance of her own family life as validated in a book by Jacqueline Wilson.
  Anna

Why We Wrote This Book

This is a book about the experiences of LGBTQI+ parents and their children, and their relationship with schools. In it we look at how these 'alternative' families work with schools, and at how schools do, or do not, support their children. There has previously been a range of research on and parenting books for lesbian mothers (Pollack & Vaughn, 1987; Arnup, 1995; Wright, 1998; Johnson & O'Connor, 2001; Ryan-Flood, 2009; Taylor, 2009), and research on gay male fathers, particularly those who had adopted their children (Bigner, 1999; Stacey, 2006). Often this work focused on families in big cities, and was limited to the opinions and experiences of the parents (Wienke & Hill, 2013; Shelton, 2013; Hequembourg & Farrell, 1999), rather than including children's voices directly (though see Stonewall (2010)). Much of this work remains useful despite the rapidly changing legislative and social climate. Nevertheless, much research on lesbians and gay men ignores a wider range of parents who are LGBTQI+. We wanted to discover what parenting is like for a broader group of LGBTQI+ people, and, as educators, we were especially interested in these families' relationships with the children's schools, both formally with school staff and processes, and in social contact with other parents. Schooling is a central part of life for most parents and children: we wanted

2   Introduction

to explore how LGBTQI+ parented families were visible, recognized and included in overlapping playground and classroom worlds.

Civic life in the UK has recently become more inclusive with the advent of the Gender Recognition Act, 2004, the Equality Act 2010 and the Marriage (Same-Sex Couples) Act 2013. However, these developments have mainly conformed to a binary model of gender that is at odds with the experience of many LGBTQI+ people. Trans people in particular have, in recent years, experienced an upsurge in both recognition and abuse in the media and in institutional life. We wanted to contribute to the more diverse recent discussion (Russell, McGuire, Lee, Larriva, & Laub, 2008; Bergman, 2013; Shelton, 2013; Garwood, 2016; Pallotta-Chiarolli & Rajkhowa, 2017) by addressing schools as nuanced, complex fields of research, and by attempting to be more inclusive of less binary identities and relationships and of bi, trans and intersex people. We also sought the voices of people living both inside and outside big cities, in order to see if there were any differences in their experiences. Finally, we felt that a piece of qualitative research conducted outside of the survey-based campaigning literature (Bradlow, Bartram, Guasp, & Jadva, 2017) might help to develop a deeper analysis, and offer some nuanced ideas as to how schools can continue to support diverse families in a time of flux.

A Rapidly Developing Climate

While we have been writing this book, trans people have become the topic of much debate in media and politics and the target for increasing levels of violence and abuse both in the streets and in social media (McInroy & Craig, 2015; Samer, 2017). This has become mainstream: for example, in *The Times*, Gilligan (2017) stokes a moral panic about trans activists lobbying to abolish birth certificates and hand out free hormones to children on demand. Trans celebrities such as Caitlyn Jenner and Laverne Cox have huge transatlantic exposure (Samer, 2017), while at the same time, the UK government is attempting to update gender recognition legislation. Meanwhile, there is an increasingly visible presence of lesbian- and gay-parented nuclear families in schools, the media and other institutions, a development underpinned by the recent legal changes noted above. This corporate and institutional acceptance of the apparently well-behaved, affluent homonormative lesbian and gay family, however, can act to exclude other, less normative queer, polyamorous or activist LGBTQI+ parented families. We unpick some of these dilemmas and contradictions from parents' and children's points of view, within the specific context of schooling.

Empirical Basis for the Book

The findings we report in this book come from four different sets of data, all but one collected specifically for the book. They are linked by our overall interest in how LGBTQI+ parented families experience and interact with their children's schools, and by our overarching theoretical framework, which we discuss in Chapter 2. At the centre of the book is a set of in-depth interviews with 26 parents and carers (referred to as 'parents' throughout) and 19 children, all from LGBTQI+ parented families. Some of the children and parents come from the same families, but in other cases we interviewed the parents but not the children, or vice versa. Family members chose whether or not they wanted to be interviewed alone or as a group. The findings from these interviews are juxtaposed with three other studies: an analysis of media reports concerning LGBTQI+ parented families over four discrete time periods; an analysis of policies found on school websites in two contrasting English Local Authority areas, alongside responses to a survey of schools in or near London; and an evaluation of the England-wide Educate & Celebrate intervention to support schools in becoming more inclusive of LGBTQI+ people. We hope that this will give a more rounded picture of the factors involved in how LGBTQI+ parented families are able to be recognized by, interact and work with schools.

We discuss the methods used and the respondent or data samples for each study in more detail in the specific chapters that focus on each. We should, however, make a few overarching ethical comments at this point. All participants were given full information about the study in which they were involved, using a participant information sheet tailored to their situation, plus, where appropriate, additional information and consent check from whichever one of us was conducting that interview or focus group. Participants, and, where appropriate, parents and other relevant authorities (such as a child's social worker) completed and signed consent forms for the research. Both audio recordings and written transcriptions were stored in a secure file on Goldsmiths' university servers, and all participants, their partners, parents, children and schools have been given pseudonyms. Although some parents and children were interviewed together, or children interviewed in the presence of their parents, where this was not the case, we were particularly concerned that parents should, as far as possible, not be able to identify what their children had said to us in their own confidential interviews. We have therefore not associated parents with their children in the text, and removed contextual clues that might otherwise make this possible. For the same reason, we do not offer an appendix with a table of the various family members we interviewed. While this has its drawbacks, we felt that it was essential in order to protect the confidentiality and anonymity of participants, especially child participants.

Insider Positions and Their Effects

We come to this research as insiders, but to different extents and with different standpoints (Acker, 2000; Breen, 2007; Dwyer & Buckle, 2009;

Keval, 2009; Paechter, 2012b; Perryman, 2011; Taylor, 2011). While writing together from our different positions has been fruitful, our differences may also have had some effects on some of the data collected and on our analytical positions. Anna is a half Catholic, half Jewish, cisgender lesbian parent of four children aged 2 to 25, married to a woman. Whilst focused clearly on social justice (and with a keen eye for injustice), in her early career she wanted to avoid being pigeonholed as a lesbian academic conducting research on lesbians. However, she has spent the last four years conducting research with the LGBTQI+ schools charity Educate & Celebrate, and collecting data for this book. Her early research (Carlile, 2012a) was on permanent exclusion from school and institutional prejudice, looking at inclusion and exclusion more broadly, such as in the case of gender (Carlile, 2009) and ethnicity (Carlile, 2012c); she has also addressed student voice (Carlile, 2012b), multilingualism, and creative and critical pedagogies (Carlile, 2016). Her four children are variously mixed heritage Jamaican, Irish Traveller and white British; as a parent she has visited their schools on several occasions to address the racist, homophobic and heteronormative pressures on them. Anna has a history as a school teacher, and was asked to leave her first teaching position after a parent complained about her presentation as an out and visible lesbian on the staff. She saw multiple transgressions of children's rights and of institutional and personal racism, homophobia and sexism during her school-based career. In collecting, coding and analyzing data for this book, Anna has, therefore, tried to think intersectionally, foregrounding respondent voice in the process. Carrie is a cisgender, Jewish, heterosexual parent whose mother came out as a lesbian when Carrie was 14. Carrie has therefore been part of an LGBTQI+ blended family for 45 years, and went to school while part of such a family (Paechter, 2000), but has no direct experience of LGBTQI+ parenting or what it is like to be part of such a family interacting with schools today. She is also a former school teacher, and her interest in gender and identities related to education (Francis & Paechter, 2015; Paechter, 2007, 2012a, 2017) stems from this period. She presents as conventionally feminine, and was previously unknown to most of the parents and all of the children she interviewed.

It is difficult to unpick the effects of these multiple differences in our positions, but we have attempted to be mindful of them when gathering and analyzing our data. For Anna, her full insider position allowed an exchange of experiences and an assumption of shared perspectives which may have resulted in parents speaking more openly with her than with Carrie, whose sexual orientation was only known to some participants. On the other hand, some things which Anna's own experience led her to ask about, such as whether Mothers' Day or Fathers' Day was a problem, were not explicitly mentioned by Carrie, who was then struck by how much some common issues were raised by parents unprompted.

All the children interviewed by Anna were aware that she was a lesbian parent herself, and several had met Anna's children; those interviewed by Carrie had no information about her position. We do not know how much this affected children's responses. However, it is interesting to note that the two children who said that when 'gay' was used as a derogatory term in the playground it was not intended as abusive were talking to Carrie, and it was clear from her interviews with their parents that they would not have shared this view. Several of Anna's interviews with both adults and children also took place at Rainbow Families camps, in which LGBTQI+ parented families gather together on holiday. This context may have had an effect on children's responses, particularly to the question we asked about the benefits of being in an LGBTQI+ parented family. The fact that these children were recruited in this setting may also point to a difference between them and some of those interviewed elsewhere, in that they came from families in which being LGBTQI+ was an important aspect of their parents' identities and networks. Not all of the children we interviewed came from families that were so embedded in such connections.

Language

We should also say something at this stage about some of the terminology we have chosen to use. We spent some time discussing whether or not to use the full acronym LGBTQI+ and decided, on balance, that it would not be inclusive to leave out any of the various identities it encompasses.[1] We do need, however, to add some clarifications about T, Q and I. We understand T as indicating trans, which includes non-binary identities as well as those which involve movement across a binary divide. In doing so, however, we are mindful of the specific identities and preferences of our respondents. In particular, we discussed for some time how to refer to parents who had a trans history but did not identify as trans at the time we interviewed them. This applied specifically to women who had been assigned male at birth but who identify as women. While we do not want in any way to deny the status of these women *as women*, we do need to distinguish them from cis women in our analysis as our data suggest that they can experience very specific difficulties in working with their children's schools. Following the usage of one of our respondents we refer to them as 'women of trans history'. We refer to the men of trans history as 'trans men' as that was how they indicated that they currently identify.

Our own understanding of Q, and that of most of our respondents, is that it refers to a 'queer' identity that is related to, but not synonymous with, non-binariness, or, at least, to a position dissociated from binary gender narratives. However, one older respondent, a woman of trans history, was clear that she was very uncomfortable with the term being used in this way, and thought that it would be better if it stood for 'questioning'. This was due to her own previous experience, as someone growing up in the 1970s, when it was used repeatedly to bully her:

> Right, so I fully understand that some people embrace that world and want to be described that way. What I also know, for me personally, and for most gay people that I know of a similar age to me, specifically, quite a big chunk of us find it grossly offensive. . . . I mean, when I was at school, I was taunted as being a queer one, and there wasn't really a day went by that that wasn't thrown at me.

While many younger LGBTQI+ people feel able to reclaim the word 'queer' as an identity, it is important to be aware that for others it brings back painful memories.

The inclusion of I, or intersex, was also something that we discussed. Intersex is both a condition and an identity, and many intersex people identify as one or other binary gender. However, related to the increase in intersex activism in recent years (Accord Alliance, 2017; Organization Intersex International, 2017; Viloria, 2017) more people with intersex conditions are taking up intersex as an identity. One of our respondents identifies as intersex, so we felt that it was important to include their identity as part of our overall acronym. Similarly, given that identifications around gender appear, at time of writing, to be changing with considerable rapidity, the use of '+' to denote any that might arise after we go to press seemed to us to be important. Throughout, we have been careful to use the preferred pronouns of our different respondents: while most are 'he' or 'she', some use the non-binary pronoun 'they', and we have respected this.

What Is in the Book

We begin with an outline as to the societal and ideological context within which LGBTQI+ parented families and schools exist in the England and Wales, and of the theoretical approach we take to analyze our findings in this context. This includes the way in which the heterosexual matrix (Butler, 1990) is related to homonormative family structures (Garwood, 2016) which align closely with their heterosexual counterparts, and therefore may become more amenable to governmental disciplinary technologies (Repo, 2016). Related to this, we consider established ideologies of motherhood and fatherhood, and how they relate to the spectrum of LGBTQI+ parents and parenting forms. We also consider how these ideologies affect the visibility and invisibility of family members such as trans, biological and non-biological parents in LGBTQI+ parented families.

Chapter 3 addresses the media context surrounding LGBTQI+ parented families, and the impact of media on policy. We trace one potential source of the recent 'transgender moment' (Samer, 2017) to a key media event featuring an LGBTQI+ parent: when US transgender father Thomas Beatie was pictured as a 'pregnant man' in 'maternity pose' in *The Advocate* in 2008 (Norwood, 2013). It was important to understand how social ideas and misconceptions about LGBTQI+ parented families might have developed in schools since then, so we analyzed a UK and Ireland newspaper sample gathered across four weeks in 2015 and 2016, finding disturbing evidence that UK media is only positive about LGBTQI+ parents who happen to be wealthy consumers within a neoliberal paradigm (Caviedes, 2015; Littler, 2013). The remaining parents who feature tend to stand accused of horrific child murders, grooming, drug use, molestation and even mind control and witchcraft. We describe the ways in which many ethnically and religiously diverse school children learn about LGBTQI+ people (often celebrities) through their status as confident, open minded social and online media 'digital residents' (White & Le Cornu, 2011), and compare this with the sparse and fearful knowledge base which 'digital visitor' (White & Le Cornu, 2011) teachers often develop.

The next chapter focuses on those school policies which impact on LGBTQI+ parented families and how they can illuminate schools' attitudes towards them. We draw on two sources of data: responses to a survey of teachers across a large number of schools around London, and a collection of school policies drawn from rural and urban school websites over two geographically diverse local authority areas. While it remains the case that the drafting of a policy may inadvertently become a means by which an institution avoids positive action (Ahmed, 2012), the extent to which they are present in school policies does give an indication of how much LGBTQI+ parented families are visible and valued in a school.

Chapter 5 examines, through an analysis of interviews with 26 LGBTQI+ parents, their relationship with the schools attended by their children. A key theme emerging from the interviews concerns the tensions and contradictions inherent in the parents' thoughts, feelings and strategic practices of visibility and invisibility (Brown, 2012; Cloughessy, Waniganayake, & Blatterer, 2017; Dalton & Belby, 2000; Holman & Oswald, 2011; Taylor, 2009). Our analysis reveals a range of tactics and desired positions of visibility and invisibility which vary across rural and urban contexts, and between lesbian/gay/bisexual parents, women of trans history, trans men, intersex people, activists and non-activists.

We then move on to examine what the children of LGBTQI+ parents said in their interviews. Children's stories about school are characterized by more stress and negative experience than those of their parents; they could, in some cases, be seen to be protecting their parents from knowledge of these. We discuss the concern some children have for their parents, which resides alongside their somewhat contradictory desire to visibly advocate for their families and queer communities. We look at peer relationships, including friends, bullying, microaggressions (Kosciw,

Greytak, Diaz, & Bartkiewicz, 2010) and violence, and consider how children 'come out' as the offspring of LGBTQI+ parents (Taylor, 2009). Finally, we examine how schools address LGBTQI+ parented families in their work on friendship, bullying and curriculum.

Chapter 7 draws on data collected during an evaluation of the LGBTQI+ education charity Educate & Celebrate. We are primarily interested here in how the charity successfully addresses some of the problems identified in our research, particularly relating to school policies; the development of an LGBTQI+ friendly environment and community; and how it works to embed LGBTQI+ people and issues across the curriculum. We also consider whether or not the Educate & Celebrate model problematizes heteronormative constructions of LGBTQI+ families, and conclude that its approach is generally more nuanced than appears to be the case in many schools.

Note

1 We reluctantly omitted the + from the title on the advice of the publisher. This was because special characters such as + cause problems with online searches, and so the book might not have come up in search results. While we are strongly committed to the inclusivity of the +, we felt that it was also important that our research be found and read.

References

Accord Alliance. (2017). *Homepage*. Retrieved from www.accordalliance.org/
Acker, S. (2000). In/out/side: Positioning the researcher in feminist research. *Resources for Feminist Research*, 28(1–2), 189–210.
Ahmed, S. (2012). *On being included: Racism and diversity in institutional life*. Durham, NC: Duke University Press.
Arnup, K. (1995). *Lesbian parenting: Living with pride and prejudice*. Charlottetown, Canada: Gynergy Books.
Bergman, S. B. (2013). *Blood, marriage, wine and glitter*. Vancouver: Arsenal Pulp Press.
Bigner, J. J. (1999). Raising our sons: Gay men as fathers. *Gay and Lesbian Social Services*, 10(1), 61–77.
Bradlow, J., Bartram, F., Guasp, A., & Jadva, V. (2017). *School report: The exeriences of lesbian, gay, bi and trans young people in Britain's schools in 2017*. London: Stonewall and University of Cambridge.
Breen, L. J. (2007). The researcher "in the middle": Negotiating the insider/outsider dichotomy. *Australian Community Psychologist*, 19(1), 163–174.
Brown, G. (2012). Homonormativity: A metropolitan concept that denigrates "ordinary" gay lives. *Journal of Homosexuality*, 59, 1065–1072.
Butler, J. (1990). *Gender trouble: Feminism and the subversion of identity*. London: Routledge.
Carlile, A. (2009). "Bitchy girls and silly boys": Gender and exclusion from school. *International Journal on School Disaffection*, 6(2), 30–36.

Carlile, A. (2012a). *Permanent exclusion from school and institutional prejudice: Creating change through critical bureaucracy*. Rotterdam: Sense Publishers.
Carlile, A. (2012b). "Critical bureaucracy" in action: Embedding student voice into school governance. *Pedagogy Culture and Society, 20*(3), 393–412.
Carlile, A. (2012c). An ethnography of permanent exclusion from school: Revealing and untangling the threads of institutionalised racism. *Race Ethnicity and Education, 15*(2), 175–194.
Carlile, A. (2016). Student Participant-Researchers: Learner agency and creative engagement. In J. Anderson & V. Macleroy (Eds.), *Multilingual Digital Storytelling: Engaging creatively and critically with literacy*. London: Routledge, 87–105.
Caviedes, A. (2015). An emerging "European" news portrayal of immigration? *Journal of Ethnic and Migration Studies, 41*(6), 897–917.
Cloughessy, K., Waniganayake, M., & Blatterer, H. (2017). "This is our family: We do not hide who we are." Stigma and disclosure decisions of lesbian parents in Australian early childhood settings. *Journal of GLBT Family Studies*, online advance publication.
Dalton, S. E., & Belby, D. D. (2000). "That's our kind of constellation": Lesbian mothers negotiate institutionalized understandings of gender within the family. *Gender and Society, 14*(1), 36–61.
Dwyer, S. C., & Buckle, J. L. (2009). The space between: On being an insider-outsider in qualitative research. *International Journal of Qualitative Methods, 8*(1), 54–63.
Francis, B., & Paechter, C. (2015). The problem of gender categorisation: Addressing dilemmas past and present in gender and education research. *Gender and Education, 27*(7), 776–790.
Garwood, E. (2016). Reproducing the homonormative family: Neoliberalism, queer theory and same-sex reproductive law. *Journal of International Women's Studies, 17*(2), 5–17.
Gender Recognition Act 2004. London: HMSO.
Gilligan, A. (2017, December 17). Action for Trans Health activists want free sex-change hormones for children. *The Times*. Retrieved December 19, 2017, from www.thetimes.co.uk/edition/news/action-for-trans-health-activists-want-free-sex-change-hormones-for-children-dhvv5c52v
Hequembourg, A. L., & Farrell, M. P. (1999). Lesbian motherhood: Negotiating marginal-mainstream identities. *Gender and Society, 13*(4), 540–557.
Holman, E. G., & Oswald, R. F. (2011). Nonmetropolitan GLBTQ parents: When and where does their sexuality matter. *Journal of GLBT Family Studies, 7*(5), 436–456.
Johnson, A. M., & O'Connor, E. (2001). *For lesbian parents: Your guide to helping your family grow up happy, healthy and proud*. New York: The Guilford Press.
Keval, H. C. (2009). Negotiating constructions of "insider"/"outsider" status and explaining the significance of dis/connections. *Enquire, 4*, 51–72.
Kosciw, J. G., Greytak, E. A., Diaz, E. M., & Bartkiewicz, M. J. (2010). *The 2009 national school climate survey: The experiences of lesbian, gay, bisexual, and transgender youth in our nation's schools*. New York: GLSEN.
Littler, J. (2013). Meritocracy as plutocracy: The marketising of "equality" within neoliberalism. *New Formations: A Journal of Culture/Theory/Politics, 80*, 52–72.

Marriage (Same Sex Couples) Act 2013. London: HMSO.
Martin, A. (1993). *The guide to lesbian and gay parenting*. London: HarperCollins Publishers.
McInroy, L. B., & Craig, S. L. (2015). Transgender representation in offline and online media: LGBTQ youth perspectives. *Journal of Human Behavior in the Social Environment, 25*(6), 606–617.
Norwood, K. (2013). A pregnant pause, a transgender look: Thomas Beatie in the maternity pose. In J. Campbell & T. Carilli (Eds.), *Queer media images* (pp. 65–76). Plymouth: Lexington Books.
Organization Intersex International. (2017). Home Page. Retrieved from http://oiiinternational.com/
Paechter, C. (2000). Growing up with a lesbian mother: A theoretically based analysis of personal experience. *Sexualities, 3*(4), 395–408.
Paechter, C. (2007). *Being boys, being girls: Learning masculinities and femininities*. Maidenhead, Berks: Open University Press.
Paechter, C. (2012a). Bodies, identities and performances: Reconfiguring the language of gender and schooling. *Gender and Education, 24*(2), 229–241.
Paechter, C. (2012b). Researching sensitive issues online: Implications of a hybrid insider/outsider position in a retrospective ethnographic study. *Qualitative Research, 13*(1), 71–86.
Paechter, C. (2017). Young children, gender and the heterosexual matrix. *Discourse: Studies in the Cultural Politics of Education, 38*(2), 277–291.
Pallotta-Chiarolli, M., & Rajkhowa, A. (2017). Systemic invisibilities, institutional culpabilities and multicultural-multifaith LGBTIQ resistances. *Journal of Intercultural Studies, 38*(4), 429–442.
Perryman, J. (2011). The return of the native: The blurred boundaries of insider/outsider research in an English secondary school. *International Journal of Qualitative Studies in Education, 24*(7), 857–874.
Pollack, S., & Vaughn, J. (Eds.), (1987). *Politics of the heart: A lesbian parenting anthology*. New York: Firebrand Books.
Repo, J. (2016). *The biopolitics of gender*. Oxford: Oxford University Press.
Russell, S. T., McGuire, J. K., Lee, S., Larriva, J. C., & Laub, C. (2008). Adolescent perceptions of school safety for transgender parents. *Journal of LGBT Youth, 5*(4), 11–27.
Ryan-Flood, R. (2009). *Lesbian motherhood: Gender, families and sexual citizenship*. Basingstoke, Hants: Palgrave Macmillan.
Samer, R. (2017). Editor's introduction: Transgender media studies. *Spectator 37*(2), 5–8.
Shelton, M. (2013). *Family pride: What LGBT families should know about navigating home, school, and safety in their neighborhoods*. Boston: Beacon Press.
Stacey, J. (2006). Gay parenthood and the decline of parenting as we knew it. *Sexualities, 9*(1), 27–55.
Stonewall. (2010). *Different Families: The experiences of children with lesbian and gay parents*. London: Stonewall.
Taylor, J. (2011). The intimate insider: Negotiating the ethics of friendship when doing insider research. *Qualitative Research, 11*(1), 3–22.
Taylor, Y. (2009). *Lesbian and gay parenting: Securing social and educational capital*. Basingstoke, Hants: Palgrave Macmillan.
Viloria, H. (2017). *Born both: An intersex life*. New York: Hatchette Books.

White, D. S., & Le Cornu, A. (2011, September 5). Visitors and residents: A new typology for online engagement. *First Monday*, *16*(9). Retrieved December 19, 2017, from http://firstmonday.org/ojs/index.php/fm/article/view/3171/3049

Wienke, C., & Hill, G. J. (2013). Does place of residence matter? Rural—urban differences and the wellbeing of gay men and lesbians. *Journal of Homosexuality*, *60*(9), 1256–1279.

Wilson, J., Illustrated by Sharratt, N. (1999). *The Illustrated Mum*. London: Doubleday.

Wright, J. M. (1998). *Lesbian step families: An ethnography of love*. New York: Harrington Park Press.

2 Ideologies of Parenting and Schooling
Visibility, Invisibility and Alternative Family Forms

When I was a young teacher in the 1980s, we had a residential training event on equalities. As part of this there was a session on lesbian and gay students. Before the session, I asked the trainer whether there would be anything about people with lesbian and gay parents 'as we also have problems'. He replied briskly that no, there would not. I don't think he even heard the 'we' in my question: I think he assumed that I was hoping to distract the session onto a discussion how unfair gay parenting was on the children—though it may also have just been that he knew absolutely nothing about us. For me, it was yet another example of my family's complete invisibility, even in inclusive contexts.

Carrie

Introduction

It is impossible to investigate the experiences of LGBTQI+ families in relation to schools and schooling without a strong theoretical understanding of some of the key aspects of the society in which this relationship is played out. In this chapter we are going to explain some of the fundamental ways in which schools and families are located within wider societal forms and assumptions. We will start by explaining and developing our understanding of the heterosexual matrix (Butler, 2009) and its relationship to civil society, including schools. We will discuss the ways that changes in civil society, in tandem with the heterosexual matrix, are leading to the development of forms of homonormativity that parallel long-established heteronormative arrangements. We will then briefly discuss ideologies of motherhood and fatherhood and their relationship to different forms of LGBTQI+ parenting, and to female and male bodies. Finally, we examine visibility and invisibility and the question of who is acknowledged in schools' relationships with parents, and who is erased. Both the heterosexual matrix and ideologies of motherhood and fatherhood have complex visibility/erasure effects, so that individuals and families can be rendered either hypervisible or (and frequently simultaneously) invisible by the effects of both heteronormativity and homonormativity, coupled with the general tendency of schools to erase both bodies and sexuality. We will argue that the greater incorporation of gay and lesbian partnerships into wider civil society, while clearly important in social-justice terms, can serve to render homonormatively structured LGBTQI+ families less visible, and therefore potentially less well served, than before, and that there is a concomitant increased visibility, and potential pathologization, for those families who do not conform to these new norms. We will also suggest that this incorporation of more families into the body politic makes them more amenable to disciplinary forces of the contemporary state (Repo, 2016).

LGBTQI+ parented families remain very much in the minority, even in affluent areas of the globe and particularly outside of major cities. For example, UK figures for 2016 indicate that same-sex couple families with children comprise 1.8% of all families with children in the UK (Office for National Statistics, 2016). This suggests that, even as civil society makes available mainstream family forms to a wider range of people, such families may continue to stand partially outside, and ignored by, wider assumptions about what it is to be a mother or father, particularly in relation to schooling. Furthermore, lone parent LGBTQI+ parented families are not even visible in these statistics, as they are not differentiated from lone heterosexual parented families in the data.

Heteronormativity, Homonormativity and the Heterosexual Matrix

A key aspect of the social, cultural and civil context in which both LGBTQI+ families and schools operate is the heterosexual matrix. This concept was introduced by Butler (1990), as a way of thinking about how society structures gender identities and performances through an assumption of heterosexuality. She argues that gender is constructed through a complex matrix in which gender and sexuality are inextricably linked, defining her use of the term as being

> to designate that grid of cultural intelligibility through which bodies, genders, and desires are naturalized. I am drawing from Monique Wittig's notion of the "heterosexual contract" and, to a lesser extent, on Adrienne Rich's notion of "compulsory heterosexuality" to characterize a hegemonic discursive/epistemic model of gender intelligibility that assumes that for bodies to cohere and make sense there must be a stable sex expressed through a stable gender (masculine expresses male, feminine expresses female) that is oppositionally and hierarchically defined through the compulsory practice of heterosexuality.

(151)

What Butler means here is that there is an underpinning assumption that applies to all bodies, genders and desires, which is that they are heterosexual, and that this is assumed to be the 'natural' way to be. This of course has a number of quite problematic implications, which we will come to later.

Butler's conception of the heterosexual matrix stems, as she points out, from the work of Wittig (1989/1992), who claims that the unspoken social contract, which underpins civil society, is inherently heterosexual. Wittig argues that the assumption of heterosexuality is so fundamental to society that the social contract is, in effect, a heterosexual contract:

> Being tied together by a social link, we can consider that each and every one of us stands within the social contract—the social contract being then the fact of having come together, of being together, of living as social beings. This notion is relevant for the philosophical mind . . . through the established fact that we live, function, talk, work, marry together. Indeed, the conventions and the language show on a dotted line the bulk of the social contract—which consists in living in heterosexuality. For to live in society is to live in heterosexuality.
>
> (40)

This idea that to live in society entails living in heterosexuality develops an argument from an earlier essay in which Wittig suggests that the discourses emanating from 'the straight mind' function to eliminate non-heterosexuals: 'you-will-be-straight-or-you-will-not-be' (Wittig, 1980/1992: 28). This foreshadows even more closely Butler's (1990) conception of the hegemonic heterosexual matrix. To stand outside of heterosexuality, is, on such a formulation, to repudiate or exclude oneself from the social contract; equally, by stepping outside of, or refusing, the social contract one is at the same time enabled to remove oneself, and refuse, from the heterosexual matrix.

Unfortunately, as Wittig herself admits, the heterosexual social contract is so embedded in civil society that it is more or less impossible to avoid living within its forms, including the heterosexual matrix. It is also the case that, despite certain problems, in particular with respect to its application to children, the heterosexual matrix is a useful concept for summing up the complex assumptions underpinning life in a social world that assumes heterosexuality as a norm. Furthermore, because of its foundation in civil society, the heterosexual matrix is a central aspect of how schools, as public institutions, as well as individuals and families, are constructed and construct themselves as part of that society. We have, therefore, to explore what living within the heterosexual matrix might mean for the LGBTQI+ parented families that are the focus of this book.

A key and obvious aspect of the heterosexual matrix is the assumption of heterosexuality. This is not quite an underpinning belief that everyone is heterosexual, but more that heterosexual ways of living are treated as taken-for-granted and normal, so that anything that stands outside of this is in some way not just different, but deviant. This idea encompasses not just compulsory heterosexuality, but also particular ways of living one's heterosexuality, so that there is, for example, an expectation in many cultures that adults will form an exclusive partnership with one and only one person of the opposite binary gender and aim to have children with them. These particular ways of living out (heterosexual) lives are collectively referred to as 'heteronormativity' and underpin not just assumptions about social life but also such things as national legal, tax and medical systems, which are structured around the heteronormative family to different extents in different jurisdictions (Browne, 2011; Neary, 2016; Ryan-Flood, 2009). Civil life, as Wittig (1989/1992) points out, is founded on heteronormative assumptions about people and their relationship to society. As a result, social policies place heterosexual monogamous relationships at the heart of the social, despite evident diversity (Pallotta-Chiarolli, 2010).

Another important feature of the heterosexual matrix, and one on which Butler (1990) is particularly keen to focus, is the assumption of 'a stable sex expressed through a stable gender (masculine expresses male, feminine expresses female)' (151). For Butler, this is important for her understanding of identity as in some ways fragmented and performative, and for her argument that this stability is an illusion. It is also significant, however, simply in terms of the underpinning assumptions about what it is to be a person. The heterosexual matrix, as defined by Butler, assumes that sex/gender is binary (there are two and only two, opposing sexes/genders), that it is stable (you are only one sex/gender, and always have and will be) and that our (sexed) bodies conform to our (gendered) identities. The heterosexual matrix, through which society perceives and understands individual human identities, therefore assumes binary cisgendering. Such taken-for-granted assumptions will obviously have a variety of effects on families with parents who are not cisgender, or, indeed, committed to binary gender identities or performances.

Since Wittig and Butler developed these concepts, however, there have been significant formal changes to the ways in which civil society operates with respect to LGBTQI+ citizens. In particular, the spread of legislation enabling gay marriage, in the affluent global North and West at least (Brown, 2012), could be seen as introducing a new set of norms which encompass many, but not all, LGBTQI+ people. Various writers (Ashford, 2011; Duggan, 2002; Garwood, 2016; Santos, 2013; Stryker, 2008) argue that new legal labels and processes enabling, for example, LGBTQI+ couples to legitimately claim the right to use terms such as 'husband', 'wife' and 'parent', are symptomatic of a new homonormative legal discourse focused around stable, monogamous, mainly lesbian and gay couples. They suggest that such 'concessions' reflect an assumption that one can be included in heteronormative civil society only if one lives in ways that are modelled on and parallel its forms.

The participants in our research are variously situated in relation to these new forms and structures, so it is important to discuss the concept of homonormativity and the tensions inherent in both its theorization and its practice. Although the term has been used for longer, much of the more recent writing about homonormativity stems from the work of Duggan, who argues that homonormative discourse is a political and theoretical form

> that does not contest dominant heteronormative assumptions and institutions, but upholds and sustains them, while promising the possibility of a demobilized gay constituency and a privatized, depoliticized gay culture anchored in domesticity and consumption.
> (Duggan, 2002: 179)

Duggan and others (Croce, 2015; Garwood, 2016; Stryker, 2008; Taylor, 2012) argue that homonormativity is allied to liberal or even neoconservative tendencies in wider society, through which 'gay or lesbian, cisgender, middle-class, white, western, able-bodied, monogamous, family-oriented, married' (Garwood, 2016: 9) people are able to have heteronormative privilege extended to them in return for giving up the struggle for radical social change. It is argued by critics of campaigns for inclusion in such civil institutions as marriage and family life that lesbian and gay activists, in particular, abandoned bisexual, queer and trans allies to present themselves as 'normal', good citizens who should be included in mainstream society (Richardson, 2004).

The move from a wider struggle for social change to campaigns for inclusion in key civil institutions such as marriage and parenting has caused considerable and often heated debate, which reflects and is reflected in tensions between the wish to challenge heteronormative assumptions and institutions (Atkinson & DePalma, 2008) and parallel desires for love, family and children (Stacey, 2006). Brown (2012), speaks clearly to this tension in critiquing the way that homonormativity as a term is both conceptualized and applied. Distinguishing homonormativity as an assemblage of social changes and Homonormativity as the theorization of this, he argues that, while there are indeed problems with the way the former entrenches privilege, the latter treats homonormativity as if it were 'a homogeneous, global external entity that exists outside all of us and exerts its terrifying, normative power on gay lives everywhere' (1066). Of particular relevance for this book, he notes that 'Homonormativity overlooks the lived experience of many lesbians and gay men outside of the metropolitan milieu in which these theoretical debates circulate' (1067). Brown points out that these developments have taken place because of cumulative changes in everyday practices in which even queer theorists are complicit, and suggests that, while the costs of change have certainly been borne by many trans people and LGBTQI+ people of colour, we should not ignore either the importance of these new freedoms or the emotional power that comes from being recognized, while remaining alive to negative consequences. Similarly, Weeks (2007) argues that, although such things as same-sex marriage and access to reproductive rights absorb LGBTQI+ relationships into heteronormativity and normalize particular forms of couple relationship while marginalizing others, without this inclusion even more people are marginalized with respect to parenting rights, recognition as next of kin and other central aspects of ordinary citizenship. The value of these rights and the possibilities they bring, including, for example, access to fostering and adoption for gay men (and the benefits to the children they parent) (Stacey, 2006) should not be disregarded. As Weeks (2007) points out, we should 'never underestimate the importance of being ordinary' (9).

This valuing of 'ordinariness' has been reflected in campaigns for equal marriage and parenting rights in particular, which stress the 'sameness' of stable heterosexual and homosexual partnerships (Ryan-Flood, 2009). Taylor (2009) describes this 'ordinariness strategy' as one in which LGBTQI+ families focus on mundane aspects of family life in order to make themselves recognizable as similar to heterosexual families (Clarke, 2008; Croce, 2015), dissipating any suggestion of the 'wrong' kind of difference, and associating themselves with the apparent heteronormativity of parenthood (Richardson, 2004; Ryan-Flood, 2009). While such strategies have been useful in attaining civil rights, they are also salient, as we shall see, in how LGBTQI+ parented families operate in their relationships with schools, particularly in establishing recognition as 'good parents' (Taylor, 2009).

Clearly, the fight for equal rights involves accepting and even embracing some normative frameworks, which is not always what campaigners originally intended. Ashford (2011) argues that homonormativity, rather than contesting heteronormative assumptions and institutions (as envisaged, for example, by Atkinson and DePalma (2008)) instead upholds and sustains them, as part of the demobilization of gay culture, with the homosexual constructed as 'one of us'. Ryan-Flood (2009) further notes that while this assimilative perspective is politically expedient, it not only reinforces (hetero)norms but also ignores the role of sexuality in LGBTQI+ families, rendering invisible gay and lesbian desire within the family. Ryan-Flood (2009) suggests that the effects of this include the implicit stigmatization of butch/femme lesbian couples as part of the requirement to erase sexuality within the normative family. A further result of this increase in homonormative moves towards the mainstream, at least in the metropolitan North (Brown, 2012), is that there has been a shift in specific positionings that fall outside the heterosexual matrix, and are therefore marginal to civil society, with a redefinition of what constitutes a transgressive sexual act (Ashford, 2011).

These compromises and redefinitions can lead to tensions not just between those who are included and those who are not but also between different aspects of identity. People who have previously been active in challenging heteronormative family forms and structures may experience dissonance between their identity as outsiders and their lived experience as part of 'ordinary' LGBTQI+ parented families. For example this can be problematic for lesbian-identified partners of trans men who now find themselves in what appear to the outside world to be heterosexual relationships. For women who have previously considered themselves on the margins of mainstream society, this incorporation into heterosexuality and heteronormative privilege can be dislocating and disruptive of self-identity, while marginalizing them within the wider LGBTQI+ community (McGuire, Kuvalanka, Catalpa, & Toomey, 2016; Platt & Bolland, 2017). Furthermore, in more material terms, the success of campaigns for inclusion may inadvertently disadvantage some already marginalized families by, for example, making lesbian couples subject to dual income means testing for benefits (Browne, 2011).

One significant effect of the legitimatizing of homonormative family forms is that a greater proportion of individuals and families fall into the enlarged compass of the body politic. Repo (2016) argues that this is in part because of the emergence of neoliberalism as the dominant mode of governmentality, redefining the social sphere as an economic domain. In a context in which more women have been entering the workplace, Repo argues that this has led European governments in particular to put into place gender equality legislation in an attempt to prevent women's paid employment from causing a decline in population. While this has mainly focused on attempts to encourage more men to be involved in everyday childcare, releasing heterosexual women to spend more time in paid work, it has also, she suggests, led to a shift from a negative discourse of family breakdown to a more positive one of family diversity. This, she argues, allows governmental institutions to incorporate increasing numbers of families and relationships into their disciplinary ambit:

> While gender equality is clearly still modeled as a restorative response to the re/production crisis of the nuclear family, at the same time the nuclear family is no longer being reterritorialized on a number of "family forms"—homosexual, unmarried cohabitation, and single parenting are all becoming increasingly encapsulated within the scope of biopolitical governmentality. The gradual transformation and expansion of the definition of family enables the EU to target new forms of intimate relationships, such as queer families and

single-parent households that previously fell outside sovereign control because they were not recognized as families.

(Repo, 2016: 151)

The result of this is not just that previously excluded family forms are recognized and recorded in official statistics. It is also that through this they become governable, incorporated into and subject to the disciplinary norms of the state. Thus, in exchange for recognition and a social invisibility consequent of and alongside institutional visibility, homonormative families lose their transgressive positioning and become subject to neoliberal disciplinary forces.

The inclusion of homonormative families alongside heteronormative ones within mainstream civil society does little, of course, to alleviate or prevent the exclusion of those people who cannot easily fit into, or resist such structures: people who are trans, genderqueer, living in polyamorous relationships, or even just single. Indeed, Taylor (2009) suggests that single LGBTQI+ parents regard their singleness as the most salient aspect of their parenting. Pallotta-Chiarolli (2010) argues that a hierarchy has developed in which the social acceptance of white, middle-class, monogamously coupled, exclusively homosexual parents leaves non-heteronormative families with other relationship patterns marginalized. She suggests that heteronormativity, homonormativity and opposite-sex and same-sex couple families are three unequal systems of power that frame and marginalize bisexual and queerly-mixed families. For the children of multisexual/polyamorous parents, she argues, school remains a site of absence and isolation, in which they have to choose between silence and openly challenging the status quo. Pallotta-Chiarolli points to the continued marginalization of bisexuality within both LGBTQI+ communities and in wider society, noting that even the prefix 'bi' rests upon a binary system of classification of desire, and that the subsumation of bisexuality within lesbian and gay sexual orientations can be problematic. This is exacerbated for polyamorously parented families by the normativity of the monogamous couple bond. Pallotta-Chiarolli (2010) notes also that polyamorously parented families tend to be white middle-class and use this privilege as a way to circumvent or overcome marginalization.

Similarly, Taylor (2009) suggests that middle-class lesbian and gay couples can use their financial capital to participate in heteronormative structures: surrogate babies and donor insemination through clinics are expensive to procure. The ability to achieve familyhood, she argues, is differentially distributed and easier for the affluent (Stacey, 2006). Furthermore, a combination of finances, social capital and prejudice makes it harder for working-class LGBTQI+ parents to access the same entitlements and privileges of heterosexual and middle-class LGBTQI+ parents, such as 'good' schools, and themselves being regarded as 'good' parents and citizens. Because they are less able to mobilize resources to secure and legitimize their parenting, working-class LGBTQI+ parents have less access to the benefits of homonormativity than their middle-class counterparts.

At the same time, the rise of homonormativity has the potential to render children of homonormative couples invisible within school, because their families appear to have so much in common with those of heterosexual parents. Taylor (2009) argues that one problem for LGBTQI+ parented families in relation to schools is the requirement to negotiate the taken-for-granted invisibility of heterosexuality as a structuring presence in the school experience. This, she argues, formally silences lesbian/gay sexuality. The rise and recognition of homonormative family forms may, however, lead to their incorporation into this taken-for-granted invisibility, treated as just another monogamously parented family grouping. If homonormative parenting really is more or less the same as heteronormative parenting but with same-gendered parents (Clarke, 2008; Farrr, Tasker, & Goldberg, 2017; Martino & Cumming-Potvin, 2011; Richardson, 2004; Tasker & Golombok, 1997; Taylor, 2009), it could appear as though there were no need to make special provision for the children involved, once this basic recognition of the parents has taken place. While this invisibility can, of course, bring benefits (one is less likely to be bullied for being different), it can also mean that images of even homonormative LGBTQI+ families are absent from the school context, while making it even less likely that representations of non-normative families are available.

The inclusion and invisibility of some LGBTQI+ parented families also emphasizes the issue of geographies of sexuality (Brown, 2012). The acceptance of homonormative family forms has historically been seen as a mainly urban phenomenon. Ryan-Flood (2009) points out that the history of sexuality has a hidden geography in which institutions regulating sexualities are concentrated in geographic and political centres, with metropolitan areas being seen as centres for both regulation and liberation. She suggests that the spatiality of lesbian parenting has evolved differently in different countries, pointing out, for example, that, at the time of her research, Irish lesbians were both outside the law and invisible, rarely congregating and with no support group, whereas lesbian and gay parents were much more visible within Swedish society. This has differential effects concerning where LGBTQI+ parents choose to locate themselves: while in many countries cities are preferred, because of the expected greater concentration of similar families, the Irish lesbian parents Ryan-Flood studied felt that they had more privacy in the countryside. Taylor (2009) points out, however, that the choice, for example, of moving to a location where there are other LGBTQI+ families or a particularly supportive school, remains, for financial reasons, a middle-class prerogative.

Ideologies of Motherhood and Fatherhood

Images of the 'good parent' (Taylor, 2009) and their relation to heteronormative family forms and the 'good homosexual' are intimately connected with concepts of motherhood and fatherhood. Ideologies of motherhood and fatherhood are rooted in traditional gender ideologies and assumptions, including the heterosexual matrix. Indeed, if the heterosexual matrix is, as Butler (1990) suggests, based in the social contract, it is founded on an idea which was, in its origins, a contract between adult males, with this conception persisting into the late twentieth century with Rawls's (1972) influential understanding of it as a contract between (male) heads of households. Furthermore, social understandings of parenting are located within an assumption of heterosexuality: Marshall (1991) notes, for example, that childcare manuals only mention heterosexual parents. Thus, within the heterosexual social contract, fathers and mothers are understood to have particular roles, and these unwritten assumptions continue to affect notions of family life even within the context of LGBTQI+ parenting.

Ideologies of motherhood are associated with particular forms of femininity as qualities of the personality (Giddens, 1992), emphasizing caring and responsiveness to children (Burman, 1994, 1995). Mother-love is seen as natural and inevitable (Johnston & Swanson, 2003; Marshall, 1991) and it is assumed that the 'good mother' will want to care for her children herself as far as possible. Taylor (2009) points out, however, that mothering is not a classless practice (Johnston & Swanson, 2003), and working-class ways of mothering are sometimes seen as the antithesis of good parenting. In particular, the need for working-class mothers to engage in full-time paid work may cut across these ideologies of maternal devotion to children. Connolly (2004) found that working-class boys were expected to become streetwise at an early age and consequently given more responsibilities younger than middle-class children, and that the comparative lack of emphasis given by these working-class parents to organization and control led teachers to consider that they were unable to support their children effectively. It is therefore important, when considering how ideologies of motherhood and fatherhood impact on LGBTQI+ parents, to be aware that different race and class positions may lead to different effects.

The emphasis on the mother-child bond and the devotion of mothers to children as a priority above all others suggests that lesbian couples would have more equal parenting practices, as both would be subject to the ideologies of motherhood. To some extent this is borne out by research findings: for example, Dunne (1997) found that lesbian couples had more equal childcare and housework arrangements than those of heterosexuals, for whom there is a well-documented bias towards women doing a large proportion of the work (Baxter, 2000; Bianchi,

Sayer, Milkie, & Robinson, 2012; Carriero, 2011; Gager & Hohmann-Marriott, 2006; Hochschild, 1989; Lachance-Grzela & Bouchard, 2010; Legerski & Cornwall, 2010; Taylor, Bennett, & Sung, 2010; van Hooff, 2011). However, this is not a universal occurrence (Hicks, 2013), and, indeed, we had both gay and lesbian couples among our respondents whose family lives were structured, at least partially, around distinct earner/homemaker roles more typical of traditional middle-class heterosexual partnerships (Dalton & Belby, 2000; Stacey, 2006). Furthermore, Biblarz and Savci (2010) report that the commitment to a high degree of egalitarianism is a white middle-class phenomenon. Their review of research from the early 2000s suggests that among lesbian couples the biological mother both did more housework and childcare and got more responsibility and power in decision making, and that working-class lesbian couples frequently had one partner (usually the biological mother) taking the primary caretaker role. Hicks (2013) also notes that black women in lesbian partnerships tend to value autonomy over equality and suggests that this may be related to a greater likelihood of poverty. Findings on gay fathers are contradictory. Patterson (1992), reviewing the research on gay men as fathers, suggests that, while at that time few gay fathers lived in the same households as their children, they seemed to parent similarly to straight men (Bigner, 1999). Most of these earlier studies, however, focus on gay men whose children were born into heterosexual partnerships. Biblarz and Savci's more recent review (2010) found, by contrast, that gay men co-parenting with each other appear to do so in a style more typical of women than of straight fathers. Hicks (2013) argues that gay fathers have to contend with the maternal image of parenting and the strongly gendered assumptions about fathering roles. They have to decide how much they are prepared to challenge external assumptions about gender, and some felt resented by other men because their level of participation in childcare and housework showed up the lower involvement of many heterosexual fathers. Stacey (2006) suggests that paternity is always more of a social status than maternity, and that gay parenting intensifies this, especially given the prevalence of adoption for family formation, meaning that children may very visibly have no biological relationship to either parent.

Ideologies of motherhood are also associated with the feminized body as a bearer and nourisher of children, in a state of maternal bliss (Johnston & Swanson, 2003). However, this is assumed to take place within a heterosexual context. Romans (1992) argues that simply appearing in public with children invokes a presumption of heterosexuality; lesbian motherhood therefore challenges and disrupts dominant ideologies of gender, motherhood and family. Smart (1996: 37) argues that motherhood is:

> an institution that *presents* itself as a natural outcome of biologically given gender differences, as a natural consequence of (hetero) sexual

activity, and as a natural manifestation of an innate female characteristic, namely the maternal instinct.

The lesbian mother is, as Ryan-Flood (2009) points out, both an icon and a conundrum, upsetting the normative relationship between heterosexuality and parenting. She found that even co-parents were invested in the traditional idea of a special connection between the biological parent and the child during the breastfeeding period, despite consanguinity not generally being an issue between couples.

The iconic status of the birth mother and her relationship to the child produced by her body has a number of effects. First, it can lead to the differential perception of birth mothers and their partners, with the birth mother being treated as the 'real' mother due to her role as the physical bearer of a particular child. Hequembourg and Farrell (1999) note that this can even extend to co-mothers being sidelined as parents by their own families of origin, particularly if they have no formal legal parenting status. Birth mothers may also be perceived as more committed to the children, particularly given the assumed relationship between motherhood and nurturing. Ryan-Flood (2009) notes that even researchers have tended to ignore co-parents, again due to the taken-for-granted status of birth mothers. In some jurisdictions this status has significance in legal terms (Dalton & Belby, 2000; Garwood, 2016; Sifris, 2014), which may in turn have consequences for how each parent is perceived and treated by schools (Ryan-Flood, 2009). Furthermore, the relatively precarious situation of co-mothers in some countries may make it harder to be taken seriously as parents (Dalton & Belby, 2000): for example, Ryan-Flood (2009) found that none of her co-parent respondents became primary carers after relationship breakdown. At the same time, because birth mothers are automatically given parental status, and are therefore able to choose whether to share parenting with their partner, this leads many positively to assert their partner's parental status, in compensation (Dalton & Belby, 2000; Hequembourg & Farrell, 1999). However, the possibility of other people being involved in caring for the children, particularly if donors and their parents took an active role, could be challenging for co-parents (Ryan-Flood, 2009).

The association of motherhood with particular feminized bodily forms also marginalizes and problematizes the position of birth mothers who take up butch or genderqueer identities, which are perceived as transgressive in this regard; one of the requirements of homonormativity, like heteronormativity, is that members of homonormative partnerships should present as typically cisgendered. Such maternal ideologies are particularly challenged by those people who identify and/or present as male while pregnant and/or chestfeeding (McDonald, Noel-Weiss, Walks, Biener, & Kibbe, 2016; Moore, 1998). The masculine body is strongly at odds with traditional images of motherhood and such bodies may therefore be experienced by others, including their healthcare providers, as unreadable.

Ideologies of fatherhood as a more distant, less caring, but also more physically boisterous practice (Ross & Taylor, 1989) may also be challenged by the phenomenon of male couples co-parenting (Hicks, 2013). These families not only challenge conventional understandings of masculinity but also undercut many unspoken assumptions about fathers' relationships with schools. Reay (1998), for example, found that, in working-class families, women were usually the main communicator with their children's schools, only involving the father if there were serious concerns. Schools may therefore have to adjust their expectations of fathers in the light of these different parenting structures, including those which involve extended family groupings in which lesbian and gay couples and/or polyamorous groupings parent together.

How this is played out varies, of course, between different locations. Ryan-Flood (2009), for example, argues that in Ireland, marriage and motherhood are related to a post-colonial nationalist political heritage in which women are seen as symbolic representations of the nation. She suggests that the prohibitive nature of Irish anti-abortion laws demonstrate that women only exist there as a function of their maternity, so that they are simultaneously symbolically invoked, and excluded. Neary (2016) suggests that LGBTQI+ rights in Ireland are shaped by the relationship between church and state and that religiosity is an inextricable part of (hetero)normal Irish life. In Sweden, by contrast, the prevalent and officially backed equality discourse highlights the benefits of shared parenting, joint custody after separation is strongly supported, and fathers have official decision-making rights with respect to children. At the same time, however, an ideology of mothers' availability to children remains, in line with wider ideologies of motherhood. Furthermore, the official importance of biological fathers in Sweden makes it harder for lesbian co-parents to gain parental recognition (Ryan-Flood, 2009). Such arrangements strongly support heteronormative coupled parenting, even between LGBTQI+ biological parents, above other family structures. Meanwhile, LGBTQI+ parents are also subject to expectations from their own communities: Taylor (2009) argues that decisions about whether or not to reproduce signify identities and allegiances with respect to traditional 'scene' spaces, and that gay fathers may be seen as freakish by both gay and straight communities. Stacey (2006) notes that gay men who want to parent challenge gender/sexual norms of gay culture and that becoming a parent may require the ending of relationships with reluctant partners.

It is important to be aware that dominant ideologies of masculinity and femininity, as well as of motherhood and fatherhood, can affect perceptions of LGBTQI+ parents, who may stand in transgressive, normative or mixed positions in relation to school structures and expectations.

So, for example, a gay male couple with a parenting setup typical of a traditional heterosexual marriage may appear transgressive in the school context, due to the wider social expectations of masculinity as not fully nurturant, and of the family home as a feminine space (Connell, 2011). Again, however, there may be significant geographic and policy-led differences. Ryan-Flood (2009) notes, for example, that the greater Swedish expectations of paternal involvement with children, and the emphasis there on biological fatherhood and a child's right to know their biological father, mean that gay sperm donors known to the mothers are likely to stay involved with their children, and are therefore preferred by lesbian couples. In other countries, however, lesbian mothers may actively choose anonymous donors in order to prevent future contact or the assertion of paternal rights. This might be a particularly salient issue where female co-parents have no legal parenting status and fear losing the child if anything were to happen to the birth mother (Dalton & Belby, 2000).

Visibility and Invisibility in the Schooling Context

These various ideologies come together to bring about patterns of visibility and invisibility that affect and are affected by LGBTQI+ parented families in relation to schools. One of our tasks in this book is to examine how these patterns operate and to explore who and what is rendered visible or invisible, and when, and the implications of this.

Ryan-Flood (2009) argues that public spaces, such as hospitals, schools and neighbourhoods, are heteronormative in multiple ways. This means that parenthood is supported within clearly heteronormative parameters, and becoming a LGBTQI+ parent requires a repeated coming out in new environments, where it is never certain how service providers will react (Taylor, 2009). While sexualities and identities are produced in particular spaces, sexuality is socially regarded as a private matter, so bringing it into the public domain can be seen as threatening to the social order (Ashford, 2011). Normative heterosexuality is invisible because it is the default position: because children are seen as an unproblematically expected outcome of heterosexual partnerships, the sexual nature of these partnerships is rendered invisible. Non-heteronormative parenting, however, brings sexuality into the public sphere, through the contrast between non-procreative sexuality and the presence of children. Ryan-Flood (2009) argues that lesbian mothers are placed in a no-person's land between the subversions of gay communities and the apparent heteronormativity of parenthood (Taylor, 2009). The overt transgressiveness of some LGBTQI+ parents, coupled with the invisibility of others, work in complex ways with the relationship between schooling and the body, to render some LGBTQI+ parented families invisible, and others hypervisible, in the school context. This is of course exacerbated by the disciplinary forces of the neoliberal state, which, through the encouragement of and support for homonormativity, work to incorporate as many families as possible within normative social structures.

Schools are places where the body and sexuality are largely invisible, to the extent that they are effaced for much of the time; any leaching of sexuality into the school arena is therefore disruptive (Paechter, 2004, 2006, 2007; 1996). This erasure arises partly from the requirements of the heterosexual matrix, which assumes a constant sexuality that is simultaneously catered for and denied, through attempts to prevent its expression. Compulsory heterosexuality produces a problem for schools, which are supposed to operate not just in a sexuality-free zone (because of ideologies of childhood innocence) but also to work mainly with children's minds, as opposed to their bodies, the latter being largely excluded as part of a deeply embedded Cartesian legacy in which learning and knowledge are associated solely with the disembodied mind.

This drive to sideline bodies and make them invisible in school is closely related to a parallel exclusion of sex and sexuality, except at the very specific times and places of sex and relationship education. Sex as such has no place in school, and this means that the sexualized aspects of children's bodies are expected to disappear in order to allow a focus on the education of the mind (Paechter, 2004). Children's and young people's bodies also discomfort adults, partly because of their awareness that adolescents, at least, are often preoccupied with their emergent sexualities. While pre-pubertal children are not supposed to have any sexual interest in each other's bodies (despite evidence that they do (Renold, 2005, 2006)), at the same time these bodies are controlled in such a way as to prevent any interest that does appear from developing further (Foucault, 1978). There is, therefore, a discourse which treats the child's body as being without or outside of sex, while at the same time an unacknowledged awareness that it is nothing of the kind. In order for the ideology to prevail, the sexual aspects and urges of children have to be disciplined so that they cannot be expressed within the school. This disciplining cannot be overt, as this would require an acknowledgement that children's bodies are sexual. Consequently, what is regimented and denied is the body itself. If it is kept outside the framing of schooling, then its sexuality cannot creep back to undermine the discourse. Furthermore, while adults cannot so easily deny the sexuality of adolescent bodies, these bodies are seen as unpredictable and their increasingly sexualized development as polluting their former identity as innocent children. Consequently, there is an even greater urge to control their expression, effacing the body as a way of avoiding any focus on desire.

This need on the part of schools to render bodies and therefore sexuality invisible is threatened by the presence of LGBTQI+ parented families, particularly at the earlier stages of education. Adult, and in particular parental, sexualities are not usually a problem for schools, as long as they are straight sexualities: in a heteronormative society these are sufficiently taken for granted to be ignored. Taylor (2009) points out that all the lesbian and gay parents in her study had to negotiate the invisibility of heterosexuality as a structuring presence in school experience, and the concomitant silencing of lesbian and gay sexuality. LGBTQI+ parents are still too much of a minority group for even homonormative sexualities to disappear from view easily and immediately in all schools, so they have the potential to constitute a threat to the effacement of the body, particularly in primary schools where parents (and therefore family forms) are likely to be visible in the playground on a daily basis.

Until recently, schools dealt with this simply by ignoring the existence of these families, effacing their existence entirely (Casper, Schultz, & Wickens, 1992; DePalma & Atkinson, 2009; Kosciw & Diaz, 2008; Malins, 2016; Martino & Cumming-Potvin, 2011). Changes in statutory provision, and consequent greater public recognition and legitimation of homonormative relationships, however, have brought the potential, and, to some extent the requirement, for alternative approaches. Homonormative family forms, particularly in localities where such families are relatively numerous, can be incorporated into the curriculum and practices of schools in the same way as heteronormative families are, thereby rendering them analogously invisible. Thus sex and relationship education, instead of focusing on heterosexual marriage and longstanding committed relationships, might involve discussion of marriage and committed relationships more generally. While this inclusion is welcome on many levels, it both reinforces the disciplinary results of homonormativity, and has several effects in terms of visibility and invisibility.

First, it maintains the invisibility of groups of parents who do not fall into heteronormative categories but who at the same time do not stand out in other ways during their contacts with schools. These parents would in any case have to declare themselves to schools in order to be seen, but it is arguable that, with the decreased visibility of homonormative parents, this will become harder. Single LGBTQI+ parents, for example, are likely to be treated as if they were straight, and their particular experiences, and those of their children, ignored. In order to make themselves and their families visible, these parents have explicitly to come out to schools, as their sexual orientation cannot easily be inferred from the presence of, for example, two people of the same gender at parents' evenings. Similarly, if a single lesbian and a gay man co-parent, even if not living together, they will appear to their children's schools as a straight couple (or former couple), unless they consciously take steps to explain their parenting situation. Trans men, unless their transition has taken place while their children are at (the same) school, or unless they temporarily become the highly transgressive (and unusual) figure of the pregnant man (Riggs, 2013), are also likely to be completely invisible, particularly if they are continuously parenting with the same partner (Hines, 2006). Such families may therefore experience a decrease in visibility as they move from having, for example, a lesbian couple as parents to one that appears to involve normative heterosexual parenting (McGuire, Kuvalanka, Catalpa, & Toomey, 2016). This decreased visibility may or may not be beneficial to the children of what remains an unusual family arrangement.

At the same time, however, the (admittedly still rare) incorporation of homonormative families into mainstream aspects of school policies and curricula makes those people who have non-homonormative bodies, presentations and family forms potentially far more visible, because even more in the minority. In some cases this leaves them with the need to make decisions about how open they wish to be with schools and other parents; in others it gives them a forced visibility that may become problematic. Those for whom there is less choice may include women of trans history, who, because it is harder to transition to a physical form that looks unproblematically and convincingly cisgender female, may find they have to be at least partially out to teachers and other parents, or to take great care over their self-presentation when visiting their children's schools. Similarly, those people presenting as genderqueer or non-binary will also be highly visible, and may find that (correct or incorrect) assumptions are made about their sexual orientation as a result of this. Those for whom decisions have to be made about visibility (and remade as their children get older) include those with family structures that do not fit single-parent or two-parent expectations. For example, gay men (and gay couples) co-parenting with lesbian couples may have to be quite explicit with schools about their relationship to the children and their right, for example, to school information. This situation is even more complicated for those parents involved with alternative family structures, such as polyamory, which may involve both same-sex and heterosexual partnerships. These parents will have to decide whether (and when) to be upfront with schools about the relationships between the adults involved, their children and who is primarily responsible for parenting (Pallotta-Chiarolli, 2010). It remains unlikely that these non-hetero- or homonormative ways of constructing families will become incorporated either into school policies or into the curriculum even to the extent to which homonormative forms have been.

Previous research suggests that families deal with questions about visibility and invisibility in a variety of ways. These, however, are constrained by several factors, including social class and the family form involved, and there are also questions about to whom one is, or might want to be, visible or invisible. Taylor (2009) points out that for many parents the choice about whether to be out to schools or to other families is in effect forced on them by their children talking about family life, and others had been outed by former partners post-separation. Many of Taylor's respondents kept a deliberately low profile at the school gates, coming out at the 'right' time (for example, after important examinations were over). Others were deliberately out to their children's schools as a precaution against bullying. Most parents in Taylor's sample felt that it was dangerous and potentially damaging to tell lies to maintain the boundary between home and school, as these could too easily go wrong, and would mean that children could not bring friends home. However, the ways in which they dealt with the home/school boundary varied by social class, with middle-class parents seeking to minimize risks to their children, while working-class parents, by contrast, sought to toughen them up so that they could deal with any problems.

Pallotta-Chiarolli (2010) argues that polyamorous families adopt one of three visibility/invisibility strategies with respect to schools: passing, bordering and polluting. Parents using passing as a strategy kept their family structures closeted, choosing two adults from a group relationship to act as the parents in public situations, or using terms such as 'step-mum' to name some of the partners, implying an amicable post-divorce heterosexual setup. This strategy could be relatively easy to carry out, given their outward similarity to heteronormative monogamous families, and schools were found not to ask questions as long as the children were doing fine. This did have the disadvantage, however, that children would either have not to know about their parents' sexual arrangements, or would have themselves to be discreet or secret, and parents varied in their beliefs about which of these was least problematic. Pallotta-Chiarolli notes that children of bisexual or polyamorous parents could find it difficult to connect the worlds of home and school, as school imposes silence about such relationships. In the US, she reports, some families resorted to home education to avoid scrutiny, though there was some concern that this might make one more visible by drawing attention to difference.

Parents using bordering as a strategy were neither fully open nor fully closeted, neither lying about nor broadcasting their family structure. While the children would know about their parents' relationships, there might be discussions about what were private and what public matters, with strong boundaries between the two. Families taking a polluting strategy deliberately set out to be 'out and proud' about their family structures. They were aware that schools saw them as problematic and their children as contaminating, but were nevertheless highly public about their situation, making strong challenges, including resorting to law, if their children were harassed. In this way, they explicitly called into question both heteronormative and homonormative assumptions, presenting themselves and their families in positive terms as socially and sexually transgressive, embracing and encouraging their visibility. At the same time, however, they undercut and softened this polluting strategy, by seeking to present themselves as committed and involved parents, volunteering at schools, always attending parent-teacher meetings and becoming involved in school governance (Ryan-Flood, 2009), thereby attempting to reinsert themselves into the school body politic, resisting the exclusion resulting from their refusal to embrace the disciplinary forces of hetero- and homonormativity. Pallotta-Chiarolli (2010) describes this as 'hypernormalization' (214) and notes that it could cause pressure on the children also to perform perfectly and successfully at all times, in order to forestall criticism. Taylor (2009), argues, however, that this 'good parent' presentation is only open to some families, as it is strongly socially classed, and that it is mainly middle-class parents who are active in schools. She suggests that these parents are more confident in dealing with teachers, and consider their differences from the norm as benefitting other children. Middle-class parents were also in a stronger position, compared to working-class families to find 'good' schools where they would be accepted, to move to recognizably lesbian/gay areas where their child would not be the only one with LGBTQI+ parents, or even to send their children to private schools, where, as parents, they might have more influence. Nevertheless, even in 'good' places, the parents in Taylor's (2009) study were sometimes subject to microaggressions (Kosciw & Diaz, 2008), such as not being greeted or people being awkward around them. Some of Taylor's respondents also felt that what was seen by schools as inclusion of their families was merely tokenistic, such as buying books with lesbian/gay themes rather than full inclusion in the curriculum.

It is also important to be aware that visibility and invisibility are relative terms, and the question of who is visible or invisible to whom needs to be considered. Parents' sexualities may be visible to a school in a minimal way, in that all parents are recorded as such on official information, but this may go no further, so that, for example, class teachers may not be aware of the family structure, particularly if only one parent (or maybe two, in the case, for example, of two lesbians co-parenting with a gay male couple) attends parent-teacher meetings, or if one of the parents is trans. In these cases, while the family may be visible to at least some parts of the school, it may remain invisible to many if not all of the other parents. Visibility to the children's classmates and friends may also vary according to age and the closeness of the friendship, with children regulating how much they are out to their peers. In addition, as discussed earlier, single parents may not be visible at all as LGBTQI+, nor may gay men co-parenting with lesbians if the children live mainly or entirely with the latter.

The increased incorporation of homonormative family structures into civil society, and therefore schools, therefore makes these families both more socially incorporated and more invisible. Homonormative families, while still in the minority, are sufficiently part of the everyday social world, at least in some localities, that they have become part of the taken-for-granted, alongside those parented by straight couples. This is likely to have some positive results in that neither parents nor children will be treated as unusual, both parents will be included in school meetings, groups and events, and children are less likely to be bullied. These families may even feature, alongside straight families, in sex and relationship education as stable relationships which may involve marriage (DePalma & Atkinson, 2009). However, this incorporation into mainstream society may come at a price, even beyond the constraints of co-option into the disciplinary regulation of homonormativity. For example, there remain very few children's books that feature non-heterosexual couples, and decreasing visibility, through incorporation of homonormative families into the heterosexually based social contract, may actually make it less likely that schools will take steps to remedy this. Meanwhile, those parents who have not, for one reason or another, adopted homonormative relationship forms have been rendered more visible, and more challenging to schools. How parents and families deal with these dilemmas, and how schools respond, is the focus of the remainder of this book.

References

Ashford, C. (2011). (Homo)normative legal discourses and the queer challenge. *Durham Law Review*, 1(1), 77–97.

Atkinson, E., & DePalma, R. (2008). Imagining the homonormative: Performative subversion in education for social justice. *British Journal of Sociology of Education*, 29(1), 25–35.

Baxter, J. (2000). The joys and justice of housework. *Sociology*, 34(4), 609–631.

Bianchi, S. M., Sayer, L. C., Milkie, M. A., & Robinson, J. P. (2012). Housework: Who did, does or will do it, and how much does it matter? *Social Forces*, 91(1), 55–63.

Biblarz, T. J., & Savci, E. (2010). Lesbian, gay, bisexual and transgender famiklies. *Journal of Marriage and Family*, 72, 480–497.

Bigner, J. J. (1999). Raising our sons: Gay men as fathers. *Gay and Lesbian Social Services*, 10(1), 61–77.

Brown, G. (2012). Homonormativity: A metropolitan concept that denigrates "ordinary" gay lives. *Journal of Homosexuality*, 59, 1065–1072.

Browne, K. (2011). "By partner we mean . . .": Alternative geographies of gay marriage. *Sexualities*, 14(1), 100–122.

Burman, E. (1994). *Deconstructing developmental psychology*. London: Routledge.

Burman, E. (1995). "What is it?" Masculinity and femininity in cultural representations of childhood. In S. Wilkinson & C. Kitzinger (Eds.), *Feminism and discourse* (pp. 49–67). London: Sage.

Butler, J. (1990). *Gender trouble: Feminism and the subversion of identity*. London: Routledge.

Carriero, R. (2011). Perceived fairness and satisfaction with the division of housework among dual-earner couples in Italy. *Marriage and Family Review*, 47(7), 436–454.

Casper, V., Schultz, S., & Wickens, E. (1992). Lesbian and gay parents and the schools. *Teachers College Record*, 94(1), 109–137.

Clarke, V. (2008). From outsiders to motherhood to reinventing the family: Constructions of lesbian parenting in the psychological literature—1886–2006. *Women's Studies International Forum, 31*, 118–128.

Connell, R. (2011). *Confronting equality: Gender, knowledge and global change*. Cambridge: Polity Press.

Connolly, P. (2004). *Boys and schooling in the early years*. London: RoutledgeFalmer.

Croce, M. (2015). Homonormative dynamics and the subversion of culture. *European Journal of Social Theory, 18*(1), 3–20.

Dalton, S. E., & Belby, D. D. (2000). "That's our kind of constellation". Lesbian mothers negotiate institutionalized understandings of gender within the family. *Gender and Society, 14*(1), 36–61.

DePalma, R., & Atkinson, E. (2009). Putting queer into practice: Problems and possibilities In R. DePalma & E. Atkinson (Eds.), *Interrogating heteronormativity in schools* (pp. 1–16). Stoke on Trent: Trentham Books.

Duggan, L. (2002). The new homonormativity: The sexual politics of neoliberalism. In R. Castronovo & D. D. Nelson (Eds.), *Materialising democracy: Towards a revitalised cultural politics* (pp. 175–194). Durham and London: Duke University Press.

Dunne, G. A. (1997). *Lesbian lifestyles: Women's work and the politics of sexuality*. Basingstoke: Macmillan.

Farrr, R. H., Tasker, F., & Goldberg, A. E. (2017). Theory in highly cited studies of sexual minority parent families: Variations and implications. *Journal of Homosexuality, 64*(9), 1143–1179.

Foucault, M. (1978). *The history of sexuality volume one* (Trans. R. Hurley). London: Penguin.

Gager, C. T., & Hohmann-Marriott, B. (2006). Distributive justice in the household. *Marriage and Family Review, 40*(2–3), 5–42.

Garwood, E. (2016). Reproducing the homonormative family: Neoliberalism, queer theory and same-sex reproductive law. *Journal of International Women's Studies, 17*(2), 5–17.

Giddens, A. (1992). *The transformation of intimacy*. Cambridge: Polity Press.

Hequembourg, A. L., & Farrell, M. P. (1999). Lesbian motherhood: Negotiating marginal-mainstream identities. *Gender and Society, 13*(4), 540–557.

Hicks, S. (2013). Lesbian, gay, bisexual and transgender parents and the question of gender. In A. E. Goldberg & K. R. Allen (Eds.), *LGBT-parent families: Innovations in research and implications for practice*. New York: Springer.

Hines, S. (2006). Intimate transitions: Transgender practices of partnering and parenting. *Sociology, 40*(2), 353–371.

Hochschild, A. R. (1989). *The second shift*. New York: Avon Books.

Johnston, D. D., & Swanson, D. H. (2003). Invisible mothers: A content analysis of motherhood ideologies and myths in magazines. *Sex Roles, 49*(1/2), 21–33.

Kosciw, J., & Diaz, E. M. (2008). *Involved, invisible, ignored: The experiences of lesbian, gay, bisexual and transgender parents and their children in our nation's schools*. New York: Gay, Lesbian and Straight Education Network.

Lachance-Grzela, M., & Bouchard, G. (2010). Why do women do the lion's share of housework? *Sex Roles, 63*, 767–780.

Legerski, E. M., & Cornwall, M. (2010). Working-class job loss, gender, and the negotiation of household labor. *Gender and Society, 24*(4), 447–474.

Malins, P. (2016). How inclusive is "inclusive education" in the Ontario elementary classroom?: Teachers talk about addressing diverse gender and sexual identities. *Teaching and Teacher Education, 54*, 128–138.

Marshall, H. (1991). The social construction of motherhood: An analysis of childcare and parenting manuals. In A. Phoenix, A. Woollett, & E. Lloyd (Eds.), *Motherhood: Meanings, practices and ideologies* (pp. 66–85). London: Sage.

Martino, W., & Cumming-Potvin, W. (2011). "They didn't have *out there* gay parents—They just looked like *normal* regular parents: Investigating teachers' approaches to addressing same-sex parenting and non-normative sexuality. *Curriculum Inquiry, 41*(4), 480–501.

McDonald, T., Noel-Weiss, J., Walks, M., Biener, M., & Kibbe, A. (2016). Transmasculine individuals' experiences with lactation, chestfeeding and gender identity: A qualitative study. *BMC Pregnancy and Childbirth, 16*, 106.

McGuire, J. K., Kuvalanka, K. A., Catalpa, J. M., & Toomey, R. B. (2016). Transfamily theory: How the presence of trans* feily members informs gender development in families. *Journal of Family Theory and Review, 8*, 60–73.

Moore, S. D. (1998). The pregnant man—An oxymoron? *Journal of Gender Studies, 7*(3), 319–328.

Neary, A. (2016). Civil partnership and marriage: LGBT-Q political pragmatism and the normalisation imperative. *Sexualities, 19*(7), 757–779.

Office for National Statistics. (2016). *Statistical bulletin: Families and households in the UK 2016*. London. Retrieved from www.ons.gov.uk/people populationandcommunity/birthsdeathsandmarriages/families/bulletins/familiesandhouseholds/2016

Paechter, C. (2004). "Mens sana in corpore sano": Cartesian dualism and the marginalisation of sex education. *Discourse, 25*(3), 309–320.

Paechter, C. (2006). Gender, power and curriculum: An inevitable interconnection. In A. Moore (Ed.), *Schooling, society and curriculum* (pp. 75–86). London: Routledge.

Paechter, C. (2007). *Being boys, being girls: Learning masculinities and femininities*. Maidenhead, Berks: Open University Press.

Paechter, C., & Head, J. O. (1996). Gender, identity, status and the body: Life in a marginal subject. *Gender and Education, 8*(1), 21–30.

Pallotta-Chiarolli. (2010). *Border sexualities, border families in schools*. Plymouth: Rowman and Littlefield.

Patterson, C. J. (1992). Children of lesbian and gay parents. *Child Development, 63*, 1025–1042.

Platt, L. F., & Bolland, K. S. (2017). Relationship partners of transgender individuals: A qualitative exploration. *Journal of Social and Personal Relationships*, online advance publication.

Rawls, J. (1972). *A theory of justice*. Oxford: Oxford University Press.

Reay, D. (1998). *Class work: Mothers' involvement in their children's primary schooling*. London: UCL Press.

Renold, E. (2005). *Girls, boys and junior sexualities: Exploring children's gender and sexual relations in the primary school*. London: Routledge.

Renold, E. (2006). "They won't let us play . . . unless you're going out with one of them": Girls, boys and Butler's "heterosexual matrix" in the primary years'. *British Journal of Sociology of Education, 27*(4), 489–509.

Repo, J. (2016). *The biopolitics of gender*. Oxford: Oxford University Press.

Richardson, D. (2004). Locating sexualities: From here to normality. *Sexualities*, 7(4), 391–411.

Riggs, D. W. (2013). Transgender men's self-presentations of bearing children post-transition. In F. J. Green & M. Friedman (Eds.), *Chasing rainbows: Exploring gender fluid parenting*. Bradford, ON: Demeter Press.

Romans, P. (1992). Daring to pretend? Motherhood and lesbianism. In K. Plummer (Ed.), *Modern homosexualities: Fragments of lesbian and gay experience* (pp. 98–107). London: Routledge.

Ross, H., & Taylor, H. (1989). Do boys prefer daddy or his physical style of play? *Sex Roles*, 20(1/2), 23–33.

Ryan-Flood, R. (2009). *Lesbian motherhood: Gender, families and sexual citizenship*. Basingstoke, Hants: Palgrave Macmillan.

Santos, A. C. (2013). Are we there yet? Queer sexual encounters, legal recognition and homonormativity. *Journal of Gender Studies*, 22(1), 54–64.

Sifris, A. (2014). Gay and lesbian parenting: The legislative response. In A. I. o. F. Studies (Ed.), *Families, policy and the law*. Melbourne: Australian Institute of Family Studies.

Smart, C. (1996). Deconstructing motherhood. In E. B. Silva (Ed.), *Good enough mothering? Feminist perspectives on lone motherhood* (pp. 37–57). London: Routledge.

Stacey, J. (2006). Gay parenthood and the decline of parenting as we knew it. *Sexualities*, 9(1), 27–55.

Stryker, S. (2008). Transgender history, homonormativity and disciplinarity. *Radical History Review*, 100(Winter), 145–157.

Tasker, F. L., & Golombok, S. (1997). *Growing up in a lesbian family: Effects on child development*. New York: The Guildford Press.

Taylor, N. (2012). U.S. children's picture books and the homonormative subject. *Journal Of LGBT Youth*, 9, 136–152.

Taylor, S., Bennett, F., & Sung, S. (2010). *Unequal but "fair"? Housework and child care in a sample of low- to moderate- income British couples*. Oxford, Department of Social Policy and Social Work, University of Oxford.

Taylor, Y. (2009). *Lesbian and gay parenting: Securing social and educational capital*. Basingstoke, Hants: Palgrave Macmillan.

van Hooff, J. (2011). Rationalising inequality: Heterosexual couples' explorations and justifications for the division of housework along traditionally gendered lines. *Journal of Gender Studies*, 20(1), 19–30.

Weeks, J. (2007). *The world we have won*. London: Routledge.

Wittig, M. (1980/1992). The straight mind. In M. Wittig (Ed.), *The straight mind and other essays* (pp. 21–32). Boston, MA: Beacon Press.

Wittig, M. (1989/1992). On the social contract. In M. Wittig (Ed.), *The straight mind and other essays* (pp. 33–45). Boston, MA: Beacon Press.

3 Media Representations of LGBTQI+ Parented Families

> *In my first year at university an article appeared in one of the Sunday supplements about children with lesbian parents. Several children were interviewed and were described as 'refreshingly normal' by the reporter. I'm not sure how I would feel about this description today, but at the time I was very excited. It was only ten years since legalisation of homosexual sex in the UK, and I knew that there had been fears that my mother and her partner would 'corrupt' me into being a lesbian myself. In that context, seeing lesbians' children, young people like myself, portrayed in lovely photographs with a supportive text, was an unexpected positive visibility at a time when we were barely acknowledged to exist.*
>
> Carrie

In this chapter we discuss some of the media context relating to LGBTQI+ parents in the UK. We wanted to find out where people might get their ideas about what LGBTQI+ parents and their families are like, especially if they do not personally know anyone living in a LGBTQI+ parented family. McInroy and Craig (2015: 607) note that a 2010 study by the anti-prejudice campaigning group Trans Media Watch found that many trans people 'felt media had informed negative reactions they experienced from family and friends'. They also reported instances of participants 'being called sex workers or mentally ill, which they felt stemmed from media the perpetrators had consumed'.

Previous researchers have found that school students in the UK tend to refer to media representations when they are asked to discuss LGBTQI+ issues (Robinson, 2010). McInroy and Craig (2015: 608) note that, in which in relation to transgender people, 'media depictions consumed may include both offline and online media as well as both fictional characters and real people'. Our concern to unpick how the media may influence schools' perceptions of LGBTQI+ parented families led us to analyze a selection of media representations of LGBTQI+ parents.

We start this chapter with an overview of the media context and the ways in which it influences and is influenced by policy. We then outline the themes arising from a media survey of UK and Irish newspapers, using the ProQuest Newsstand database to sample four weeks evenly spaced between September 2014 and August 2015, and NVivo to code the themes arising from the survey. We add to this data from our focus groups and interviews with school students and teachers, in which we paid attention to any mention of LGBTQI+ parents, either fictional or non-fictional, discussed in the media. This analysis explores where children and young people get their ideas about famous LGBTQI+ parents, and the differences between what children know about LGBTQI+ people and their lives, and what teachers believe they are aware of and understand.

LGBTQI+ Parents in UK Media and Social Policy

In recent years, there has been upsurge in certain kinds of celebrity LGBTQI+ related material in popular media (McInroy & Craig, 2015). LGBTQI+ parents have not been omitted from this development. A nascent moment in the trend occurred when US transgender father Thomas Beatie was pictured as a 'pregnant man' in 'maternity pose' in *The Advocate* in 2008 (Norwood, 2013). Norwood argues that this represents a highly significant point in the development of an environment in which it became possible for others to come out as transgender. A key example one of these others is Bruce/Caitlyn Jenner, a well-known US Olympian and the stepparent of the famous US reality television star, Kim Kardashian. Jenner came out as transgender woman Caitlyn Jenner in *Vanity Fair* in 2015, seven years after Beatie's 'maternity pose'. In the UK print media, the parenting arrangements of the singer Elton John have also become a frequent narrative. Elton John is a parent, with his husband David Furnish, of two children by surrogacy (Andrews, 2013). Before discussing the media representations themselves, however, we will consider the socio-political and media conditions under which these and other LGBTQI+ parents have become well-known media figures.

Considering media representations of LGBTQI+ parents in the UK can give us an important insight into the social policy context. Rojek (2013: 134) warns of 'the under-estimation of the innovative consequences of celebrity influx upon political process'. In the UK, media and politics are intertwined in multiple ways. McNair (2011: 55) describes a traditional pattern of right-wing bias in British media, explaining that 'the overwhelming majority of the British press . . . have consistently supported the part of big business'. Most of the UK newspaper and television media is owned by a small group of very large companies, so it is unsurprising that their interests would be with a political stance that favours an approach to governance through the encouraging of market logics and the deregulation of business practices (McNair, 2011). A close alignment between media and government has been described as originating in the use of the media to support the 1987 HIV/AIDS awareness campaign.

McNair (2011: 48–49) quotes Greenaway et al. (1992) who explain that '(t)he media could be seen to legitimate government action, and then provide the channel through which policy was implemented'. Because every UK government since 2003 has been closely aligned with the UK popular media in this way (Couldry, 2010), the discussion in this chapter, although focused on media, also points strongly towards complexities inherent in the UK policy context, including education policy, for LGBTQI+ parents.

This policy context appears to favour a rights-based approach to transgender and lesbian and gay parents. This approach is underpinned by a heteronormative and binary model of gender. It does not necessarily include bisexual-, queer-, and multiple-parented families, as it has been bolted onto an understanding of parenting that assumes two and only two, binary parents. For example, the Registration of Births and Deaths (Amendment) (England and Wales) Regulations 2009 made it possible for lesbian parents to put both names on a baby's birth certificate, but did not include the possibility of further names. In consequence, a lesbian couple might conceive a child with a male friend, but will then have to choose which two names go on the birth certificate: the biological mother's and the biological father's names, or the biological mother's name and her female partner's name. Either way, one of the child's three parents would then be left without any immediate legal connection to the child, despite an obvious parenting relationship. However, whilst tied rather too tightly to a policy which assumes a maximum of two parents, some semblance of protection has been instituted, and in 2013 the Marriage (Same-Sex Couples) Act added further protections to what were termed 'same-sex' parents.

Building on the parenting and marriage rights legislation, the Equality Act 2010 (UK Government, 2010) brought together protections for people on the basis of gender, disability and race, and added age, disability, gender reassignment, pregnancy and maternity, race, religion or belief, sex and sexual orientation as protected characteristics. The Act also introduced a new public sector equality duty (Equality and Human Rights Commission, 2017). This requires publicly funded organizations such as schools to 'eliminate unlawful discrimination'; 'advance equality of opportunity'; and 'foster good relations between people who share a protected characteristic and people who do not share it'. Because of this duty, the schools inspection body, OFSTED (Office for Standards in Education, Children's Services and Skills), now looks at and promotes schools' implementation of these imperatives as part of their inspections.

The Equality Act 2010 and OFSTED's support materials point towards an approach which advances opportunity and fosters good relations. Most of the national policy directives, however, have focused on the more pathologizing relationship between gender identity and sexual orientation and 'bullying' (see Chapter 4). While the negative connotations of risk, danger and misery are not unproblematic, it is nevertheless the case that there has been political will in the UK to address LGBTQI+ rights in limited ways. In 2017, as trans people began to become a target for transphobic abuse (Samer, 2017) both in the streets and in the media (Gilligan, 2017), the Department for Education continued to promote inclusion, but stalled on producing adequate guidance for schools to welcome and support trans students.

However, as will be seen in the discussion of specific representations of LGBTQI+ parents, this seeming turn to a celebration of diversity is problematic, because it takes place within a media and, at times, policy context of vilification of people who have other forms of 'diversity', including ethnicity, socioeconomic class and disability. This is of note especially in the light of the similar positive treatment of 'race' and 'disability' in the Equality Act 2010 (UK Government, 2010), mentioned previously. However, as Caviedes (2015: 909) explains, race and ethnicity are narrated in the UK through a negative media view of immigration, partly on the grounds of national security, but mainly on the basis of 'concerns containing an economic dimension . . . so that if any menace is suggested, it is limited to threatened prosperity'. Similarly, Valentine and Harris (2014: 87) describe the ways in which working-class people on low wages or those on welfare benefits are denounced as 'lazy, undisciplined, criminal'. They demonstrate '(t)he importance of agency, self-management and personal responsibility in a meritocratic society in which poverty and disadvantage were implicitly regarded as individual failings', offering evidence that 'people receiving welfare benefits were blamed for their own social position'. People living with a disability or terminal illness are not exempt from vilification: even during the positive atmosphere of the London 2012 Paralympics, such groups were still being recast as 'scroungers' (Crow, 2014). Refugee and asylum-seeker, disability and job-seeker welfare benefits were concurrently eroded over the course of the centre-right UK Coalition government of 2010–2015 and the subsequent Conservative government.

In this context, the rights of lesbian, gay, transgender and sometimes bisexual people seem to stand alone with a status of special protection. They are even invoked against the rights of others: in July 2015 the Education Secretary Nicky Morgan suggested that Muslim children in schools who express homophobic views might be read as 'extremist' and therefore investigated under the 'Prevent' (Cabinet Office, Foreign and Commonwealth Office, Home Office, & Ministry of Justice, 2015) guidelines to schools for the prevention of terrorism (Her Majesty's Government, 2015). Puar (2013) calls this kind of privileging of co-opted pro-gay nationalism 'homonationalism'. The UK media did not miss the irony that Morgan had herself voted against same-sex marriage only a few months before, with one headline asking 'Is Nicky Morgan going to investigate herself for extremism?' (Dunt, 2015). These contradictions suggest an uneasy relationship with diversity, and raise the question: why are LGBTQI+ rights (albeit those which align to an idea of gender and relationships as binary, monogamous, and long-term) apparently so firmly on the UK political and media agendas, when other rights are not?

LGBTQI+ Parents as a Trope of Self-Actualization

Carter and Steiner (2004: 3) argue that 'as critical feminist media research has shown, the mainstream media have increasingly incorporated or co-opted [a] counter-hegemonic view, particularly when it has proven to be in their economic interest'. This reading is especially relevant to researching media representations with a focus on schools. We suggest that the apparent UK government policy and media's favouring of lesbian, gay and transgender rights over others may stem from the notion that certain kinds of transgender, lesbian and gay parents fit solidly within a late capitalist model, sometimes enfolded into what is described as a 'neoliberal' discourse, which promotes lifestyle choice and the self-made person-as-product. At first glance, the pursuance of rights and support for family structures which might appear to undermine a patriarchal model could be read as left-wing, radical and subversive. However, right-wing political discourses both in the UK and in the US tend to oppose social liberalism whilst increasingly favouring economic liberalism. This apparent contradiction results in a low level of financial regulation alongside high trust in market forces to solve social problems.

In the early 21st century, some theorists have suggested that the capitalist imperative appears to suffuse young people's identity work through a process of 'self-branding'. This identity work is often rebellious or counter-hegemonic in intent, and is informed by media coverage of celebrity lifestyles (Allen & Mendick, 2013; Couldry, 2010). Closely related is the identity work young people conduct through engagement with reality television, an archetypal performance of the 'project of self-actualization' (Allen & Mendick, 2012). Couldry (2010) identifies reality television as normalizing the notion that self-improvement is more important than caring for others. Some of the expensive medical processes often linked with celebrity LGBTQI+ people (for example, gender transition surgery, surrogacy and IVF) might also be viewed as archetypal 'self-improvement projects'.

Wacquant's (1995) notion of 'bodily capital' may be useful here. This idea lends itself to understanding the very queerness of LGBTQI+ people as specifically embodying the potential for the generation of economic capital. In this model, market logics, in the process of self-branding, become central to one's process of identity development (Couldry, 2010; Allen & Mendick, 2012). In other words, the surgical and clinical interventions which LGBTQI+ parents sometimes need (or choose) can generate financial income. Furthermore, whilst some celebrity LGBTQI+

parents are represented as making money out of their LGBTQI+ status, they are, additionally, important economic actors in that they are often required to spend money on creating their families. This might, for example, involve spending thousands of pounds on IVF treatment or an expensive surrogacy procedure.

Caitlyn Jenner's transition represents a key example of queer bodily capital. Jenner was originally a bit-part actor in the Kardashian reality television enterprise. She was the second husband of the Kardashian matriarch; most of the show was dedicated to the glamour model Kim Kardashian and her sisters. Caitlyn Jenner's gender transition, however, seemed to generate a parallel career transition, as she became star of her own reality television show. In a discussion of Jenner's transition, *Vanity Fair* wondered whether 'it's all just fodder for a "docu-series"', asking, '[c]an you hear the thunder of a Kardashian spin-off?' (Bissinger, 2015). In 2015, the transgender self-actualization trope was already in circulation: several of the children and young people we interviewed in schools in that year had learned the popular media's transgender narrative of 'becoming the person I always wanted to be' through viewing documentaries on YouTube. One focus group of primary-aged children in a multicultural urban setting discussed it with their teacher:

VICTOR (11): I don't think I should be watching this, but on *Keeping Up with the Kardashians*, I realized, I watched that Bruce Jenner, he's turned into Caitlyn Jenner, so he's transgender, and now he's living as a girl, so yeah.
KIRSTIN (teacher): has anybody else seen that, on TV?
SOLLY (9, laughing at the idea that anyone might have missed the revelations): Well, it's all over the news and everything!
KIRSTIN: So—do you understand?
SOLLY: Yes that people should just accept who they are and they can make life changes if they want to . . .
KIRSTIN: Do you think that's been happening to her to—well Bruce that's now Caitlyn?
VICTOR: Well some people accept her like, her family accepts her and they're saying, it may not be, like, right, but we still need to encourage her to be who she wants.
SOLLY: Like why would you care about somebody's opinion if it's someone you barely know . . . I would even think, like, I don't know you, so I don't care.

Caitlyn Jenner's transition here is recognized by the children as a process of identity development. This process can be read as a self-actualizing narrative (Allen & Mendick, 2012): Victor says 'she can be who she wants'. Using her considerable wealth, she has, as Victor explains just *'turned into* Caitlyn Jenner', like magic. She can 'make life changes' if she wants to, according to Solly. Possibly influenced by some haziness around the actual mechanics of transition, the children involved in these focus groups appear to read this self-branding process as a genuinely available possibility. Their belief may be influenced by the ubiquity of market logics (Couldry, 2010): if someone wants to buy a new feminized face and breasts, then someone will be willing to sell them. Caitlyn Jenner fits solidly within a capitalist agenda. She is white and rich, and does not challenge socioeconomic hierarchies. In her expensive transition, she has performed the ultimate act of self-actualization. The children in the focus groups appeared to be influenced by the fact that media representations of rich white people tend to be positive, regardless of gender identity or sexual orientation.

We argue, then, that our data were collected within a context of the marketization of a nationalistic notion of 'equality' at the beginning of the 21st century (Littler, 2013; Puar, 2013). This suggests that self-actualizing stories of LGBTQI+ parenting would be key themes arising in the UK media of the time.

Newspaper Media Representations of LGBTQI+ Parents

To investigate some newspaper media representations (all available online) of LGBTQI+ parents in the UK, we conducted a ProQuest Newsstand search of four evenly spaced weeks over a year. This looked for mention of LGBTQI+ parents across both national and local newspapers, during the first weeks of December 2014, March 2015, June 2015 and September 2015. Search terms used are outlined in Table 3.1.

Table 3.1 Search terms used and results obtained from newspaper survey

Search terms	Lesbian AND mother OR mum Lesbian parents	Gay AND father OR dad Gay parents	Bisexual AND parents Bisexual AND mum OR mother Bisexual AND dad OR father	Transgender AND parents Transgender AND mum OR mother Transgender AND dad OR father	'LGBT parents' 'Queer parents' Polyamorous AND parents 'Intersex parent' OR 'Intersex parents'
Total number of articles found in all four sample weeks (N = 144)	74	42	23	5	0

Our search delivered a sample of 144 newspaper articles from across the news media in the UK and Ireland. Within the sample, we found a series of themes which ran through each of the four weeks, and which reveal patterns in the UK newspaper media's representation of LGBTQI+ parented families. One striking tendency was that, except in the case of those who were conspicuously wealthy and privileged, news reports only appeared to acknowledge lesbian mothers in shocking stories of child abuse and death. A very high socioeconomic status tended to protect some people (mainly gay and bisexual men) from censure. News reports consistently passed negative moral judgement on LGBTQI+ parents on average or low incomes, despite also reporting a set of often benign or positive facts. When reporters were not censuring LGBTQI+ parents directly, they were claiming that they were too old to understand, implying that LGBTQI+ families are an entirely new phenomenon of which only the young would be aware. Reports of LGBTQI+ parented families also often tended towards the spectacle or carnivalesque. These themes are discussed in more detail below.

Witchcraft, Hypnosis and Deception: The Evil Lesbian Lover

The sample collected revealed a trend in stories about lesbian mothers: those living on an ordinary income were acknowledged, but only in shocking news stories of children's deaths. Within the four-week sample, there were three separate stories relating to the violent abuse and death of children at the hands of their mothers. The stories all demonstrate the media's problem with allowing a woman to be both a 'lesbian' and what is usually described as a 'mum' (as opposed to a mother). In all three cases, the biological parent was described as a 'mum' whilst the non-biological parent was a 'lesbian' or a 'lover', or often 'a lesbian lover'. In September 2015 there was a story about two Scottish women who murdered their son entitled 'Mum and her lesbian partner deny killing two-year-old son and blaming death on boy, 7' (Riley, 2015). Another story, about a woman previously convicted with her male partner and his brother, of causing the death of her 17-month-old son in a notorious case of abuse and neglect (her child was named 'Baby P' by the courts, and this pseudonym became popularly recognized shorthand for the story), was entitled 'Baby P mum: I'll live with lesbian torturer: evil pair get close while locked up in same jail' (Dorman, 2015). In these stories, the partner of the biological mother is represented as a nefarious lesbian: Dorman's story features a 'lesbian torturer'. In a third story about a child's death (Robinson & Greenwood, 2015) the female partner of the biological mother is described as 'sadistic'. Biological mothers in these stories are not acknowledged as gay or bisexual, but as a 'mum'; even a 'perfect mum' (Robinson & Greenwood, 2015). The woman partners of the biological mothers in these news stories were also sometimes metaphorically cast as witches. The biological mothers were described as being placed under a spell or fantasy, hypnotized or deceived by their female partners. It is almost as if a mother cannot be a lesbian unless she has somehow been tricked into it. For example, one article is headed 'The lesbian lover who brainwashed the 'perfect mum' into killing her daughter: Sadistic neighbour span a web of fantasy online ending in eight-year-old's death' (Robinson & Greenwood, 2015). In it, the 'lover' was described as having 'groomed' the mother next door for sex and then persuaded her to beat and kill her daughter. The writers report a 'source' stating 'their actions were utterly inhuman . . . it was as if she was bewitched.' The media's framing of women in this way could be understood as the result of an inability to conceive of a woman as both a 'sexual being' and a 'good mother' (see Chapter 2).

Even wealthy and influential mothers who were associated with same-sex relationships could be tarnished by this. The popular bisexual singer Madonna featured strongly in the December 2014 sample. In the Express, Nicholas (2014) describes her in a review of her show in Abu Dhabi:

> Despite having her then 12-year old son Rocco on stage with her . . . she dropped the F-word from the off. . . . Some have applauded her for championing nudity as a middle-aged woman. For others the irony is that it has all become boringly predictable behaviour from the mother of four . . . Then again, she wouldn't be Madonna if she didn't at least try to raise eyebrows. It has been her brand for 30 years. There have been illicit liaisons with famous men . . . lesbian love affairs and admissions of getting high on drugs.

Madonna is described here as boring despite her 'eyebrow raising' behaviour. Her 'lesbian' affairs are listed alongside 'illicit liaisons' and drug taking as if sex with another woman is equally deceitful or illegal. All of these are presented in conjunction with her status as a mother, something her name and her curated image may deliberately or consciously invite, albeit not in these scornful tones.

Acceptable LGBTQI+ Parents: Wealth, Consumer Power and Aristocracy

Madonna's wealth did not protect her from criticism in the story described above. This does, however, seem to be the case for men. There were several stories in the sample which admiringly described evidence of the economic, social and cultural capital possessed by some gay or bisexual men. In these cases, gay parents were generally represented positively. Rich gay men's surrogacy arrangements were explained as further evidence of their consumer power. For example, a story appeared in the *Express* in June 2015 about 'multimillionaire entrepreneur' Ivan Massow, an out gay rights campaigner tipped at the time as the next Mayor of London (Helliker, 2015). Massow had a surrogacy arrangement with a lesbian couple who had split up during the pregnancy, and the pregnant woman had moved into Massow's apartment. Helliker explains,

> Brighton-born Ivan survived a difficult childhood, is a recovering alcoholic and twice attempted suicide. *But* he went on to make a fortune through financial services. . . . He has a number of celebrity friends including Joan Collins, who has already volunteered to be a godmother.
>
> [our emphasis]

That 'but' is significant. The 'fortune' and the 'celebrity' status make up for the alcoholism and the suicide attempts; Massow is recognized as a legitimate parent. A 'friend' quoted in the article adds:

> He has forged a great relationship with the mother . . . (h)e's just over the moon. He never dreamed he would become *a proper father* with his own child living with him.
>
> [our emphasis]

In the sample, there were also several obituaries of wealthy and/or aristocratic people who had both male and female lovers: in these articles, their wealth was described alongside their social lives. Bisexuality was often narrated as an accoutrement to such wealth. In an obituary of a hereditary aristocrat, Lord Beaulieu, Barker (2015) describes him as a known bisexual and

> a gentle-mannered aristocrat who put his stately home and interest in motoring to good use by establishing the National Motor Museum at Beaulieu, in Hampshire. He also became a leader in the promotion of country houses to the public, a chairman of English Heritage.

Lord Beaulieu had been imprisoned for 'unnatural acts' with two airmen before homosexuality was legalized in the UK in 1967. This, however, appears to have been a minor inconvenience: Barker reports,

> On his release from prison after eight months, Montagu resumed building up the family business. His success at attracting visitors to Palace House, part of the former Beaulieu Abbey, and its collection of cars was such that the numbers were at one time beaten only by the Tower of London.

As with Massow, the conspicuous wealth is a validating factor. Aristocracy and bisexuality tend to be accepted as a familiar combination. In

March, a film about the writer Vita Sackville-West came out, and following this, in June, there were several reviews of a memoir by her granddaughter Vanessa Nicholson. One review explains:

> Her background is certainly unusual, even by aristocratic standards. Her grandparents were the gardeners and writers Vita Sackville-West and Harold Nicolson, both of whom were gay, and her father was the homosexual art historian Ben Nicolson. Vanessa grew up in the shadow of her family's notoriety and success.
>
> (Field, 2015)

It is of note that the word 'gay' is often used where the subject of a story is a parent. The concept and identity of bisexuality can be subject to erasure where a person happens to have had sex with a person of the same sex, even if their marriage and status as parents suggest otherwise.

Acceptance by Family Members Is Often Questioned or Remarked Upon

Apart from those stories about the very wealthy, newspaper articles about gay parents often express a kind of moral judgement on how the narrative *should* be conveyed, despite the facts. The children of gay men, in particular, tend to be represented as being more positive about their parents than commentators expect. In one popular and frequently repeated story in the sample, the children of out gay rugby player Keegan Hirst were often treated as notable for their failure to have a negative reaction to their father's coming out. In an article in the *Express* entitled, 'Gay rugby league star Keegan Hirst's wife proud of his courage after first "wanting to kill him"', Hill (2015) portrays the children as a key catalyst in their parents' good relationship:

> Sara worried how her three children would react. She says: "I was with my seven-year-old and turned the TV on. Keegan was on screen and she said 'why's Daddy on the telly?'"
>
> "I could have lied, but I thought no. It's not a big dirty secret and I don't want my kids to grow up thinking it is. My youngest is only three, but I had to sit my daughter and 11-year-old son down and explain it. I told my daughter, 'Mummy and Daddy are getting divorced. Daddy might meet somebody new and it might be a boy or a girl'. Her attitude has been very grown up. I'm proud of her." It is their children who have helped her to emerge from her anger and be supportive of Keegan.

Another repeatedly reported news story in March and June 2015 consisted of commentary and analysis of a series of Irish parliamentary discussions about the upcoming law change that allowed same-sex marriage. Commentators were often quoted without criticism when they claimed that an 'ideal family' involves one father and one mother. One newspaper investigation (Byrne, 2015) argued that one radio channel had shown considerable bias:

> The three main groups leading the campaign against gay marriage are closely linked and share key personnel, an Irish Mail on Sunday investigation has found.
> The same six representatives from the three organisations have been given hours of airtime on RTE [a popular Irish radio channel] and elsewhere to argue the case against same-sex marriage. Three of them are from the same family.
> The three groups are the Iona Institute, Catholic Comment and Mothers And Fathers Matter.
>
> (MAFM)

Despite the comparatively high number of articles about this topic during the sample weeks, just one reported a child's own words. In it, the daughter of two gay fathers was interviewed for an article entitled 'My gay dads are great, says Safia, 15' (Ring, 2015). The article states:

> Colm O'Gorman's daughter, Safia, gets upset and very angry when she hears people talk about how her family is not "ideal".
> The teenager wants people to know that her dads—two married gay men—are like any other good parents.
> "They want me to be happy; they're strict, but only because they want the best for me. But, most importantly, they really, really love me," she wrote.

The children of LGBTQI+ parents mentioned in the media seem to be far more accepting than the adult reporters and judges describing and commenting on their family lives. By contrast, negative views of LGBTQI+ parents were often introduced anonymously, with terms such as 'calls for' or 'commentators say'. In one story entitled 'EXCLUSIVE—A mum, her son and THEIR baby: Mother reveals how she became a surrogate for gay supermarket worker who was desperate to become a father' (Duffin, 2015), the reporter manages to cast aspersions on the choices of everyone involved despite rather sensible comments from the people themselves. For example, she writes:

> Miles, now eight months old, is Mr Casson's biological son created by his sperm and an anonymous donor egg implanted into Mrs Casson's womb. In the eyes of the law, he is also Miles's brother.

Shrugging off the potential ethical and moral dilemmas posed by his actions, Mr Casson, 27, said last night: 'I understand that not everyone will agree with it, but they can have their opinions. I have a son and I am very happy.

To some extent, and in line with the media's favouring of economic success, Mr Casson's decisions are mitigated by his financial self-sufficiency. He explains, 'Regardless of sexuality, gender, as long as you can provide for the child, I don't see what the problem is. I paid for it myself, it's not taxpayers' money, I own my own home, I am going back to work.' The tabloid newspaper cannot therefore critique his choices on this basis. The writer instead resorts to quoting unnamed commentators, remarking 'but critics described the procedure as 'dubious' and called for urgent reforms to prevent abuses of fertility law' (Duffin, 2015). It is not made clear exactly who these critics are.

'Too old' to Cope with the Confusion: A Benign Silencing

Outside of the right-wing tabloids, when reporters and commentators are not being moral and ethical critics, they are 'confused'. In a media environment where stories about transgender people are becoming more frequent, there are some complaints that people just feel 'too old' to cope with these supposedly new ideas, identities and relationships. This amounts to a benign-looking practice of silencing and exclusion. For example, in an article in the *Mail on Sunday* entitled 'Changing sex is so brave, but you can't blame us oldies for being a bit baffled' (Johnson, 2015), the reporter claimed she was 'a little confused' when she

> tried to absorb the details of a court case last week headlined: 'Girl has gay dad, 2 lesbian mums and a transsexual stepdad'. It was about 'Alice', who was conceived with donor sperm from a homosexual male, and one of whose lesbian mothers became involved with a woman who was changing gender to male, who was seeking access to the little girl. It all made me want to wrap a wet towel around my head.

The article also comments on the Caitlyn Jenner case, complaining:

> As for Jenner, I don't think I'm narrow-minded. Trans Media Watch can come after me for saying this, but I'm just too OLD for someone choosing to change sex, then undergoing ten hours of facial feminisation surgery and then doing a cover shoot to show off her new boobs and boat race [face], to be an everyday occurrence, that's all.

In an another article, in *The Independent*, Edwards (2015) describes the way in which James Naughtie, a successful, well respected, senior member of the BBC Radio 4 news team, succumbed to this 'old and confused' narrative in his introduction to a story about Caitlyn Jenner. Edwards (2015) explains the scenario:

> Naughtie indulged those of his listeners who are getting on a bit by giving this introduction:
> "Now, this is complicated. He used to be called Bruce but he's now a woman. I realize some of you will never have heard of Kim Kardashian, let alone her stepfather, who was Bruce and is now a woman but, anyway, they are very well known on television."

Naughtie later apologized for calling Jenner 'he', but it was actually his jokey description of the situation as 'complicated' which more tellingly revealed his analysis of the situation.

Bizarre Freaks

This approach to discussing stories about LGBTQI+ parenthood implies, like the stories about children's 'surprising' acceptance discussed above, that living outside cisgender heteronormativity is a transitory and experimental phenomenon that older people cannot reasonably be expected to understand. In general, where the protagonists were not extremely rich, stories about LGBTQI+ parents found in the sample could be seen as representing a vicarious peep into an apparently freakish, sometimes sordid world. In one example drawn from the selection, the headline reads: 'Revealed: The bizarre family tree at the heart of an extraordinary court battle over one little girl—involving two lesbian mothers, a gay sperm donor and a transsexual lover now living with a man' (Allen, 2015). It describes how the child's transgender stepfather 'claims she called him 'daddy''. He had asked the court for contact, but was refused this by the court amid concern 'that he encouraged Alice to wear boys' clothes and told her to avoid playing with 'gender appropriate toys''. This article is typical in a use of language across the sample which appears to sexualize LGBTQI+ parents, particularly in using the word 'lover' to describe a non-biological parent.

As McInroy and Craig (2015:614) explain, 'representations have a direct impact on transgender people's lives as the perceptions and behavior of people they encounter are influenced by the media'. The ambiguity in current media treatment of transgender parents is significant in a context which allows for LGBTQI+ parent identities as long as they fit within a white, income-generating hetero- or homonormative framework. LGBTQI+ parents are treated relatively positively if they fit the basic model of economic generation: the nuclear family. Where celebrity LGBTQI+ parents were discussed positively in the media, they had all formed nuclear family units, with children planned as accoutrements to their already successful lives. There is plenty of analysis indicating the assimilation of queer families into homonormative nuclear family models resulting from recent advances in same-sex marriage legislation (Rodgers, 2010; West, 2014; Michaels, 2006; Sears, 2005; Cloud, 2001). This assimilation, together with LGBTQI+ parents' participation as consumers and generators of capital, gives a certain kind of LGBTQI+ parent institutional validity. The group of positively represented LGBTQI+ parents have also created their families in a way which indicates it was a feature of their projects of self-actualization. They are, therefore, adhering to the characteristics of successful self-actualizing celebrities identified by Allen and Mendick (2013). Reflecting our newspaper survey findings, white, wealthy, self-actualized and nuclear, the celebrity parents positively represented in the media are a particularly monocultural set of diversity icons.

Children, New Media and What Parents and Teachers Think They Know

We turn now to the question of where the school students we interviewed get their ideas about LGBTQI+ parents. The data collected in schools indicated that children and young people know far more about LGBTQI+ parents and particularly about transgender stories than their parents and teachers appear to believe that they know. For example, a Year 6 (age 10–11) focus group of children in an urban multicultural school discussed with Anna and their teacher what we might call 'YouTube pedagogy'. We started by asking about whether the children knew anyone at the school who had come out as lesbian, gay or transgender. Victor, whose family belongs to an African Christian Evangelist church, discussed his thoughts with his classmate Solly and their teacher, Kirstin:

VICTOR: It happened at lunchtime . . . everyone was starting to gossip about her, she just announced that she was a lesbian 'oh I'm a lesbian, I don't mind', so some people were like 'oh, I can't be your friend because you're lesbian' and she was like 'why do you hate me?' And some people were saying 'because it's wrong.' But technically [pause] it's not that wrong. Well it kind of is, cos God made you as you are, but you can like feel . . .
SOLLY: choose to be who you are
VICTOR: yeah. Because like sometimes your hormones are different because like, you might be a boy but you're born in a girl's body and you might be a girl but you're born in a boy's body

Victor was bringing his church's discourse into play here, but with Solly's help was framing his own ideas about the topic. The interviewer, Anna, decided to try and find out the other sources of Victor's ideas:

ANNA: Hm. It sounds like you've thought quite a lot about it and have quite a lot of information. Where do you get your ideas from?

VICTOR: um . . . I watch a lot of TV and YouTube and I just flick through everything. And I watched this one documentary about this girl that was living as a boy . . . when she was a bit young, she turned into a girl, because her parents encouraged her and I think that's a good thing, and now, she's living as a nice girl, and this other documentary about a girl that was living—well, a boy that was living as a girl, and now she is, or he is a boy, now.

The fact that Victor had been watching transgender people's stories on television and YouTube was not a surprise. We found that, in a context in which little is taught about LGBTQI+ people (see Chapter 4), many children and young people had been busily educating themselves using their internet-enabled phones and tablets. Anna mentioned this, thinking that perhaps their teacher Kirstin was looking a little worried. Kirstin responded:

Hmm, it might not be something that's talked about at home or at school so much, well, not in the past, so we all need to get more factual information so that we know what we're talking about . . . cos I think there's a lot of question marks.

Here Kirstin's cheeks coloured and she paused for a long time. Finally, she added slowly, thinking aloud:

it's very interesting to listen to this actually . . . sometimes we hear things in the classroom but we don't hear this in the classroom. And when you are in the playground we are not there . . . so these kind of conversations we sometimes don't hear about . . . and we think we know what's going on . . . but actually when it goes a little bit further there's other things that we find out about too which is good.

This conversation between Victor and Kirstin was one of many similar discussions we heard during the school focus groups. Each time, the children and young people spoke about things they had learned about LGBTQI+ people's experiences through YouTube and television, accessing the internet through mobile devices. Each time, it became apparent that the anxiety the teachers were feeling about addressing LGBTQI+ issues at school was rooted in a lack of familiarity with the subject matter, and that the students were frequently more familiar with the material than were the teachers.

If we need to challenge homophobia, transphobia and biphobia in schools, then it is important to know that teachers and school students get their ideas about what LGBTQI+ parents are like, if they don't know any personally, from multiple media sources: television; newspapers; YouTube; music videos; and film. Representations of LGBTQI+ parents in the media tend to be stereotypes, but positive ones as long as they align themselves with celebrity wealth and consumerist paradigms and do not challenge structural inequity: an easy start for a heteronormative world. However, those visible and positively represented are limited in their ethnic, socioeconomic and gender diversity. As Norwood (2013: 73) explains,

> Stone (1992) calls for transsexuals to cease attempts to pass as *either* male or female. By making the trans-body complicit with heteronormative notions of sex and gender, Stone argues the trans-identified person forecloses possibilities of polyvocality, and in effect commits violent erasures of subjectivity.
>
> Norwood (2013: 73)

Our findings confirm the valorization of these 'heteronormative notions of sex and gender' across the media landscape of LGBTQI+ parents.

In view of this, we suggest that schools wanting to teach about LGBTQI+ parents and their families could start with these 'acceptable' representations, but use them only as a starting point for a more nuanced, creative and meaningful discussion. Thomas Beatie's pregnant body 'forces us to see how sex is written, unwritten, and rewritten on the body, and incites confusion that creates a space for questions, leading us closer to a re-evaluation of sex and gender' (Norwood, 2013: 74). Nonnormative family forms can be a useful focus for this questioning and re-evaluation. Through this process, more empathic, inclusive institutions may be developed, leading to schools which demonstrate understanding about who LGBTQI+ parents and their families really are, and what they need.

References

Allen, K., & Mendick, H. (2012). Keeping it real? Social class, young people and authenticity in reality TV. *Sociology, 47*(3), 1–17.

Allen, K., & Mendick, H. (2013). Young people's uses of celebrity: Class, gender and "improper" celebrity. *Discourse, 34*(1), 77–93.

Allen, V. (2015, June 3). Revealed: The bizarre family tree at the heart of an extraordinary court battle over one little girl—Involving two lesbian mothers, a gay sperm donor and a transsexual lover now living with a man. *Daily Mail*. Retrieved January 25, 2016, from www.dailymail.co.uk/news/article-3109128/Modern-family-life-complicated-says-judge-case-involving-four-parents.html#ixzz3yXVrDoqO

Andrews, E. (2013, January 28). "You find new depths of love and experience pure joy": Sir Elton John and David Furnish proudly show off new baby son Elijah. *MailOnline*. Retrieved July 14, 2015, from www.dailymail.co.uk/tvshowbiz/article-2269318/Sir-Elton-John-David-Furnish-proudly-new-baby-son-Elijah.html

Barker, D. (2015, August 31). Lord Montague of Beaulieu. *The Guardian*. Retrieved January 8, 2016, from www.theguardian.com/uk-news/2015/aug/31/lord-montagu-of-beaulieu

Bissinger, B. (2015). Caitlyn Jenner: The full story. *Vanity Fair*. Retrieved July 14, 2015, from www.vanityfair.com/hollywood/2015/06/caitlyn-jenner-bruce-cover-annie-leibovitz

Byrne, N. (2015, March 1). How voices of anti gay marriage are linked: Massive airtime for three groups that share same handful of activists. *Mail on Sunday*.

Cabinet Office, Foreign and Commonwealth Office, Home Office, and Ministry of Justice (2015, May 8). 2010 to 2015 government policy: Counter-terrorism (policy paper). Retrieved July 14, 2015, from www.gov.uk/government/publications/2010-to-2015-government-policy-counter-terrorism/2010-to-2015-government-policy-counter-terrorism

Carter, C., & Steiner, L. (2004). Introduction to critical readings: Media and gender. In Carter, C., & Steiner, L. (Eds.), *Critical readings: Media and gender* (pp. 1–10). Berkshire, UK: OUP.

Caviedes, A. (2015). An emerging "European" news portrayal of immigration? *Journal of Ethnic and Migration Studies*, 41(6), 897–917.

Cloud, D. (2001). Queer theory and "family values": Capitalism's utopias of self-invention. *Transformation*, 2, 71–114.

Couldry, N. (2010). *Why voice matters: Culture and politics after neoliberalism*. Sage: London.

Crow, L. (2014). Scroungers and superhumans: Images of disability from the summer of 2012: A visual inquiry. *Journal of Visual Culture*, 13(2), 168–181.

Dorman, N. (2015, March 1). Baby P mum: I'll live with lesbian torturer: EVIL PAIR GET CLOSE WHILE LOCKED UP IN SAME JAIL. *Sunday Mirror*. Retrieved January 7, 2016, from http://search.proquest.com/uknews/docview/1658915479/DE47CD4289014B4FPQ/1?accountid=11149

Duffin, C. (2015, March 6). EXCLUSIVE—A mum, her son and THEIR baby: Mother reveals how she became a surrogate for gay supermarket worker who was desperate to become a father. *Daily Mail*. Retrieved January 25, 2016, from www.dailymail.co.uk/news/article-2983380/EXCLUSIVE-mum-son-baby-Mother-reveals-surrogate-gay-supermarket-worker-desperate-father.html#ixzz3yXs9hXCH

Dunt, I. (2015). Is Nicky Morgan going to investigate herself for extremism? *Politics.co.uk*. Retrieved July 14, 2015, from www.politics.co.uk/blogs/2015/06/30/is-nicky-morgan-going-to-investigate-herself-for-extremism

Edwards, R. D. (2015, June 7). At all costs, get the pronouns right: With celebrity transsexualism such big news, we'd better take the issue seriously. *The Independent*. Retrieved January 25, 2016, from www.independent.ie/opinion/independent-journalists/ruth-dudley-edwards/

Equality and Human Rights Commission. (2017). Public sector equality duties. Retrieved January 4, 2018, from www.equalityhumanrights.com/en/advice-and-guidance/public-sector-equality-duty

Field, M. (2015, June 2). Have you been good?: A memoir by Vanessa Nicolson—Book review: An affecting memoir of grief, loneliness and dysfunction. *Independent*. Retrieved January 7, 2016, from www.independent.co.uk/arts-entertainment/books/reviews/have-you-been-good-a-memoir-by-vanessa-nicolson-book-review-an-affecting-memoir-of-grief-loneliness-10292836.html

Gilligan, A. (2017, December 17). Action for Trans Health activists want free sex-change hormones for children. *The Times.* Retrieved December 19, 2017, from www.thetimes.co.uk/edition/news/action-for-trans-health-activists-want-free-sex-change-hormones-for-children-dhvv5c52v

Helliker, A. (2015, June 7). Ivan Massow moves in with lesbian mother. *Express.* Retrieved January 8, 2016, from www.express.co.uk/comment/columnists/adam-helliker/582786/Adam-Helliker-opinion-Ivan-Massow-baby-joy

Hill, P. (2015, September 7). Gay rugby league star Keegan Hirst's wife proud of his courage after first "wanting to kill him". *Express.* Retrieved January 8, 2015, from www.mirror.co.uk/sport/rugby-league/gay-rugby-league-star-keegan-6390448

Her Majesty's Government. (2015). *Prevent duty guidance: For England and Wales. Guidance for specified authorities in England and Wales on the duty in the Counter-Terrorism and Security Act 2015 to have due regard to the need to prevent people from being drawn into terrorism.* Retrieved July 14, 2015, from www.gov.uk/government/uploads/system/uploads/attachment_data/file/417943/Prevent_Duty_Guidance_England_Wales.pdf

Johnson, R. (2015, June 7). Changing sex is so brave, but you can't blame us oldies for being a bit baffled. *The Mail on Sunday.* Retrieved January 28, 2016, from www.dailymail.co.uk/news/article-3113998/Changing-sex-brave-t-blame-oldies-bit-baffled.html#ixzz3yYisorWJ

Littler, J. (2013). Meritocracy as plutocracy: The marketising of "equality" within neoliberalism. *New Formations: A Journal of Culture/Theory/Politics, 80,* 52–72.

Marriage (Same Sex Couples) Act. 2013. London: HMSO.

Mcinroy, L. B., & Craig, S. L. (2015). Transgender representation in offline and online media: LGBTQI+ youth perspectives. *Journal of Human Behavior in the Social Environment, 25*(6), 606–617.

McNair, B. (2011). *An introduction to political communication.* London: Taylor and Francis.

Michaels, W. B. (2006). *The trouble with diversity: How we learned to love identity and ignore inequality.* New York: Henry Holt.

Nicholas, S. (2014, December 4). Madonna: Material girl still loves to shock in provocative new photo shoot. *Express.* Retrieved January 8, 2016, from www.express.co.uk/entertainment/music/543228/Madonna-new-photo-shoot-shock

Norwood, K. (2013). A pregnant pause, a transgender look: Thomas Beatie in the maternity pose. In Campbell, J. & Carilli, T. (Eds.), *Queer media images* (pp. 65–76). Plymouth: Lexington Books.

Puar, J. (2013). Rethinking homonationalism. *International Journal of Middle East Studies, 45*(2), 336–339.

Registration of Births and Deaths (Amendment) (England and Wales) Regulations. (2009). London: HMSO.

Riley, W. (2015, September 5). Mum and her lesbian partner deny killing two-year-old son and blaming death on boy. *Daily Record,* 7. Retrieved January 7, 2016, from www.dailyrecord.co.uk/incoming/mum-lesbian-partner-deny-killing-6385657

Ring, E. (2015, March 7). My gay dads are great, says Safia. *Irish Examiner,* 15. Retrieved January 8, 2016, from www.irishexaminer.com/ireland/my-gay-dads-are-great-says-safia-15-316936.html

Robinson, K. (2010). A study of young lesbian and gay people's school experiences. *Educational Psychology in Practice, 26*(4) 331–351.

Robinson, M., & Greenwood, C. (2015, March 4, March 7). The lesbian lover who brainwashed the "perfect mum" into killing her daughter: Sadistic neighbour span a web of fantasy online ending in eight-year-old's death. *Daily Mail*. Retrieved January 7, 2016, from www.dailymail.co.uk/news/article-2979111/Lesbian-tortured-eight-year-old-daughter-death-behest-vampire-loving-girlfriend-thought-stop-gates-hell-opening.html#ixzz3wZWoqNw9

Rodgers, J. (2010). "Live your liberation—Don't lobby for it": Australian queer student activists' perspectives of same-sex marriage. *Continuum: Journal of Media & Cultural Studies, 24*(4), 601–617.

Rojek, C. (2013). Celanthropy, music therapy and "big-citizen" Samaritans. *Celebrity Studies, 4*(2), 129–143.

Samer, R. (2017). Transgender media studies: Editor's Introduction. *The Spectator, 37*(2), 5–8.

Sears, A. (2005). Queer anti-capitalism: What's left of lesbian and gay liberation? *Science and Society, 69*, 92–112.

UK Government. (2010). *Equality Act*.

Valentine, G., & Harris, C. (2014). Strivers vs skivers: Class prejudice and the demonisation of dependency in everyday life. *Geoforum, 53*, 84–92.

Wacquant, L. J. D. (1995). Pugs at work: bodily capital and bodily labour among professional boxers. *Body and Society, 1*(65).

West, I. (2014). *Transforming citizenships: Transgender articulations of the law*. New York: New York Press.

4 LGBTQI+ Parented Families and Their Visibility/Invisibility in School Policies

Shortly after my mother came out, we were at Parents' Evening. We came down the main stairs, to where the headmistress was standing regally at the bottom, smiling and greeting parents as they came by. As we approached, she turned coldly away.

Carrie

Introduction: Why Do Policies Matter?

Most schools in developed countries have at least some policies to guide how they work with students, parents, communities and staff. These policies provide a window onto their attitudes to different individuals and groups in the narrower and wider school communities, indicating how they are perceived, treated and valued. In recent years there has been a proliferation of school policy development in England, driven at least partly by Government legislation. For example, maintained schools[1] are required by law to have nine separate policies, covering matters from capability of staff to sex education and data protection, plus 19 other documents about such diverse topics as premises management, equality information and objectives, and child protection (Department for Education, 2014). While compliance with this seems to be patchy at best (for example, we found that, though most of the school websites we examined included some kind of equality policy, it was rare to have the mandatory annual update of how they were meeting the aims of the public sector equality duty (UK Government, 2010)), the requirement to have such documentation gives schools who take it seriously an opportunity to reflect on what they are doing in these areas and why. While we have to bear in mind Ahmed's (2012) caveat that commitments in equality policies frequently mainly reflect legal obligations and may even cover up discriminatory practices, we can nevertheless treat them, and how they are produced, as illuminating the discourses around equality within individual schools and, to some extent, the localities within which they are situated.

The discourses embedded in these policy documents and the visibility or invisibility of LGBTQI+ parented families within them are indications of how these families are perceived in schools and the extent to which a particular school is aware that there may be children from such families in their intake and community. Where children from LGBTQI+ families are mentioned, how they appear is also a reflection of the school's attitude to and positioning of them: are they perceived as problems, exceptions, victims, legalistically as people with 'protected characteristics' (UK Government, 2010) or as members of the local community who need explicitly to be included? This is partly indicated by the policies within which clauses about LGBTQI+ individuals and families sit. We only found one school which had a separate policy for LBGTQI parented families, though a few did mention them in broader policies, such as those about equality, sex and relationships or bullying. These different locations reflect different positionings of parents and students who are LGBTQI+.

While it is important to examine school policies and the sources from which they obtain or develop them, we also have to acknowledge the limitations of this approach. Having a policy does not necessarily entail a commitment to implementing it, particularly if it has not been developed by the staff involved. Ahmed (2012), indeed, suggests that devising legislation to promote equality can act as a substitute for action. She notes that how a document is written affects how it is taken up, so that involvement in policy writing offers people a stake in its enactment. Simply consulting staff, however, can give a document the legitimated appearance of having a collective origin when it does not. The end result of the process may, Ahmed argues, simply be auditable documents which institutions can use to appear to make commitments without necessarily being behind them (Braun, Ball, Maguire, & Hoskins, 2011). Similarly, Webb and Vulliamy (1996) point out that staff have to be involved in the development of a policy for it to have any impact on practice. There is some evidence, however, that overseeing authorities are beginning to be aware that having a policy does not necessarily mean that a school is taking steps actually to reduce or eradicate prejudice. For example, guidance to inspectors in England and Wales is specific about the sorts of questions that might be asked of students to see whether schools were taking LGBTQI+ issues seriously, for example:

> With primary pupils inspectors might explore whether . . . pupils have had any lessons about different types of families (single parent, living with grandparents, having step-parents, having two mums or two dads).
> (Office for Standards in Education, Children's Services and Schools, 2013: 3)

Given the all-pervasiveness of the inspection regime in England, if inspectors really do ask and act on such questions, this may lead to changes in schools in the medium term.

It is also important to consider the different forms of help that schools can call on when producing the various policies they require. It is evident from our research that school teachers and governors use a variety of sources and resources when developing policies: these can range from basing their work on guidelines and related material provided by local and national governments, LGBTQI+ charities and pressure groups (for example: (Gay Lesbian and Straight Education Network, 2012; Jennett, 2004; Jones & Hillier, 2012; Kosciw & Diaz, 2008; Safe Schools Coalition Australia & Minus18 Foundation, nd; Stonewall, 2010; Stonewall & University of Cambridge Centre for Family Research, 2012; Vancouver School Board, nd)) to adapting or adopting templates provided by local authorities or other schools (Webb & Vulliamy, 1996). There are also companies offering off-the-peg policies to schools in return for an annual subscription, though we have no evidence about how much such services are used. All these sources have, of course, their own internal discourses about LGBTQI+ parented families, which are likely to be carried over to those school policies they influence.

Data Set and Methods for the Policy Study

In considering how school policy documentation includes or otherwise covers LGBTQI+ parented families, we used two distinct sources. The first was a survey conducted via an email link to all the individuals and schools on the mailing list of Goldsmiths Teachers' Centre, some 1381 people. From these, we had 66 responses to the survey itself, and seven schools sent us the policies which they considered to cover LGBTQ-parented families. Apart from asking respondents what age range their school covered, the survey consisted of two questions: 'Do you have a school policy covering lesbian, gay, bisexual, transgender or queer (LGBTQ) parented families?' and 'Do you have, to your knowledge, any families with LGBTQ parents in your school?' Each question had a range of responses, so that schools could both indicate under which policy they felt that LGBTQ parents would sit, and whether they had had LGBTQ-parented families in their school in the past, if they did not have any now. There were also options for respondents to make free comments.

Of the 66 respondents, only one indicated that their school had a separate policy on LGBTQ parents. Of the other main categories offered, 33 said that they were covered under the equalities policy and ten under the anti-bullying policy. Eight said that such a policy was under discussion, and seven that they did not think they needed one; this was supported in the comments sections by statements such as 'We do not feel the need for a separate policy, all families are supported according to whatever needs they have/circumstances they are in' and 'As a headteacher with a diverse community and as a lesbian I have never felt the need for a separate policy. All my families are treated equally'. We also asked the schools surveyed if they would be prepared to send us examples of policies covering LGBTQ-parented families, and seven did so. These policies were analyzed alongside those coming from our wider sample.

There were two main problems with this initial survey: first, the response rate was very low; and second, because of the source of the contacts used, it covered a geographic area focused on South-East London and the areas immediately beyond that. We felt that we needed to consider policy documents from a wider cross-section of schools, away from London, where there is a higher proportion of LGBTQI+ parented families than in much of the rest of the UK. Accordingly, we chose two local authority areas, a rural county in Eastern England and a metropolitan authority in the West Midlands, both with a wide range of school sizes and types. For each of these areas, we visited the school websites of all non-private nursery, infant, junior, primary, secondary and special schools and analyzed the relevant policies to be found on each site. Thus, for each school, we considered any equality policy, any policy for sex and relationship education and any policy concerning bullying. If we could not find any of these policies on a school's website, we instead examined the Behaviour policy.

The availability of policies on the school websites varied enormously, with some schools publishing a wide range, including those relating to employment, with others having only a handful on their sites. Altogether, from these two authorities, we examined the websites of 169 schools; we could not access the websites of a further six, all from the metropolitan authority. For each school, we noted in which policy (if in any), LGBTQI+ issues of any sort were addressed, and if LGBTQI+ parents were mentioned at any point. We also considered the general characteristics of each policy, for example whether it appeared to have been adapted (and to what extent) from one provided from elsewhere, or whether it seemed to have been specifically drawn up by the school.

Contexts of School Policy Formation and Development

Before discussing the discourses and content of school policies, it is important to remind ourselves that the presence of policies does not necessarily imply actual engagement with the people and ideas on which they are focused (Ahmed, 2012; Martino & Cumming-Potvin, 2011). Schools operate within a national policy and legal context (Braun, Ball, Maguire, & Hoskins 2011), and what is found on their websites reflects this. For example, in the UK, all organizations are subject to the Equality Act 2010 (UK Government, 2010), which protects people from direct or indirect discrimination on the basis of eight 'protected characteristics': age; disability; gender reassignment; marriage and civil partnership; race; religion or belief; sex; or sexual orientation. Furthermore, as public bodies, schools are subject to the public sector equality duty, which requires them to go further and 'take steps not just to eliminate unlawful discrimination and harassment, but also to actively promote equality' (Equality and Human Rights Commission, 2017) with regard to all of the protected characteristics. This means that inspections of schools in England and Wales include scrutiny not just of the policies they have in this area but also of the steps they have taken to monitor equality and mitigate discrepancy in opportunities and outcomes.

However, as pointed out above, schools in England and Wales also have to have a considerable number of policies which are signed off by their governing bodies and made available to parents and others. This can be particularly problematic for small schools (of which there were several in our rural sample) which have few staff yet still have to have the same number of policies as larger ones. In order to have something available, school governing bodies and head teachers may feel that they do not have time to put together policies with the full involvement of the wider school community (Webb & Vulliamy, 1996), even though the latter would mean that teachers and other staff would have greater understanding of, and commitment to, the principles underlying the resulting policies (Ahmed, 2012; Tondeur, van Keer, van Braak, & Valcke, 2008). This is particularly likely to be the case because statutory policies are officially the responsibility of school governing bodies, which are made up almost entirely of volunteers, although the drafting of policy can be delegated to staff (Department for Education, 2014).

In consequence, many schools obtain outline or even full policy documents from elsewhere. In our analysis we found evidence that policies had been amended, or adopted wholesale, from local authorities, who might provide schools with a model policy for adaptation, and from other schools. Some had also clearly obtained them from Continuing Professional Development courses, and, indeed, one school had adopted a set of training materials as their 'policy'. Where schools had shared policies with each other, this was often because they had an official relationship, such as membership of the same academy chain (some academy chains had common policies for all schools involved) or one school sponsoring the other, though in most cases this borrowing was not acknowledged at all. For example, one school in our sample had taken over a complete sex and relationships education policy from its sponsoring school without acknowledgement and including the paragraphs explaining that it had been developed in conjunction with students. In the rural authority, we found several schools clearly using the same template, which was occasionally acknowledged as having been developed by the local Diversity and Standards officer.

While a properly adapted and adopted model policy could lighten the load for a school while still providing a high level of engagement, we found considerable evidence that many schools had not gone through this process of consideration and adaptation. For example, several of these model policies had sections which were clearly indicated as places where schools could add in their own particular features, or say what steps they had taken so far; in many cases these were simply left blank or with the original wording and/or highlighting indicating this. A typical example is this from one school's Single Equality Policy: '[Insert reference to where specific equality actions will be set out—for e.g. Improvement Plan, self-evaluation document as well as reference to Accessibility Plans]'. Other schools, however, used these models well; a neighbouring special school had adapted the same original document to produce a strong policy adapted to children with physical disabilities and including a five-year action plan.

Schools are supposed to have not only an equality policy, but an annually updated set of objectives: several policies based on standard models referred to these but they were nowhere to be found on the schools' website and in one case all we could find was a commitment (in 2016) to publish them by 2012. Thus, while those who had originally devised a model policy may have seen it as part of an interlocking and interdependent network of documents including anti-bullying, behavioural and sex and relationships policies plus action plans, what might actually be in place in a school (or, at least, on its website) would only be one of these, with indications of links but nothing to link to.

In some cases, it was clear that model policies, or those from other schools, had been adopted wholesale without being properly checked for sense, accuracy or even legality. In one of our local authorities, several schools had adapted or adopted a policy devised centrally by a local authority officer, which contained the statement: 'Culture is about the way we behave towards one another', which is an idiosyncratic definition, to say the least. In the other, several schools had policies which included the legally dubious statement: 'Staff are personally responsible for their own acts of discrimination, harassment or victimization carried out during their employment, whether or not the employer is liable.' Although this is strictly true, it is also the case that, as a public body, the employer remains liable for employees' actions due to the public sector equality duty. In other cases, a failure to proof-read could render a policy inapplicable to the school concerned, or even nonsensical in context. For example, one secondary day school's anti-bullying policy contained long sections (in a different font) which appeared to have been pasted in from a school with very different characteristics, making reference to a non-existent preparatory department, boarders and Matron. Another had not managed to eliminate all mentions of the school from which the policy was taken. Failure to read a standard equality policy template in the context of the school's intake could also lead to some strange statements. In particular, schools frequently listed all the protected characteristics without considering whether they might reasonably apply to the students in their care. This, from the equality policy of a nursery and children's centre catering only for children under five, is typical:

> The governors welcome all applications to join the school, whatever a child's socioeconomic background, race, sex, disability, sexual orientation, religion or belief, gender reassignment, or pregnancy.

While it is laudable that even nurseries appreciate that young children might already experience themselves as having a sexual orientation or as trans, it is highly unlikely that under-fives will become pregnant. Nevertheless, with appropriate adaptations, basing school policies on previously written models could ensure that schools remained both up to date and within the law.

Where schools had engaged directly with the process, they produced equality policies that more closely mirrored their local circumstances, though this did not necessarily lead to more sensitivity to or awareness of LGBTQI+ parented families. Indeed, one policy examined at the end of 2015 (since replaced) included a statement that the school would 'challenge stereotyping and prejudice, and celebrate diversity within the confines of Section 28'. This refers to Section 28 of the Local Government Act 1988, which stated that a local authority (not a school, or individual teacher) 'shall not intentionally promote homosexuality or publish material with the intention of promoting homosexuality' or 'promote the teaching in any maintained school of the acceptability of homosexuality as a pretended family relationship'. It was repealed in 2003, so the existence of this clause in a Sex and Relationships Education Policy in 2015 suggests a long-standing ignorance of what is legally permitted, let alone good practice, particularly in the context of the introduction of same-sex civil partnerships and, subsequently, marriage. However, this was an extreme case.

Several of the policies in the urban authority appeared to have been adapted from earlier race equality ones, reflecting long-standing priorities due to the ethnic mix of their local communities. Others had their strongest focus on disability. Unlike several of the equality policies adapted from templates, which tended to be so generic that they simply listed all the protected characteristics, bespoke or fully adapted policies drew attention to particular features of their local community, such as the urban SRE policy which mentioned the above national average teenage pregnancy rate. Church schools appeared to be more likely to do this, and several had policies specifically geared to their religious ethos, with a wide variety of effects. Mainly this resulted in an increased stress on marriage and family life, although in the UK, with the legalization of same-sex marriage, an emphasis on marriage per se has now become much more inclusive. Some schools, however, took the opportunity to emphasize particular exclusions or inclusions. At one extreme there was a Roman Catholic primary school whose 'Family Life Policy' was aimed at 'the formation of right attitudes in our children' and which stated explicitly that homosexuality, masturbation, oral sex, contraception, abortion and rape would not be 'discussed in detail'. Given that homosexuality is sometimes equated with sexual activity, this could result in the complete exclusion of LGBTQI+ issues and individuals (Martino & Cumming-Potvin, 2011). At the other extreme were church schools whose bespoke policies explicitly included LGBTQI+ people and even, in one case, families. So, for example, one Roman Catholic secondary school stated at the start of its Family Life Education policy that 'sexuality is essential to our personal identity and is God's gift to us', with 'sexual identity' taught to older students. A Church of England primary school's Sex and Relationships Policy not only covered same-sex relationships in the curriculum for older children, but also explicitly claimed to teach 'how do families with same-sex parents have babies?' In between were a few church schools which omitted some of the protected characteristics from their lists, focusing only on race, gender and disability. Others tried to strike a balance between inclusivity and explicit teaching about sex. One Roman Catholic primary school, for example, while having a thoroughly written Diversity Policy stating that children will be encouraged to challenge homophobic language, and 'discouraged from using offensive language about gender reassignment, civil partnership and marriage', also stated in its Love and Relationships policy that 'We have to bear in mind that the children are in the period of innocence—the period of latency which lasts from 5 until puberty—this period of tranquility should never be disturbed by any unnecessary information about sex' (Malins, 2016). This reflects otherwise inclusive guidance for primary schools produced more recently by the Church of England (The Church of England Education Office, 2017). It is worth noting in passing that only church schools mentioned 'love' in a policy title.

One thing that we noticed when going through the school websites was that schools which might have a relatively basic model-based policy for equality might have extremely well thought-out tailored policies for specific other things. It appeared that where a school had identified a need for a particular policy they might go to some trouble to devise one that fully suited their circumstances. One secondary school, for example, went into some detail about different kinds of home life, such as being a young carer, or a refugee, which might make a child vulnerable to bullying. Another had well-developed strategies to prevent and challenge bullying of Gypsy and Traveller children, while one primary school had a carefully worded Separated Parents policy. Other schools had inserted clauses or named groups into otherwise unremarkable policies. Several schools spoke of 'different family arrangements' without specifying what these might be. Others stressed that children should not be discriminated against due to family poverty. These examples suggest that it is only when a school has to deal explicitly with a particular kind of family or set of circumstances that it devises or amends its policies so that they work effectively in practice. This was particularly noticeable in some of the policies sent to us by people contacted through our initial survey. One of the most comprehensive documents, however, came from one of these schools but was based on guidance provided by a London local authority. It included a 19-page Gender Reassignment policy, applying to both staff and students, which set out both the legal situation and gave guidelines about how to behave towards trans people within the school community. Neither this, nor the school's Sexual Orientation Equality policy, however, referred to LGBTQI+ parents.

Discourses of Policy and Policy Support Materials

Maguire, Hoskins, Ball, and Braun (2011) note that policies can be regarded as discourses that construct a topic. A school's equality policy, therefore, reflects the power/knowledge relations that govern how equality is to be perceived and to whom it is understood as applying. Policies are themselves discourses that mobilize power through the ways in which they produce truths about individuals and groups. Grimaldi argues that analyzing policy as a discourse makes it easier to avoid simplistic analyses and allows us to see the discursive as a contested field, and where 'processes of policy production can be read as part of the struggles developing between different regimes of truth' (Grimaldi, 2012: 448). Policies socially construct their objects and, through their discourses, produce subjectivities and subject positions, which need to be uncovered and examined (Taylor, 2004). School policies relating to LGBTQI+ issues in general, and parents in particular, position LGBTQI+ parented families in specific ways, which will have different effects both in terms of their visibility as members of school communities, and of the ways they are regarded. It is therefore important to analyze the various discourses of the documents concerned, although of course it is not possible, given that we only have documents, to say to what extent this affects practices in schools and classrooms. The discourses of the documents we examined positioned LGBTQI+ parented families in three distinct ways: as invisible or excluded; as victims; and as members of the school community who need to be acknowledged. We will examine each of these in turn.

LGBTQI+ Parents as Invisible or Excluded

LGBTQI+ parented families were invisible in most of the policies we examined. The vast majority of policies did not mention them at all. This invisibility implicitly constructs LGBTQI+ parented families as not existing at all within the social and educational world of the school (Grimaldi,

2012). In many cases it was unclear whether it had simply not occurred to those constructing the policy documents that these families existed, whether they thought the family backgrounds of their students were unimportant to the work of the school, or whether there was a deliberate attempt to exclude mention of LGBTQI+ parented families from consideration. This lack of clarity extended both to equality policies and to those focused on sex and relationship education, so that it was common, for example, to find a school that had a strong statement about combatting unfair treatment of LGBTQI+ students, made clear claims (usually in the context of the equality duty relating to people with protected characteristics) to support trans teachers, but did not even mention the existence of non-stereotypical family forms. This is quite possibly due to the use of model policy documents focusing very directly on legal obligations, but does nevertheless reflect the overall invisibility, and, indeed, erasure, of LBGTQI+ parents in school contexts.

What this means in practice is that a school might have a sex and relationships education policy that is inclusive of same-sex love when considering students' current or potential relationships, but which discusses family life in such vague terms that an unthinking teacher could forget to take into account that the children or young people concerned might come from a wide range of family structures. Sex and relationship policies might, therefore, refer to teaching such things as 'why families are special for caring and sharing' or state that they would 'emphasise the role and value of family life' but say nothing about how those families might be constructed (Martino & Cumming-Potvin, 2011). This sort of indirect statement may, as Jones and Hillier (2012) point out, serve to give an illusion of inclusion where none exists in practice. Similarly, one primary school's website included a document of recommended reading for children about sex education and advice for parents, which included 'don't assume your children are heterosexual', but said nothing about people not making assumptions about the parents of their children's friends. Indeed, sex and relationships policies generally were quite vague about the extent to which the school taught about or encouraged a positive attitude to same-sex relationships, leaving a discursive disjuncture between the legally underpinned statements of their equality policies and what they claimed to cover in the classroom. Even where there were explicit statements, they were not always positive. One school, for example, stated clearly that 'We do not use sex education as a means of promoting any form of sexual orientation'. While this is open to being interpreted also as not promoting heterosexuality, in the context of the repealed Section 28 it is more likely to indicate a reluctance to discuss LGB relationships.

This is not surprising given the confused and contradictory nature of official advice on the subject. For example, many schools made it clear that they gave emphasis to the importance to 'the value of family life, marriage and stable and loving relationships for the nurture of children'. This reflects Government guidance which suggests that

> Within the context of talking about relationships, children should be taught about the nature of marriage and its importance for family life and for bringing up children. The Government recognises that there are strong and mutually supportive relationships outside marriage. Therefore, children should learn the significance of marriage and stable relationships as key building blocks of community and society.
> (Department for Education and Employment, 2000: 11)

Given the subsequent introduction of same-sex marriage, it might be assumed that, with the passing of time and the increase of homonormative relationships, this has served to move potential stigma or exclusion from same-sex parents to those who are parenting without a partner or close support community. Guidance from the Equality and Human Rights Commission, however, suggests that this is unlikely to be the case, as it is clearly stated that:

> No school, or individual teacher, is under a duty to support, promote or endorse marriage of same sex couples. Teaching should be based on facts and should enable pupils to develop an understanding of how the law applies in different relationships. . . . Any views expressed about marriage of same sex couples, by governors, teachers, other school staff, parents and pupils, may reflect the religious ethos of the school.
> (Equality and Human Rights Commission, 2014: 2–3)

Supplementary, Government-endorsed advice about sex and relationship education, intended to update the existing guidance (Blake, Emmerson, Lees, & Hayman, 2014), ignores this issue entirely, focusing mainly on safeguarding, internet safety and pornography, though it does point out that 'teachers should never assume that all intimate relationships are between opposite sexes' (12). There was not, however, much evidence that this supplementary guidance had been taken on board by schools in updating their policies. It is unsurprising, therefore, that a survey carried out by Stonewall found that 40% of respondents were 'never taught anything about LGBTQI+ issues in school or college' (Bradlow, Bartram, Guasp, & Jadva, 2017: 22)

Even where school policies, particularly those focusing on equality rather than sex and relationships education, indicated strong support mechanisms for LGBTQI+ students, this did not usually extend to mention of parents, except in the vague and all-inclusive context of 'diverse family circumstances', occasionally with same-sex parents used alongside single parents or grandparent care as an example. This is despite clear

Government guidance about the need to recognize that some children do not come from heterosexually parented families. For example, a UK Government document about challenging homophobia in schools (Jennett, 2004) states explicitly that schools should not 'use generic language that assumes parents and staff always have opposite sex partners' (17) and that a good partnership with parents requires that 'the school makes it clear to all parents and carers that any information about their personal circumstances, including their sexuality, childcare arrangements etc., would be welcome and will remain confidential', going on to suggest that 'same-sex partners are encouraged and supported to attend parents' evenings together' (22). This officially sanctioned advice appeared to have had no impact at all on schools' equality statements more than 10 years after publication. Where LGBTQI+ parents are concerned (and particularly in relation to those who are B,T,Q or I), a discourse of invisibility is the dominant theme of the school policy arena.

LGBTQI+ Parented Families as Victims

In contrast to their invisibility in sex and relationships education and equality policies, members of LGBTQI+ parented families did sometimes appear in schools' anti-bullying documentation. Most of the anti-bullying policies, where they mentioned particular categories of bullying at all, did refer to homophobic bullying, usually in the contexts of protecting LGBTQI+ students or combatting homophobic language, particularly the use of 'gay' as a term of abuse, something that was often explicitly mentioned as an issue to be addressed. There was the occasional mention that 'children and young people with family members or friends who are lesbian, gay, bisexual or transgender are also susceptible to homophobic bullying', but most anti-bullying policies focused on children being bullied about their own sexual orientation and did not appear to be aware that young people might have parents who were themselves LGBTQI+. That said, there was more visibility for LGBTQI+ students and parents in anti-bullying policies than anywhere else on school websites. While in some ways this comparative visibility is welcome, it is problematic that it is centrally located within a discourse of victimhood (Jones & Hillier, 2012). As Martino and Cumming-Potvin (2011:498) note:

> addressing name-calling directed at children from same-sex families as a safe-schools' matter does not necessarily translate into discussing the homophobia and the heterosexism that give rise to such bullying and disparagement of sexual minorities in the first place.

Furthermore, if the only place that LGBTQI+ people feature in school policies at all is in lists of people with 'protected characteristics' under the Equality Act or as potential victims of bullying, this presents a picture of LGBTQI+ life as problematic, painful and in need of special protection, rather than as another variant of human sexuality and living arrangements.

Of course, this approach does reflect the continuing prevalence of homophobic bullying in schools (Kosciw & Diaz, 2008; Malins, 2016; Martino & Cumming-Potvin, 2011; Safe Schools Coalition Australia & Minus18 Foundation, nd) and the concomitant need to combat it. There is some disagreement about the extent to which children of LGBTQI+ parents are bullied specifically as a result of their parents' sexual orientation (Clarke & Demetriou, 2016; Tasker & Golombok, 1997), and establishing what is happening is difficult due to the pressure, for both children and parents, to play down bullying in the face of accusations that LGBTQI+ parents bring this upon their children as a result of their 'choices' (Martino & Cumming-Potvin, 2011) (to either have children in a LGBTQI+ relationship or to come out after having had them in a heterosexual one) (Clarke, Kitzinger, & Potter, 2004). As will be seen in Chapter 6, accounts given by children themselves, however, suggest that actually being bullied about their parents' sexual orientation is relatively rare. Nevertheless, they are distressed when things like homophobic name-calling are not addressed in their schools, and complain that the invisibility of LGBTQI+ families in the school curriculum means that they have to educate both peers and teachers (Stonewall, 2010).

This discourse of children from LGBTQI+ families as victims arises in part from their invisibility within the taken for granted world of the school. This means that they only appear at all in relation either to LGBTQI+ students defined as requiring protection, or to this group being bullied, rather than as individuals in their own right. Because there is good evidence that LGBTQI+ students are frequently the victims of bullying, and because casual use of homophobic language remains an ongoing problem in schools, children from LGBTQI+ families are assumed, by association, to be both closeted about their parents and victimized because of their parents' identities. This may be at least in part due to an unacknowledged anti-gay agenda on the part of some schools (Clarke, 2001; Clarke, Kitzinger, & Potter, 2004), leading them to position children from LGBTQI+ parented families as victims of their parents. However, this emphasis on closeted victimhood can be found even in advice to schools (Kosciw & Diaz, 2008), where LGBTQI+ parented families, as opposed to students, frequently remain invisible. For example, in a well-meaning but sometimes bafflingly misguided document found on the website of an organization supporting anti-homophobic work in schools, there are only two mentions of LGBTQI+ parented families. One suggests that children might role play 'families where there are LGBT parents and/

or children' in drama lessons (though how they might interpret this is not explained) and the other recommends that

> schools could provide counsellors to pupils whose parents are LGBT as they may want to talk to someone about it as they may never have talked to anyone about their parent's gender or sexual orientation.
> (Barrie, 2013: no page numbers)

This both takes for granted the invisibility of LGBTQI+ families in the school context and again positions LGBTQI+ parented families as passive victims who need to be rescued by school pastoral services.

LGBTQI+ Parented Families as Members of the Community Who Should Be Acknowledged

> While most elementary educators have embraced [diversity] work and construct and conduct lessons focused on diversity, recent research suggests that intentional efforts to include explicit lessons that foster respect for differences in gender identity or gender expression or that include families with LGBT parents/caregiver, siblings, or other individuals significant in our students' lives, are less frequent. As a result, many students go through their elementary school years without positive mentions of families that include LGBT persons or friends or people who may be gender non-conforming.
> (Gay Lesbian and Straight Education Network, 2012: 1)

Finally, there are a few instances where LGBTQI+ parented families are treated as members of the school community like any others, with their presence in policy and advisory documents functioning as a means to acknowledge this. We found only six schools that explicitly mentioned LGBTQI+ parented families, five of which were from the group solicited via our survey. Some other schools did refer to 'different family arrangements' but where examples of these were given they referred only to situations such as single parenting and grandparent care (Martino & Cumming-Potvin, 2011). Where LGBTQI+ parented families were explicitly mentioned or indicated, at one end of the spectrum there were such purely inclusive statements, located in such a way that it was clear that this referred to LGBTQI+ parented families, as 'resources will reflect the full variety of families and homes that exist in society today', or that the school would 'promote a safe and inclusive learning environment for all children where they feel comfortable to talk honestly about their families'. At the other end were much more explicit commitments, such as: 'the curriculum should reflect the diversity in society and as such should avoid being heteronormative'; or the claim that 'it is incumbent on teachers to . . . challenge the stigmatisation of lesbian and gay families in lessons about families, marriage and stable relationships.' Such statements were, however, rare, only found in policies that appeared to be written in-house for specific schools, and entirely absent from even the best local authority-supplied documentation.

The advisory documents stemming from campaigning groups were more inclusive in this sense, though some still focused entirely on LGBTQI+ young people, only mentioning parents in that context, not as people who might be LGBTQI+ themselves. Those that spent most time discussing LGBTQI+ parented families were focused more on younger children, presumably because parents are more directly involved in their children's schools at this age, or were, like Stonewall's study of the experiences of children with lesbian and gay parents (Stonewall, 2010) explicitly examining this area. It was notable, however, that even campaigning groups had little advice about LGBTQI+ parents explicitly on their websites. Given this absence, it is hardly surprising that schools so rarely include them in their policies and, presumably, therefore, in their curricula. This is of concern in the light of Stonewall's finding that

> children with gay parents said that lesbian, gay or bisexual people or families are never mentioned in schools and they find this difficult and it makes them feel invisible.
>
> (Stonewall, 2010: 3)

There is a clear need, in the UK at least, for school policies, and the advice available to support their development, to be much more upfront about the existence of LGBTQI+ parented families, in order to support the children involved as they go through school.

Conclusion

Given the power of policy discourses to construct the power/knowledge relations within which schools operate, the positioning of LGBTQI+ families in schools' policy documents is of considerable concern. Where the existence of LGBTQI+ families is completely ignored, this not only renders them invisible in school but conveys an underlying heteronormative assumption that such families either do not exist at all or are not part of that particular community (Braun et al., 2011). This leads to children from LGBTQI+ parented families feeling excluded by school practices, processes and curricula. Kosciw and Diaz's (2008) US-based study found that children from LGBTQI+ parented families encountered negative responses to their having LGBTQI+ parents, were discouraged by staff about being open about their families, and that LGBTQI+ parents felt that they were not included in school activities. In the UK, Stonewall's (2010) study found that these complaints were also raised by children with LGBTQI+ parents and that they felt invisible as a result. Policies, such as the majority of those we examined, that position children from LGBTQI+ families as only existing as victims of bullying construct a negative world in which coming from such a family is seen as abnormal or problematic. Given the increasing diversity of families in Western society, schools need to engage more fully in the implications of their own policy discourses in order to include all the families in their communities.

Note

1 These are schools 'maintained' by local authorities, that is not academies or free schools. Some policies are only 'advisable' for the latter, although we found that most academies published a similar number of policies (more, in some cases) as maintained schools.

References

Ahmed, S. (2012). *On being included: Racism and diversity in institutional life.* Durham, NC: Duke University Press.

Barrie, R. (2013). *The national LGBT toolkit for schools: Meeting the educational, social and emotional wellbeing needs to pupils who identify as lesbian, gay, bisexual, trans*, genderqueer or pupils who are questioning their sexual orientation.* Birmingham: Birmingham LGBT.

Blake, S., Emmerson, L., Lees, J., & Hayman, J. (2014). *Sex and relationships education for the 21st century.* London: Brook, PSHE Association and Sex Education Forum.

Bradlow, J., Bartram, F., Guasp, A., & Jadva, V. (2017). *School Report: The exeriences of lesbian, gay, bi and trans young people in Britain's schools in 2017.* London: Stonewall and University of Cambridge.

Braun, A., Ball, S. J., Maguire, M., & Hoskins, K. (2011). Taking context seriously: Towards explaining policy enactments in the secondary school. *Discourse, 32*(4), 585–596.

The Church of England Education Office. (2017). *Valuing all God's children: Guidance for church of England schools on challenging homophobic, biphobic and transphobic bullying* (2nd ed.) London: The Church of England Education Office.

Clarke, V. (2001). What about the children? Arguments against lesbian and gay parenting. *Women's Studies International Forum, 24*(5), 555–570.

Clarke, V., & Demetriou, E. (2016). "Not a big deal": Explaining the accounts of adult children of lesbian, gay and trans parents. *Psychology and Sexuality,* online publication 13/1/16.

Clarke, V., Kitzinger, C., & Potter, J. (2004). "Kids are just cruel anyway": Lesbian and gay parents' talk about homophobic bullying. *British Journal of Social Psychology, 43*(4), 531–550.

Department for Education. (2014). *Statutory policies for schools: Advice on the policies and documents that governing bodies and proprietors of schools are required to have by law.* London: Department for Education Retrieved from www.gov.uk/government/uploads/system/uploads/attachment_data/file/ 357068/statutory_schools_policies_Sept_14_FINAL.pdf.

Department for Education and Employment. (2000). *Sex and relationship education guidance*. London: Department for Education and Employment.
Equality and Human Rights Commission. (2014). *The Marriage (Same Sex Couples) Act 2013: The equality and human rights implications for the provision of school education*. London: Equality and Human Rights Commission.
Equality and Human Rights Commission. (2017). *Public sector equality duties*. Retrieved January 4, 2018, from www.equalityhumanrights.com/en/advice-and-guidance/public-sector-equality-duty
Gay Lesbian and Straight Education Network. (2012). *Ready, set, respect!: GLSEN's elementary school toolkit*. New York: GLSEN.
Grimaldi, E. (2012). Analysing policy in the context(s) of practice: A theoretical puzzle. *Journal of Education Policy, 27*(4), 445–465.
Jennett, M. (2004). *Stand up for us: Challenging homophobia in schools*. Wetherby, Yorkshire: Department for Education and Skills and NHS Health Development Agency.
Jones, T. M., & Hillier, L. (2012). Sexuality educaton school policy for Australian LGBTIQ students. *Sex Education, 12*(4), 237–254.
Kosciw, J., & Diaz, E. M. (2008). *Involved, invisible, ignored: The experiences of lesbian, gay, bisexual and transgender parents and their children in our nation's schools*. New York: Gay, Lesbian and Straight Education Network.
Maguire, M., Hoskins, K., Ball, S., & Braun, A. (2011). Policy discourses in school texts. *Discourse, 32*(4), 597–609.
Malins, P. (2016). How inclusive is "inclusive education" in the Ontario elementary classroom?: Teachers talk about addressing diverse gender and sexual identities. *Teaching and Teacher Education, 54*, 128–138.
Martino, W., & Cumming-Potvin, W. (2011). They didn't have *out there* gay parents—They just looked like *normal* regular parents: Investigating teachers' approaches to addressing same-sex parenting and non-normative sexuality. *Curriculum Inquiry, 41*(4), 480–501.
Office for Standards in Education, Children's Services and Schools. (2013). *Exploring the school's actions to prevent and tackle homophobic and transphobic bullying: Briefing for section 5 inspection*. Manchester: Office for Standards in Education, Children's Services and Schools.
Safe Schools Coalition Australia, & Minus18 Foundation. (nd). *All of Us: Health and physical education resource understanding gender diversity, sexual diversity and intersex topics for years 7 and 8*. Victoria: Safe Schools Coalition.
Stonewall. (2010). *Different families: The experiences of children with lesbian and gay parents*. London: Stonewall.
Stonewall, & University of Cambridge Centre for Family Research. (2012). *The experiences of gay young people in Britain's schools in 2012*. London: Stonewall.
Tasker, F. L., & Golombok, S. (1997). *Growing up in a lesbian family: Effects on child development*. New York: The Guildford Press.
Taylor, S. (2004). Researching educational policy and change in "new times" using critical discourse analysis. *Journal of Education Policy, 19*(4), 433–451.
Tondeur, J., van Keer, H., van Braak, J., & Valcke, M. (2008). ICT integration in the classroom: Challenging the potential of a school policy. *Computers and Education, 51*, 212–223.
UK Government. (2010). *Equality Act*.

Vancouver School Board. (nd). *Making school safe for everyone*. Vancouver: Vancouver School Board. Retrieved January 4, 2018, from www.safeschoolscoalition.org/Making%20School%20Safe%20For%20Everyone.pdf

Webb, R., & Vulliamy, G. (1996). A deluge of directives: Conflict between collegiality and managerialsim in the post-ERA primary school. *British Education Research Journal, 22*(4), 441–458.

5 LGBTQI+ Parents' Perspectives on Their Children's Schools

I wasn't out about my mother at school, at all. It was difficult enough being out about my parents being divorced: I didn't even know anyone else in that situation. I had also been brought up to be very open-minded about things like sexual orientation and had already had a lot of arguments with other students about this—so I was worried that people would think that this was just because my mother was a lesbian, rather than my own previously existing principled position. When I got to university, I moved in the opposite direction, and told everyone at every opportunity. I enjoyed the frisson of difference and specialness. In my second year I met someone else with a lesbian mother, which was amazing, and we became good friends. His mother (a school librarian) was completely in the closet, and I always felt sorry about that.

Carrie

Introduction

In this chapter we examine the relationship between LGBTQI+ parented families and schools from the point of view of the parents. We consider this specifically through the lens of visibility/invisibility and how that affects relationships with schools. We note that some parents chose a highly active and distinct visibility within the school context, while others sought to minimize the differences between their families and others by being visible in a more low-key sense. Other parents' LGBTQI+ status was involuntarily invisible, and some took steps to remedy this. Two parents chose invisibility as a strategy to protect themselves and their children: this was a high-risk approach which caused significant stress to these parents in particular. Overall, and in contrast to some previous studies of LGBTQI+ parented families (Kosciw & Diaz, 2008; Pyne, Bauer, & Bradley, 2015; Ryan-Flood, 2009), we found that family forms and sexual orientations were not experienced as problematic in the school context, though several parents felt that schools could do more actively to include their families, and, in a few cases, to support their children.

The data source for this chapter is 23 interviews with 26 LGBTQI+ parents and carers, mainly in England and Wales, although two lived elsewhere in Europe. Locations varied from suburbs of major cities to small villages. Most people were interviewed alone, even when part of a couple parenting together, though in two cases we interviewed both parents together. One couple was interviewed twice, before and after they had left London for a more rural location, and in three cases parents and children were interviewed together. Sixteen interviews were conducted face-to-face, five via Skype, one via instant messaging, and one via email. The face-to-face and Skype interviews were audio-recorded and transcribed for analysis. This range of approaches allowed us to have a wider geographical reach than might otherwise have been the case, and also in some cases to give additional level of confidentiality to respondents.

The families were recruited via a combination of convenience and snowball sampling. We set up a Facebook page early in the project, for general discussion of LGBTQI+ parenting and school issues, being upfront from the start about the fact that we were conducting research. Some respondents were recruited through this. Others came from contacts made at Rainbow Families camps, and others via personal contacts or names passed on by respondents. We deliberately sought a wide range of LGBTQI+ parents, so that although our respondent sample is relatively small, it reflects a variety of identity positions, family structures and approaches. However, all but one of our respondents was white (though not all white parents had white children), and most could be described as middle-class. Family composition and origin ranged from single parenting by a lesbian with an unknown donor, to children who had a male and a female couple involved in their upbringing, though not to an equal extent. In all cases except three we interviewed the parent(s) who were the main or equally shared carers for the children. This obviously means that we only have the perspective of these parents, and their co-parents are invisible. However, the evidence from both the non-resident parents and the equal co-parents whom we interviewed suggests, with regard to schools, that non-resident LGBTQI+ parents are similarly situated to heterosexual/cisgender parents in this position, for example, with regard to access to information about their children's progress, invitations to parents' evenings and so on (Brown, Lundgren, Stevens, & Boadle, 2010).

Most of our respondents were cisgender. However, two identified as trans men, four as women of trans history, one as genderqueer, one as non-binary and one as intersex. We did not ask about the sexual orientation of our respondents, other than they fell into the broad LGBTQI+ category. However, one described herself as bisexual and one couple as polyamorous (though no-one else was involved in their child's parenting). One of the trans men was parenting (and interviewed) with his partner, a cis woman who identifies as a lesbian (Platt & Bolland, 2017), and one of the women of trans history told us she was now in a heterosexual relationship, though she had previously been married to (and conceived her children with) a woman.

Parenting arrangements were not always entirely clear-cut, and the descriptions here are simplifications to some extent. However, 14 respondents (10 families) were parenting birth, adopted, or fostered children as a couple. Eleven could described as single parents, eight of whom were co-parenting to a varying extent (up to equally shared time) with their former partner; two of these had two children, one living solely or mainly with her, and one who lived mainly with her ex-partner. Three of the lesbian-parented families had involved male donors who saw the children on a regular basis. Three families had only cis male parents (two couples, one parenting alone) and one child was parented by a single trans man. The two children of one of the women of trans history were now adults.

The ages of the children in our respondents' families ranged from two to adult, with the majority of compulsory school age. Of the 35 children in total, seven were adopted (three by cis men, two by a lesbian couple, two by a lesbian/non-binary couple), four fostered, 11 born into conventionally heterosexual families (in one family, the mother came out as a lesbian, while in the other five one parent subsequently transitioned). In one family with a trans male parent, the child was born to the couple by donor insemination, and the trans man is the child's birth parent. The remaining 12 children were born to lesbian, binary/lesbian or intersex/lesbian couples or single parents through donor insemination, which in some cases included IVF.

Strategies of Visibility and Invisibility

Questions of visibility and invisibility emerged as a clear theme from our interviews, with different parents taking different approaches. This was partly a result of the situation of individual parents and families, but was also connected with views about the importance (or not) of being a visible example of a member of a particular group (Brown, 2012; Cloughessy, Waniganayake, & Blatterer, 2017; Dalton & Belby, 2000; Holman & Oswald, 2011; Taylor, 2009). We discuss this in detail as follows, considering parents who had a strategy of active visibility, those who were unwillingly visible, those who saw themselves as just a family like any other and wanted to be treated that way by schools, and those who aimed for an (albeit precarious) invisibility.

It is important to be aware that being visible and being out are not the same thing. In fact, for some parents, coming out to schools and to other parents was an explicit strategy for relative invisibility. Those parents who came into our 'just a family like any other' category, generally outed themselves at an early stage so that the issue had been dealt with and in order that it could subsequently be ignored (Cloughessy et al., 2017).

This distinction is important because there were other parents for whom invisibility was felt to require *not* being out to their children's schools. This particularly applied to two of the women of trans history, one of whom was not out to her children's schools, and the other of whom had delayed transitioning until her children had grown up. We discuss the problems they face later.

We should also at this point mention locality as a factor in parental relationships with and discussions about schools. Although our respondents came from a wide range of locations, from suburbs of cities to small villages, several seemed to feel that their generally good relationships with their children's schools and school community was partly to do with the relative safety of that particular location (Cloughessy et al., 2017). For example, Rachael spoke of her and her partner's decision to remain in London because they might be 'one of the only strange people in the class alongside lots of heteronormative nuclear families' if they moved to a commuter town. Similarly, though, Kristy remarked that it had been easier for her to transition in a village, compared with a small market town 'where you're more likely to run into trouble'. David and Peter, however, had relocated from London to just such a town, and again affirmed their new semi-rural location as being particularly welcoming and non-judgemental. While many of these were at least partly middle-class neighbourhoods, Jess, whose foster daughter had remained in her previous school, talked about her positive inclusion by other parents in an area she described as 'very socially deprived. Lots of people excluded, long-term unemployment, higher crime area, lots of alcohol, drugs and lots of kids in care'. It appears that while LGBTQI+ parents may *believe* that their location is important to their acceptance within a school community, this may not be the case in practice.

Active Visibility

> GRAY: I made a choice to be out and fighting for people's rights.

For some parents, being highly visible as LGBTQI+ was extremely important. This was usually related to wanting to provide children and schools with a clear alternative image of the variety of humanity. For some parents this was about sexual orientation, but for others it was more a matter of ensuring that alternative ways of being gendered were placed in front of children and other parents and seen as a viable way of life. Sylvie, for example, said explicitly that they thought their gender-queer presentation was an important aspect of being out and proud:

> I value being visibly queer and I feel there is a benefit to that. I've been visibly queer in both schools. So although I don't spend a lot

of time in secondary school, parents see me and my ex around, the teachers. . . . I have sons who say 'these are my mums'. They see me as gender-nonconforming, so there is that visibility and I think that's really valuable for other kids, apart from my kids, that they see those relationships. They see people who don't gender conform proudly getting on with their lives.

Sylvie also felt that their own visibility attending school events and parents' evenings with their ex-partner made it easier for their children: the family situation was thereby made obvious so it was unnecessary for the children themselves to explain it (Ryan-Flood, 2009). This did not mean, however, that their children were never embarrassed by them. Sylvie was particularly disappointed by the sex education at their children's school, describing it as 'put a condom on a banana and what types of contraception there were'. They were so vocal about this that their children complained:

> Anyway, there was a point when my kids told me to stop talking about sex because I constantly wanted to be saying that sex is not penis/vagina sex. Everybody does other sorts of things or probably want to, or it's more fun if you do.

It was not clear whether these discussions took place at school or at home, or in front of friends, but, wherever they occurred, the potential for adolescent embarrassment is obvious.

As well as wanting to be visibly out and proud, other parents had active visibility strategies that were specific to their children's situation. Peter and Jane, both of whom had adopted children, joined their school governing bodies, partly because of the particular needs of their children and partly because, as Jane put it, 'I thought, if anything starts coming up, it's best to be on the inside'. Active involvement of this sort could also be a strategy for presenting oneself as a 'good' parent (Pallotta-Chiarolli, 2010; Ryan-Flood, 2009; Taylor, 2009), which put one in a strong position with the school and with other parents if difficulties arose. Jess, foster parent to a child on long-term placement, felt that her daughter's problematic history was already well known to other parents and that anything other than her own complete visibility as a lesbian was 'yet another layer of her potentially complicated upbringing'. She had an explicit strategy of making herself visible by joining the parent-teacher association (PTA) in order to give parents and children a different image of parenthood from the one usually seen at this school:

> I joined the PTA, which is really funny. I never thought I would join the PTA and I was very conscious about it. I wanted to be seen. I wanted to be a different representative of what a parent or carer looks like. I don't have the standard long hair. I don't wear the usual clothing.

> I'm fairly masculine in appearance and I've got short hair. I have tattoos. Lots of the women at school have tattoos but they're different than mine. I wanted to be as out as possible and have a name.

Jess was particularly keen that she present an alternative way of being in a locality where there were few women who looked like she did. Such concerns were especially salient for parents whose gender or whose children's origin was unusual. Julian, a trans man who had given birth to his son after already having taken testosterone and had top surgery, felt that their family story was something that could explicitly be used by the school as part of equality training. Similarly, Jo, who is an intersex activist living in Sweden, thought that it was important to educate other parents about the existence of intersex people in general and their own situation in particular. Jo, who is frequently perceived as male, has the explicit intersex-reflecting parent name of Mapa, and wanted both children and other parents to recognize this and what it meant. Their children's nursery suggested they write to parents and explain:

> I'm a mapa and shortly after Mina started . . . Mina's friends, the other classmates would say, 'here comes your papa', and I would say, 'Mina's mapa', and I would try to explain in my bad Swedish that I was a mapa and they were like . . . and I talked to the teachers and they said, maybe you should write a letter. . . . So I wrote a letter that they send out every year, and I say, when your child comes home and says that Mina and Nell have a mapa, they're not saying something wrong: I am. That is the name; and then I go onto explain that I am an intersex activist, that I come from a queer background, and that it's very important to me that people understand that there are people in the world that can embody both male and female or either. So it's kind of simple, rather long, but simple explanation.

This approach by Jo reflected their wider concern with what they described as cisnormativity even within lesbian and gay life in Sweden. They felt that it was important to challenge this, and that 'you have to be gender queer, or queer, to really open things up', for themselves, their children and for society more generally.

Unwanted Invisibility

Some of the more actively visible parents took this stance partly because they were otherwise in danger of becoming completely invisible as LGBTQI+ and were unhappy about this (Platt & Bolland, 2017). This was particularly an issue for those people who could be perceived as part of a heterosexual couple. Julian and his partner Elizabeth, for example, had explicitly to tell people about Julian's trans status, as it was otherwise invisible. Similarly, Jo, who has a beard and so is frequently read as male, despite not binding their breasts and having a not particularly deep voice, suggested that because of this they have to be very active in insisting on their intersex identification. In some cases, these concerns could be specific to the school context. Sylvie, who in other situations quite enjoys the transgressiveness of being addressed as male, described an incident at a school open day for prospective parents when they experienced this as much more problematic:

> One of the things I felt strange about was, sitting in the assembly putting my hand up to ask something about language teaching. 'Sir, what's your question?' Then feeling like always seen as this heterosexual couple, me and my ex, because they'd read me as a man, and feeling like I'd like to be a bit more visibly queer in that situation. . . . Because I suppose I like being queer. That's part of my identity, that I like being queer, although I like being read as male as well.

It was presumably also problematic for Sylvie's lesbian-identified ex-partner that she was also read as heterosexual in this situation.

Single parents also complained about their invisibility as LGBTQI+, as it meant that their family structure might not be recognized at all by the school or by other parents. Dawn found that, because she and her ex had already split up by the time he started school, the parents of her son's friends saw her as a single parent rather than a lesbian. Even parents who did know about her situation, however, might make her further invisible through insensitive remarks, in this case about all children having a father. Dawn's children were conceived via an unknown donor, so they have no-one identified in this way:

> There was a comment in the playground once, from one of the mums, who knew about their parentage. I can't remember what it centred around, but they made a comment, 'well, everyone's got a dad'. And you know, I didn't say anything, but in my mind I was like, well, actually, no, not everyone.

Similarly, Sam, who had left her husband for another woman, was only visible as a lesbian within her children's school because she worked there, as her former husband, with whom she shared care of their two children, joined her for parents' evenings. Even then, she found that, because she and her children no longer shared a surname, when she attended as a parent not all her children's teachers were aware of her sexual orientation:

> We do give the outer appearance that we're just a divorced set of parents. It's a big secondary school so I don't know all of the teachers personally but a lot of them know that I'm gay. Not all of them,

particularly new members of staff, because I reverted back to my old maiden name, sometimes they don't even know that they're teaching my kid, so that was a bit of a shock to start off with. I would definitely say that it maybe isn't as visible as some of the parents where we do have two mums turn up or two dads turn up to parents' evening.

Single LGBTQI+ parents not being recognized as such might also mean that homophobia, which could have a greater impact on their children, might not be dealt with, and there might not be any attempt to provide books and other materials that included LGBTQI+ families.

Parents who were not the main carer could also be invisible, or less visible, to schools. For example, while Rachael's child's father did pick up his son from school, he did not come to parents' evenings, so he was less well known to the school than Callum's mothers were, and his partner, who acted as a parent when Callum visited at weekends, was not seen by the school at all. We did not generally interview non-resident parents, so we are not aware the extent to which this is an issue for them. It was definitely a problem for Cal, however, who was the resident parent of her younger child but not of his elder brother, who lived with her ex-partner in a rural village. The child went to the tiny village school his birth mother had attended and where his grandmother had worked as a teaching assistant. This meant that the school felt very much 'like it was their territory and I wasn't to encroach into it'. The situation was further complicated because Cal was unclear about the extent to which her ex was herself out to the school. Cal and her ex were already separated by the time Thomas started school, and although Cal was as involved with school matters as she could be, she sometimes felt that, in the face of obstruction from her ex-partner, this put the teachers in an impossible position, caught between two parents giving out different messages. This extended quotation illustrates the kinds of conflict that could arise:

> There was certainly one incident where he got these kind of things called Wow Tokens which parents could take home. . . : they're basically like a sheet of paper that said 'Wow my child did . . .' and then you filled it in, and the teacher gave me some of those. And there was one time when he was with me and he'd just learned to write and he wrote a postcard to her saying what he'd done, and he wrote all of it, and wrote her address and everything and it took him about two hours but he was so proud of himself that I took a photograph of it. And then I filled in one of these Wow things, saying, 'Wow, Thomas wrote a postcard to his other Mamma and even did the address', and then the teacher put it on a noticeboard with all the other Wow things, and when they kind of changed them they put them in his, like, learning journal, or whatever they called it, and in that learning

journal there's all of the other Wow things that I had done. And then there was one parents' evening where I went in, and I was just flicking through his thing and there was a clear gap where one of them had been and there was, like, Pritt Stick marks. So it had been stuck in and it had been ripped out. And I kind of said to the teacher, 'what happened to this one?', and, like, I knew which one it was, because I could remember what all the other ones said, and the teacher was like, 'oh, I don't know, I thought it was in there', and so she had clearly taken it out because I think she objected to me kind of naming myself as his other parent and kind of essentially outing her as being a lesbian. . . . But the teacher kind of. . . . I could see the teacher didn't know what to do. I didn't know what to do and it was just like . . . it was just a really horrible scenario for everyone.

Cal's account adds a further layer of complication to the already well-documented problems experienced by non-resident parents and their relative invisibility in relation to their children's schools (Brown et al., 2010).

Just a Family Like Any Other

SIMON: I don't think I have had any [experiences with the school] as a *gay* parent.

Several of our respondents made it clear that they just wanted to be seen and treated by the school as ordinary parents with ordinary families (Santos, 2013; Taylor, 2009; Weeks, 2007). Unlike those who thought visibility was important to demonstrate how different people might live, these parents disavowed such roles. Kevin, for example, who was both a primary school head teacher and, with his husband, the foster parent of a teenage boy, was explicit that not only did he not want to be involved in such activities, but that also that he was not supportive of them in general:

I've never been a great flag waver. The fostering service want to wheel you out at every event now, because they've got gay fostering parents. The NUT [National Union of Teachers] want me to go on the flipping bus at Pride in Brighton and it's not about that for me. If we want to integrate it's just . . . it's not highlighting the differences.

Sometimes such statements were made in response to our question about the possible advantages of being an LGBTQI+ parented family. Rachael, for example, found even the question irrelevant to her situation:

I don't. . . . I find it quite hard to answer that question. . . . It's just my life. It doesn't have any benefits.

Harriet and Catherine, a lesbian couple with one child, were similarly resistant to the question, suggesting that it was essentialist. When they did come to reflect on it, they continued to challenge the underlying premise, suggesting that it might not be the sexual orientation of the parents that would confer the benefits that other parents perceived. Harriet expressed this very clearly:

> So he's got a very strong sense of injustice around gender which I hope, I would have hoped that being raised by two socialist parents would do that anyway.... I haven't really thought about it from that point of view. I hadn't really thought about it as an advantage or not.

These parents who emphasized their status as a family like any other appeared to take the view that society had now moved on to such an extent that it was not just unnecessary but inappropriate to draw attention to their differences. They wanted to be accepted in their children's schools but did not feel the need to make a stand about their LGBTQI+ status.

In order to achieve this position it was, however, necessary for these parents to come out early, both to the school and to other parents, and to be extremely matter-of-fact about this. This reflects the findings of Cloughessy et al. (2017). They report that 89% of the Australian lesbian parents they studied mentioned their family composition at the first meeting with an early years' provider, and expected this information to be shared with other educators, children and families. For our respondents, the idea seemed to be that if they got their sexual orientation out into the open immediately, then it was dealt with as an issue and everyone could get on with their lives. This was typically done not by explicitly announcing their LGBTQI+ status, but by deliberately dropping names and pronouns of both parents into conversations with staff and other parents.

Rachael, for example, was very clear about her approach, and saw it as partially self-protective:

> And I mean, naturally, just kind of mentioning my partner in a not.... I don't go around going 'hello I'm a lesbian'. I go around saying, you know, 'oh, my partner, she does this'. And I do it as soon as I can because I actually think, well, if people are homophobic then they can just decide to diss me now. I don't want to get to know people and then find they have dodgy views and all that sort of stuff.

This tactic of dropping the name of one's partner into conversation, referred to by Cloughessy et al. (2017: 10) as 'display tools' emphasized these people's desire for a visible invisibility: it treated same-gender partnerships as not significantly unusual for comment.

Being upfront about one's status by talking frequently about one's partner also had the effect of emphasizing a couple's collaborative approach to parenting (Dunne, 1997), even when one parent had given up work and so was more frequently seen at school. Jess, for example, always referred to her partner in conversations about their child:

> I made it clear that any conversation was 'Laura and I': 'Laura and I had a conversation last night and this is what we came up with'. . . . It was never 'I'. I wanted to be as out as possible in the school.

Jess was also anxious to protect her foster daughter, whose difficult background was well known to other parents, and viewed her openness about herself and her partner being lesbians as proactively working against bullying, using humour to connect with other parents about the issue:

> It's not about me ramming it down people's throats. I just really want to be clear that Saika doesn't have to be subject to any form of bullying, either by teachers or by pupils or by parents. I was really clear with other mums and grandparents who joined the PTA. I was like, 'I'm joining the PTA because Saika is a looked-after kid, she's a Muslim, she's black, and now she's being raised by two lesbians, oh my god, isn't that funny?'

For Jess, parenting a particularly vulnerable child, simple openness was not enough. While she wanted her relationship with her partner to be treated as unremarkable, in order to achieve this, she took trouble to make it highly obvious from an early stage.

Other parents had an overt strategy of modelling visible ordinariness (Brown, 2012; Santos, 2013; Weeks, 2007). David and Peter, for example, took the view that they should behave in similar ways to heterosexual couples when visiting the school for parents' evenings and other events:

> I do go in acting and doing the same as every heterosexual parent. I will hold his hand. I will touch his shoulder or put an arm around him or whatever. Because that's what other people do and I want the kids to see that I am doing that and I am gay.

While it might appear from this quotation that David and Peter chose a strategy of active visibility, and while it was the case that they felt that they were important potential role models for any gay children they might encounter, what they were really trying to achieve was a visible invisibility that allowed them to behave exactly the same as any heterosexual couple, without it being noticed or remarked upon. This was particularly clear from our interview with them after they had left London for a small rural town. Comparing their new home to London, where they felt that they were 'making a statement walking down the road',

David felt that in many ways the relative lack of identity politics in their new locality allowed them to be accepted like any other couple:

> Like London is . . . there's so many different groups vying for popularity, I don't know, vying for identity and all that kind of stuff and they're very much in your face about it, whereas here, it's just, everyone's quietly getting on with their own lives, and if you're a nice person, you're pleasant and polite and whatever, people will talk to you, and your sexuality, your background, your culture, it's just not an issue, and that, for me, has been the most refreshing thing and the thing that's given me most relief.

Being able to act as a family like any other is here shown to be central to David and Peter's ability to settle in their new home with their children, and seen as a welcome contrast to the more overt sexuality politics of the metropolis. They actively sought an unremarked life for themselves and their children and in this way embraced a homonormativity that they felt was easier to achieve in their rural town than in London (Ryan-Flood, 2009). This reflected Kristy's experience of transitioning to female in a rural village. Because she had remained in the area she was unavoidably visible locally as a woman of trans history, but felt that the local people 'just see people for who they are'.

For most of the parents in this group, being LGBTQI+ was, as Rachael put it, 'just my life'. As long as their children's schools were welcoming of them and their families, they were content to leave campaigning about LGBTQI+ issues within the school to others. This meant that their interactions with their children's schools were generally about other matters (Holman & Oswald, 2011). What these were varied, of course, from family to family, but included: children being fostered or adopted; children having disabilities; children's friendship problems; discomfort about the general atmosphere in the school, such as hearing another child being shouted at. Even where the children themselves did not have any particular difficulties that impacted on their education, parents, even if they intended to be more proactive about LGBTQI+ issues, often found that other things got in the way or took priority. This reflects Holman and Oswald's (2011) finding that sexual orientation is perceived as non-salient when it is overridden by other, more urgent matters. Parents might feel that they only have a limited number of opportunities to interact with their children's schools, and prioritize accordingly. Harriet, for example, found that she and Catherine usually had more immediately important things to discuss when in contact with their son's school:

> I often would compile stuff from the internet, or lists from schools or things from schools and get ready to give it to them, over some day when I thought, here's another occasion they could have mentioned.

They could have some better books in the library. . . . And then it always turned out that something else got in the way, because, as we were going through primary education, there's so many things you want to write, so, like, you don't want to waste your points on something that isn't absolutely top of the list, so it was always more important to say, like, why aren't you doing your times tables, or . . . what about this and what about that? And I felt like there's only a number of things, you can only speak a number of times a year. So I don't think we've, we've barely ever said anything about it.

As LGBTQI+ families have become more accepted and less unusual, it appears that family composition is not the most urgent thing that parents have to talk to schools about, so it is not raised unless something like bullying brings it to the 'top of the list'.

Although, as discussed above, some parents had told the school that they were LGBTQI+ in advance of their children joining or themselves taking over as parents, others did not have that opportunity. Foster carers, in particular, might find that they were suddenly full-time parents of children already established at school, and that they did not have any form of official meeting for some time. This meant not just that they were unable to be immediately explicit with the school about their family arrangements, but also that they were not alerted by the school to any specific policies that might be relevant to their situation. In Helen's case, for example, she and her partner had started caring for their children half way through term:

HELEN: I mean . . . it was half term when they came to us in October.
CARRIE: And you're straight in?
HELEN: Yeah, and you haven't had all those introductions that you would have had, particularly to secondary school. . . .
  I think, perhaps if we had, had a meeting . . . if we'd had a meeting with the headteacher right from the start, rather than you just turning up on day one and pick up the kids. Yeah, that would have helped, and I think . . . I think it's partly because we didn't want to make a big song and dance of being lesbian carers. We just wanted to make the children's experiences, you know, as regular as possible. So you know, I mean . . . I think, yeah, it would have been more helpful to have had some kind of welcome meeting. And maybe then they might have said, 'Well, we've got these policies around LGBTQ parents'.

Situations like this mean that opportunities to introduce oneself and inform the school about one's identity or sexual orientation simply did not occur, leaving parents with the 'dropping it in' strategy as their only clear way of outing themselves to the school. They also mean, as Helen points out, that schools do not have a clear opportunity to indicate their acceptance of such parents and their strategies for dealing with any issues that might arise. This points to what is, in many ways, a paradox inherent in the visible invisibility approach: when LGBTQI+ parented families are so normalized as to be almost invisible at school, while the curriculum remains unchanged, it may be less likely that schools will be alerted to take steps to provide greater inclusion, such as books and other teaching materials that reflect a wide variety of family formations. Such families may therefore be accepted within the school community but not be acknowledged to exist by the curriculum (Holman & Oswald, 2011).

Precarious Invisibility

There was one small group of parents who did not wish to be visible at all as LGBTQI+ within the school community. This comprised two women of trans history and one trans man. For these people, invisibility was important, even crucial, and in fact one, Patty, had delayed coming out and transitioning until her children had completed school (Hines, 2006). Jake was out to his son's school and to some of the teachers, but only because of the legal situation in Finland, where he lives:

> I'm out as transgendered to most of my son's teachers and the school office, but this wasn't fully my choice. In Finland the official records are very strongly involved in everything and there was some confusion with Benjamin having two males marked as his parents, which isn't currently possible except for situations like mine, where the mother has had their gender reassigned.

However, he pointed out that apart from this, his status was not visible within the school, and he described the teachers as 'discreet and respectful', indicating that he did not seek greater visibility to other parents.

Patty and Adele were both extremely concerned about possible bullying of their children if their trans history were discovered (Pyne et al., 2015). Unlike Julian, who, as we discuss below, believed that bullying was about uncovered secrets, they felt that transphobia itself would play a significant role. Patty had been extensively bullied at school after being discovered dressing as a woman, and was terrified of similar things happening to her children. She gave this as the reason she delayed transition until they were adults, keeping even her cross-dressing secret from them throughout their childhood:

> So in terms of my interaction with my children, I was paranoid that they should find out, that they should be harmed in any way, that they should go through any of the trauma that I went through as a child. I completely protected them.

Adele, whose son lived with her, and who had separated from his mother and moved to a different area in order to transition, lived in a state of constant fear in case Lucas's school or his friends discovered her history and he was bullied as a result. He was already being picked on because of his weight, and she was always aware that 'any one slip on my part could open Lucas up to a slew of problems'. Although she was usually read visually as female (though she said that her voice sometimes gave her away), she described herself as 'on permanent edge' taking careful precautions never to give any grounds for the school to suspect her trans history:

> I never go near the school without making my hair right, never in slobbing/androgynous clothing. I am always on edge and it is exhausting. . . . I feel like I am walking a tightrope with a BIG drop.

Adele also took her male partner to parents' evenings, which meant that 'people see what they expect to see, they saw a man and a woman', and allowed her to be treated as unproblematically female (Kessler, 1998). However, she clearly considered herself fortunate to be able to do this. A friend of hers, she told us

> has a harder time of it, her genetics were less kind to her when it comes to passing as female (tall, broad, facial shape) she just stays away from the school entirely.

Such precarious invisibility was therefore not just personally stressful for both parent and child, but also meant that these families' lives were not recognized in school at all. Furthermore, any transphobia could only be combatted by outing oneself to the school, potentially leading to further problems.

Parents and Schools

In this section we will consider the ways in which the parents in our study related to their children's schools. We will start by looking at how parents chose schools, and then examine one of the key worries for LGBTQI+ parents: bullying and homophobia. From there we will turn to some of the issues that arose from families' ongoing relationships with their children's schools, focusing in particular on those that are specific to LGBTQI+ parenting.

Choosing a School

It is important to be aware that not all parents in our study did actively choose their children's schools. As discussed earlier, in circumstances where a child moved in with new foster carers, for example, they might be kept in the same school in order to maintain that stability, particularly if the child had already had several short-term placements before arriving in their long-term family. Some parents also pointed out that, for demographic reasons, in practice they had little choice about where their children went to school, and had to deal with whatever school their child was placed in.

When choosing schools, LGBTQI+ issues were often felt to be highly salient when the children were small, becoming less so as they got older. For parents choosing nurseries or primary schools it was frequently a big deal, making them extremely anxious. There was also a tendency for parents to feel satisfied with the situation at their children's current school but to be worried about what would happen at the next educational stage: parents with children at nursery were concerned about primary school, and those with primary-aged children had anxieties about the move to secondary school. Generally, however, even among parents of the younger children, LGBTQI+ issues were not the only, or the most important consideration when choosing a school. Things that parents considered included: proximity; inspection reports; local reputation; school size; special educational needs; whether their friends had children there; academic orientation; emphasis on the outdoors; and whether the school seemed strict, friendly, relaxed or nurturing. For example, Sylvie and their partner thought it was important that their children attend local schools, unless they found a reason not to do so, so they went to the primary and secondary schools nearest to where they lived. Darcy and her partner, having initially placed their child in a 'fabulous' nursery that they felt was very sensitive to their status as lesbian parents, moved her to a nearer one about which they were less happy in this respect, because the commute to the first had been too much for the child.

As was previously found by Taylor (2009), some parents thought that general diversity was important partly to support their own inclusion and partly as something they valued, but it might not be the only, or even the overriding consideration. For example Julian and Elizabeth, who discovered only after their child was born that they were living near the most diverse primary school in the city, suggested that other factors were also important:

> It wasn't just the diversity thing, it was their approach to learning as well, that they are really, they are not driven by all their curriculum requirements and it's very play based as much as it can be—to the point where the school didn't actually have a very good reputation.

As children got older and moved to secondary schooling, their own views became more important, to the extent that the child's wishes might be the major or overriding factor in school choice.

Some parents did ask specific questions about how the school might handle LGBTQI+ issues or about their experience with LGBTQI+ parented families, and take positive or negative action according to the response. Dawn, for example, asked for anti-bullying policies when considering schools:

> There were three schools we went round. One, to this day, still haven't sent me their bullying policy, so that says a lot about that school. The other one didn't have homophobic bullying on it and I actually pointed it out. . . . But the school they attended, it was actually in their bullying policy. So I was quite . . . when choosing schools you want to make sure that if any issues do crop up.

For other parents, however, it was things specific to their child that mattered more. Jo, for example, having sent their children to daycare with 'a very progressive gender perspective' felt that it was important to find a kindergarten that supported their child's own gender expression. Jane and Paula needed a school that could appropriately support their son's specific developmental needs, while for David and Peter the overriding issue was that their older child would require a school that would be 'nurturing'.

Nevertheless, some parents did make some initial judgements about schools, often based on worries about the type of school involved. Several parents explicitly avoided church schools, partly due to beliefs about Christian attitudes to LGBTQI+ parents, and partly because of their own lack of religious belief. Jennifer, for example, a black parent who was also looking for a small, diverse school, said she had avoided Church of England schools due to concerns about homophobia:

> Because some of the things I've heard, you know, talking to people who claim to be . . . well, yeah, they're religious but then they're anti-gay. I mean, I kind of make this association in my head that, you know, religion means anti-gay. Not that it does, but it kind of pricks up my, you know, thinking, OK, what's going on here? There's some kind of discrimination happening and I feel like I'm more kind of aware of potential prejudice, you know, when it comes to religion as well.

Such initial screening-out of church schools on the part of some parents who otherwise said little about explicitly looking for LGBTQI+ friendly schools suggests that the school choice process is possibly more complex at the time than is presented by parents when recalling it several years after the fact.

Bullying and Homophobia

The potential for their children to be bullied because of their LGBTQI+ identity was an underlying worry for all the parents we interviewed. This was partly because some parents, particularly those with trans histories, had been badly bullied as children. However, only one, a woman of trans history, said that their child had actually experienced homophobic or transphobic bullying, so it remained, as Rachael put it, 'a little tiny worry' for most. Most parents, as was the case with general school matters, were concerned about what would happen to their child at the next stage of schooling, rather than the one they were in currently. Jennifer's comment was typical of what was said in interviews:

> Well, you know, nothing's happened but, you know, it could happen at secondary level.

Parents who had recently come out, either as gay or as trans, tended to be more worried than those who had been out for longer. Sam, who had left her husband for another woman while both children were at school, described herself at the time as being 'absolutely paranoid that the kids were going to be teased and their life would be awful'. Her daughter had had several problems with her friendship group, and Sam described her fears as leading to a 'knee-jerk reaction' that any bullying would be due to homophobia:

> When there is a problem my immediate thing is, are they bullying you because I'm a lesbian? That's at the back of my mind the whole time—and it will be something completely different. It's just normal teenage stuff.

Some parents also took the line that some children were just going to be bullied (Clarke, Kitzinger, & Potter, 2004) and if it was not due to their parents' sexual orientation or gender status it would be something else, so the best approach was to give their children strategies to avoid or deal with it. Some of the children had been bullied for other reasons, but homophobic bullying of their children did not come into our respondents' experience.

Parents used a variety of strategies in order to prevent or mitigate possible bullying. Several relied on strong school anti-bullying policies and asked about them when choosing schools. Indeed, Simon told us that when asked about potential bullying when going through the adoption process, his response was that 'it's the school's responsibility to tackle bullying, not mine'. Parents whose children were at particularly strict schools saw this as a source of reassurance that anything that happened would be picked up immediately. In the one case of transphobic bullying, by contrast, the school had failed to support the child at all, and he was bullied repeatedly until his mother moved house and he changed schools as a result.

Not all parents relied on the school to prevent bullying. For Julian, a trans man who had given birth to his son Sage, the most important protective strategy was complete openness. Although Sage's friends (who were still aged only four or five) did not know all the details of his parentage, it was known to staff and many parents. Julian argued that this was an essential protective strategy because 'I kind of feel like a lot of bullying is about secrets and secrets uncovered'. He and Elizabeth also, like other parents, thought that developing resilience in their children was important, as well as giving them strategies to challenge or respond to any untoward comments (Oakley, Farr, & Soherer, 2017). This reflects a strategy used by some of Pallotta-Chiarolli's (2010) polyamorous parents, who supplied their children with powerful responses to use if they were teased or bullied. Jane also argued that it was important to be open about their relationship as it meant that there was no need for secrecy on the part of the child:

> We didn't want to set up a thing where the kids were feeling that they were holding secrets or that there was something shameful about being a same sex couple.

Nevertheless, she felt that their son, coping with being adopted and having a learning disability as well as having two mothers, did often feel embarrassed about his parents, particularly as neither of the schools he attended dealt well with family diversity.

Some parents also found that they had to balance protecting their child against being seen, either by the school or by the children themselves, as making a fuss. Harriet and Catherine's son was self-conscious from an early age about his parents 'making a thing of' their family composition, so they tended not to say anything on occasions when they might otherwise have done so. Similarly, Adele had spoken to her teenage son's school when he was being bullied about his weight, and 'he was upset that I had intervened, I think he considers these things to be HIS battles'. Parents might therefore take a less interventionist strategy than they would otherwise prefer, because this was protective of their child in other ways, or out of respect for their child's wishes.

A particular issue was other children's use of 'gay' as a term of playground abuse. Parents' reactions to this varied from accepting that it took place but that their children might not feel able to challenge it, to expecting both the children and the school to take it seriously and act. Parents who were or had been teachers tended to take it for granted that such language would occur, particularly in secondary school: Gray, for example, in response to their child describing the school as being 'really good' about bullying, remarked:

> They still are quite homophobic, aren't they? They're still like normal teenagers, that playground homophobia.

In this respect, some parents distinguished between a school's ideas about LGBTQI+ and what Harriet described as 'the actual atmosphere in school'. This meant that in some cases parents felt that what really mattered was a strongly implemented anti-bullying policy, which would protect their children if anything happened, rather than a high level of understanding of the nuances of LGBTQI+ life.

Where homophobic language was allowed to go unchecked or undercover in a school, parents were aware that this might leave their children in an awkward position. Two sets of lesbian parents described their children as using homophobic language themselves, in both cases because of a need to fit in. Jane and Paula's son has learning difficulties and his special educational needs schools have not been good about dealing with homophobic abuse or LGBTQI+ inclusion. Consequently, he had picked up a lot of homophobic language from his peers, and Jane and Paula felt that he was unable to resist going along with this. After a long discussion between them in the interview, about what precisely was going on, Paula summed it up in this way:

> He loves us very much, and this is his family, and he loves all the people in our network who love him. But I think that school stuff, it appears like that, survival stuff. I've got to just be one of the lads. It's like professional footballers, there aren't many out gay professional footballers. He wouldn't have that ability to speak up. . . . He just goes with the flow.

Catherine and Harriet's son, at primary school, had also got into trouble for misusing the word 'gay' in front of a teacher. They described him as being 'surprised' to be in trouble, and felt that he had not really understood the implications and that he had seen it as 'a bit of playground banter, and maybe he was trying to fit in a little bit'.

Although some parents expressed their pride in children who had stood up to homophobic playground language, Sylvie thought that it was important for children to feel able to leave it be and not feel that they had to challenge or report it. They described an incident in which their son had felt ashamed that he had not done so:

> There had been lots of homophobic comments made in his friendship group. People telling other people they looked so gay and he felt a bit ashamed that he hadn't felt able to challenge it. There had been this point where he told me this, not in a looking for help way, but of being a bit ashamed I think, and me saying, well, you've got to look after yourself. You can't fight all those battles; sometimes it's not safe to challenge those things. You've got to look after yourself.

This example comes from a child who was at a strict school which was seen by parents as having, as Sylvie put it, 'no space where people could make negative comments without it being addressed'. Such an approach reflects the experience of most of the parents we interviewed, having an emphasis on direct bullying and in most cases clamping down on homophobic language used in front of teachers. However, because homophobia was usually dealt with as a bullying issue, and therefore something that might occur between specific children, this meant that the casual use of 'gay' as a playground term of abuse or derision was not always fully addressed.

Ongoing Relationships with Schools

Parental relationships with schools usually begin before the child even starts attending. Where this is the case, parents frequently out themselves to the school at this point, either explicitly or implicitly (Cloughessy et al., 2017). Some parents used the opportunity to ask specifically about LGBTQI+ policies, or about schools' anti-bullying policies, while others were more interested in the school's prior experience of LGBTQI+ parented families. Some parents, however, while being open with a school about the composition of their child's family, might have stronger concerns about other issues, such as their previous experience of adopted or fostered children, or of particular kinds of special need.

Schools' and teachers' reaction to parents coming out to them was usually minimal or non-existent: Jess described this as 'not even a raised eyebrow'. This lack of response, however, could indicate a lack of sophistication on the part of a school, which might see the issue entirely in relation to potential bullying. Sylvie explained the limitations she and her ex had encountered:

> So in our meeting with the headteacher, we said that we're lesbian parents of this child, and we want to know what your approach to that would be. . . . The headteacher was quite positive but she said, we've never had any parents before, but we'd deal with it in the same way that we'd deal with any other bullying issues. I don't think it occurred to her that it might take some positive action in the school, but she was quite positive about dealing with bullying.

This focus on bullying, while important, does treat LGBTQI+ parented families as potential victims rather than as contributing to the diversity of a school. It may also be blind to the importance of including images and examples of these families in the curriculum. It can also be a mask for a general lack of understanding of some of the issues involved: as Darcy remarked about her child's nursery: 'the current one said no, no, it's all fine, but they are not particularly good with it.'

One thing that happens early in parents' relationship with schools is the filling in of forms. This could cause considerable annoyance where two or more people were co-parenting. Forms tended to either have spaces for 'mother's name' and 'father's name' or for 'first contact' and 'second contact'. Some parents spent a lot of time trying to convince the school that they should change their forms or their computer systems to allow two women or two men to be registered as equal parents, but as Harriet said, 'I am always crossing it out and it always comes back the same'. The structure of official forms was also related to an assumption that a child would have one main home, even though some parents were sharing care between two homes on an equal basis. Non-resident parents were particularly likely to be excluded in this way, with only two separated parents (both sharing care equally) reporting that they both received all school communications. This situation reflects that of non-resident parents generally (Brown et al., 2010), where even those with official parental responsibility, and therefore a right to receive all documentation and be consulted in decisions about the child, might not be fully included.

Related to this is sometimes an unspoken emphasis on the greater legitimacy of the birth mother, which again caused distress to parents for whom equal parenting, and recognition as parents, were important principles (Ryan-Flood, 2009). While Sylvie told us that they had never been asked who was the birth mother of each of their children, where it was known there were sometimes more or less subtle effects. Darcy, for example, was asked by her child's nursery why her partner could not come to parents' evening alone when Darcy was unavailable at the time suggested. In other ways, children might be put under subtle pressure to see their birth mother as the main or 'real' one. Harriet recounted an incident in which their son had been on a school trip and, when asked to send a postcard home 'to your mum', ended up excluding his other mother, Catherine:

> And he just sent a postcard saying 'dear Mum, blah blah blah, and then just put my name on it. It was really quite painful.

Similarly, Rachael described an incident in which her then 5-year-old had been asked to draw a 'circle of intimacy':

RACHAEL: And he came home with this circle of intimacy diagram and I looked at it and went, hello, where am I? I wasn't on it.
CARRIE: Oh, right. You mean he had mummy and daddy?
RACHAEL: I think . . . I think he had Colton [father] somewhere quite far out. But it was mummy and then some of his little friends and stuff.

This suggested to Rachael and her partner that there had been some sort of subtle pressure to include only his birth mother, even if only because 'he was five and everybody else was probably writing mummy'. This unthinking lack of inclusion of all parents in a family was something parents found particularly distressing.

Several parents were unhappy about the ways that schools celebrated Mothers' and Fathers' Days and the expectation that children would make cards, and mentioned this spontaneously in interviews as something that had upset them. One aspect of this is that some children do not have a parent to make a card for on each of the days. This is obviously something that does not just apply to LGBTQI+ parents, but can also be an issue for single parents where the other parent is dead, unknown or otherwise uninvolved. Many schools have strategies to deal with this, most usually the child making a card for an important male or female adult in their life. While this is in many ways a reasonable approach for a busy teacher who does not have the resources to occupy a minority of children while the majority make cards, some parents felt uncomfortable about this, particularly if grandparents, usually the most obvious candidates, were not very involved. Some schools ignored Fathers' Day altogether or played it down compared to Mothers' Day, which, while fine for the lesbian parents, was the opposite for gay fathers. David and Peter's children were unusual in that they were encouraged to make two cards each on Fathers' Day, and they had a suitable person (Peter's mum) to give things to on Mothers' Day. However, their children's school had a PTA stall selling Mothers' Day gifts, but did not do the same on Fathers' Day. Peter had raised this with the school, seeing it as a basic issue of parental equality:

> They don't have a shop for Fathers' Day. . . . It's not the same, you see. So the equality is missing whether you're straight or gay, you might say. Because Fathers' Day's not there.

While Peter and Steve's children were encouraged and supported to make two cards on Fathers' Day, one for each parent, this was not a common experience. Several parents complained about their children having to stay in at playtime if they wanted to make a second card, or only bringing one card home (Kosciw & Diaz, 2008). Catherine and Harriet described this as being a problem right through their son's primary education:

CATHERINE: From nursery onwards, there's not been a single year when [child] has been able, or has been encouraged by the school to do any kind of thing that reflects both of us.
HARRIET: He did do a thing saying, I love my mums, I've got mums.
CATHERINE: Yes, he had to adapt the template.
CARRIE: Right, so the sample template says, I love my mum?
CATHERINE: Yes, and he was pleased that he'd managed to do that, but from the first year at nursery, every year at nursery we'd say

something and they would never take it on board. Of course they had other stuff to do but he always had to do it himself or he had to stay in at break to do an extra card, or had to bring home one, always something.

An additional problem when a child had only been able to make one card, and hinted at by Catherine and Harriet above, was to whom a Mothers' Day or Fathers' Day card was addressed. While Catherine and Harriet's son was able to take matters into his own hands, Darcy's daughter was too young to do so, so her card ended up only being addressed to one parent. Darcy explains that when they mentioned this to the nursery they felt that they were not being taken seriously:

> And we got a Mothers' Day card which was beautiful, you know, they had obviously made an effort with them, and on the back one of the leaders had written, Dear Mummy, Happy Mothers' Day, love from Poppy. I thought, you know, beautiful, but could it have killed you to do Mummy and Mamma? Since it's clearly an adult who wrote it on, it's not like she ran out of time to write it herself, she's only two. And when we said to them, it was lovely, but yes, we'd really like one card for both of us . . . we felt we were making a bit of a fuss about nothing.

The strength of parental feelings about this issue is something that schools generally do not seem to appreciate and stems from a concern that both (or all) a child's parents be recognized in their parenting role by the school.

Darcy and her partner Liz's problem with how their Mothers' Day card was addressed points to something that is common in both nursery and primary schools and which rests on a heteronormative assumption: the use of 'mummy' as a generic term. Such a use presupposes that a child has no more than one mother, who can be generically referred to as 'your mummy', whatever name the child actually uses for that parent. This means that when a staff member says to a child, 'your mummy's here', they are using 'mummy' as a generic term, not as a proper name. When a lesbian couple co-parent, however, 'Mummy' is usually the name the child uses for one parent. It therefore functions as a proper name which distinguishes them from the other parent, who is usually called something else. Thus when a staff member tells a child that 'your mummy's here' and the mother in question is not the one called 'Mummy', this can be experienced by that parent as excluding and insensitive. It can also (if only temporarily) be confusing for the child: Darcy reported that Poppy started referring to her as 'Daddy', presumably because that was the name that the children around her gave to the parent in their household who was not 'Mummy'.

The use of the generic 'mummy' is also related to something common to nursery and primary schools generally: the focus on the child rather than the parent, so that parents are frequently known to both teachers and other parents as 'so and so's mum/dad' rather than by their name (Sikes, 1997). Where both parents are of the same gender, this can lead to a certain amount of confusion: people tend, as Rachael put it, to

> just see a child and they see a hand holding the child. And they see a woman and they don't really look at who the woman is. . . . So there were times in the early days when I would walk in. . . . I'd walk into school and somebody would start talking to me and I'd be thinking, you think you were talking to me the other day, don't you?

Such assumptions might even extend to a child's friends, at least to start with. Catherine, for example, remarked that

> Some of his friends early on weren't, didn't actually get that there was two of us, just assumed one person, yes. . . . Tall person with short hair, you don't need to look too closely.

While this might in some ways mean that a child's family did not immediately become an object of playground gossip, it did mean that one parent (or maybe each, to some extent) can temporarily become invisible, with the result that the family structure is also invisible. The various modes of the heteronormative generic 'mummy' act both to hide the existence of these families, at least temporarily, and to distress and make invisible that parent for whom 'Mummy' is not their proper name within the family.

Informal School-Based Relationships

Relationships with Other Parents

Generally, relationships with other parents at their children's schools were not considered by our respondents to be an issue, though some pointed out that it was easy for other parents to avoid them if they wanted to do so. Jo, who is intersex, said that they had experienced problems with one other family, whom they described as 'silently seething'. Sal, who is a woman of trans history, did experience abuse from another parent at her son's school: the school did not address the issue as transphobia but as a simple difference of opinion. An American child due to visit Sal's family on an exchange visit also stayed elsewhere at the request of her family after the school informed them that Sal was in the process of transitioning. Apart from these exceptions, however, openly LGBTQI+ parents generally felt accepted by the wider school community, though occasionally other parents said ignorant things to their children, such as the parent (mentioned above) who told Patty's son that 'everyone's got a dad'.

As discussed earlier, most parents were careful to come out at an early stage, before relationships became established. This was particularly important for single lesbians, who would otherwise be assumed to be heterosexual. Sam, for example, who had left her husband and come out only relatively recently, felt that it was important to explain to unfamiliar parents before sleepovers that her partner might be staying, mainly because 'I wouldn't want to upset or freak out a child'. She had also added her lesbian status to a form about a German exchange programme her daughter was involved in, again, to pre-empt problems when her partner stayed overnight. Jennifer, whose daughter was younger, came out gradually to other parents, telling people whom she felt were 'safe' (Holman & Oswald, 2011):

> You sort of try and align yourself to the people who you see as the most broad minded and liberal thinking people [laughter]. . . . And then you find out what people do in terms of their profession and you think, OK, you know . . . or subjects that you might talk about, you know. . . . OK, this person, you know, thinks a bit beyond the box, It's not sort of restricted, you know, in a kind of small, heterosexual world.

Even then, she worried that she might be making other parents uncomfortable; it is possible that this is related to her being the only black parent among our respondents.

Kristy and Sal, both women of trans history, had no real choice about being out to other parents at their children's schools, as they remained in their rural villages during and after transition. Kristy found the process particularly unproblematic, though this may be partly because she is herself extremely tolerant of others. For example, she frequently experienced being misgendered by local people, but saw it as 'an honest mistake' arising from their previous knowledge of her:

> I don't have any issues with people misgendering me. If people do it maliciously, fine—they haven't done it yet—but most people just get it wrong because they knew me before and they know me now. It's an honest mistake.

Despite Sal and her son's problems with one other family in his school, Kristy and Sal's experience of acceptance by other people, including parents, in their rural communities, and their ability to openly be themselves when dealing with the school, form a stark contrast to the anxiety surrounding Adele's encounters with a school community in which her trans history is not known.

In localities where LGBTQI+ parented families were less common, the sight of a lesbian or gay couple might cause initial gossip among parents in the playground. Patty, living in a commuter town north of London, said that at first they had 'lots of stares' and that 'I suspect at some point we were the gossip of the playground'. In such schools in particular, parents might have active strategies to get themselves involved and accepted, such as joining the PTA or the governing body, as described above. Jess, as a new long-term foster carer in a school where there had not previously been LGBTQI+ parents, was particularly proactive in finding ways in which she could be seen as a valuable member of the school community. She spoke at length about one example of this and why she felt it was important:

> I'm the lady that sells the kids cakes at the PTA school fair, and one young girl can't eat anything with wheat in it, and of course we always buy little cakes at Sainsbury's, Tesco's, Asda . . . but this one little girl she can't have anything with wheat in it and everything we had was wheat. I saw her getting into her mum's car, and I tapped on the window and said, 'you don't know me, but I'm Jess, I'm in the PTA and I'm going to make sure that next time we have a fete, give her the money as normal and I will personally buy a cake for her that's dairy free, gluten free, everything so that she can eat it. Is there anything else she's allergic to?' and mum nearly wept. And so the next time we had a fete I had her bag waiting for her and this little girl just jumped for joy. I'm thinking, you know what, and I don't want to say, you got that from a lesbian, but all those interactions count, and it's not about me ramming it down people's throats.

This extract shows Jess's commitment not just to becoming a full part of her daughter's school community, but also an explicit strategy to facilitate this.

Nevertheless, some parents did find the social world of primary school parents difficult to negotiate, though this mainly appeared to be due to other things than their LGBTQI+ status. Jess, whose daughter goes to school in a very deprived working-class neighbourhood, reported that the first time her partner did the school pick-up, she came home saying that she 'never felt so middle-class in my entire life.' Jess herself, however, was welcomed by the other parents, and even encouraged to join the lone parent support group, on the grounds that 'Laura's off working all day, so who's looking after her? You are, you're by yourself. You're a lone parent.' Simon, whose anomalous position as a man in the playground in the mornings was compounded by his son's relatively recent adoption, so that he did not have previous experience of school gate relationships, found it particularly difficult to get involved in the parental social scene, describing himself as 'a bit of an alien'. He felt that this was partly because the school was predominantly Muslim, whereas he was 'gay and white and a single dad'. His experience of other parents was that 'everybody else seems to be sort of getting on with it; they're all sort of a tight, sort of a tight community'. Similarly, Helen, whose parenting experience began when she and her partner started long-term fostering two older children (one already at secondary school) whose difficult history was known to other parents, felt their awkwardness stemmed from this:

> We never felt all that welcomed, actually, by parents. I think partly because we hadn't been there in the beginning. So you felt a bit awkward in the playground standing waiting for your kids, and also, I think people . . . because people knew the children's history, they weren't sure who we were, and were we family members, to begin with.

In these situations it could be hard to disentangle the salience of parents' LGBTQI+ status from other factors impinging on their ability to make good relationships with other parents.

Nevertheless, even when they felt otherwise fully accepted by other parents, some people experienced exclusion that appeared to arise from their family situation not fitting heteronormative ideals. Catherine and Harriet had a particularly interesting example of this. Parents in their son's school found it hard to understand them except through the lens of a heterosexual couple relationship, which meant that they were not included in some events:

> Almost all the mums, I suppose, all the mums I see don't work, or don't work full-time. There's an awful lot of them who don't, and have got a kind of mumsy clique, so that separates into dads and mums. They don't know which of us to put into the mum's side. Which of us is the girl? Who is going to go on the girls' night out? Partly because we don't really fit into that thing anyway. So they don't ever ask us.

Such subtle incomprehensions, while minor in some ways, could nevertheless have an impact on parental school gate relationships.

Relationships with Other Children

Most of the classmates of our respondents' children appeared to take LGBTQI+ families as they found them. Some parents, such as Sam and Helen, explicitly outed themselves to parents in advance so that children could be prepared if necessary, but others did not. Most children did not seem even to have asked questions, although something did occasionally arise, as in this example from a friend of Catherine and Harriet's son:

Joshua I think said, 'so no dads around here?' actually, probably four years ago, 'so no dads here at all?' We said, 'no, no dads. OK,' we said, 'yes, he's got two mums'.

Several parents reported that their children had retained the same friends for some years, so that the situation rarely arose. Jennifer, who now had a partner who did not live with her and otherwise could appear to be just a single parent, found that her daughters' friends barely reacted to being told about Jennifer's new partner: their reported response was 'Oh, OK'.

In some respects, how things developed and what other children knew, depended on the age of the children, with teenagers being more clued up about some of the implications of LGBTQI+ status. Kristy's teenage son's friends, who were obviously aware of her transition, seemed to take it as calmly as the rest of the local population:

His friends are fine. There's no sniggering, there's no staring. They, just say, Hi Kristy, how you doing?

Younger children might be less aware of the situation, particularly if the parents' status was not obvious. This was especially the case for Julian and Elizabeth and their son. Julian is a trans man who is also the birth parent of their 4-year-old. While he was out to several of the parents of his son's friends, Elizabeth thought that these parents had not told their children about his status, for entirely benign reasons, given the young age of the children:

I don't' think those parents have told their children and probably that's coming from a good place—cos they're still little and they just blurt things out. I think they probably—I might be wrong but I don't think they've probably told their children, and that possibly is being sort of protective in a way.

Similarly, Rachael said about her 7-year-old son that 'I'm not really sure that him and his peer group have really kind of got their heads round it really.' Rachael's son had an involved father, who also had a long-term partner, so 'Callum portrays his family life as having two mummies and two daddies'. An involved donor could also mean that a child had shared experience with friends with heterosexual parents, which could make their family situation appear less remarkable. For example, Rachael's son had a friend whose parents had separated, and who also visited his father regularly:

So Callum's little friend Jacob and him talk about going to see their daddy and Callum's friend Jacob's daddy also lives in south London.

So it's just, you know . . . so they have that in common. And it doesn't matter that Callum's daddy is gay.

In this case, what Callum had in common with his friend was more salient than what separated them.

Several parents remarked that their children gained kudos at school from having a LGBTQI+ parent. Helen noted that her daughter was out at school about this but not about being in foster care. Sylvie recounted a day when their son came home particularly happy:

> He said that he'd walked home with these girls across the park and they'd said how cool it was to have two mums; it was even cooler if you had two dads.

While this coolness by association particularly applied to teenagers, it was not confined to them. Rachael described her son's friendship group as being

> all quite jealous and were particularly . . . they would particularly like to have two mummies. Because that would be better, because, when you're seven and eight, I think you're still very, very close to your mummy. And the thought of having two of them is fabulous.

This was borne out in some of our interviews with children: one 11-year-old described having two mothers as giving you 'twice the love', on the rather sexist grounds that it is mothers that do the loving in families.

Sylvie's children had also, even when very young, sometimes shared Sylvie's enjoyment of their ambiguously gendered presentation. On one occasion in particular, Sylvie went on a school trip as a helper, and was mistaken for their son's father:

> I think they must have been in Reception [age 4–5], they were going on an outing to the park for the day or something. I went along as one of the helper parents. The other kids all thought I was the dad and I didn't challenge it, and my son and his friend also didn't challenge it. They just liked the whole slightly queer thing. I think they just thought they knew more than these other kids and it was all good.

Sylvie's son had himself enjoyed confusing adults by presenting ambiguously as a young child, so maybe this was part of his delight in the shared secret. In some cases, however, a child's own ambiguous gender presentation could cause problems for children, if only because they were pestered by other children to claim a binary gender. This happened a lot to Jo's elder child, who was identified as male at birth but, at age five, used gender-neutral pronouns, had long hair, and wore skirts and dresses much of the time. In some ways, as in Jo's family, having LGBTQI+ parents was very supportive of this flexibility for a child to explore their gender, particularly if a parent had not been gender-conforming themselves when young, so could pass on strategies for dealing with other children and their prejudices. Nevertheless, Julian worried whether his son's 'controversial' approach to clothing and play might be blamed on his father's trans status. Most parents, however, if they discussed this, felt that having LGBTQI+ parents presented children with alternative ways of being that might include gender presentation and identity, as well as sexual orientation.

Parental Perceptions of How Children Presented Their Families at School

Although the interviews with children were our main source of data on how they perceived and presented their families in the school context, we also asked parents about this. Clearly a non-normative family form needs some explanation, at least to close friends or children who will be visiting the house, though the extent to which this is the case varies with the general visibility of the family or parent and with the age of the child. The parents of some of the younger children were not sure that the latter were particularly conscious that their families were unusual, particularly if their social network contained several other LGBTQI+ parented families: indeed, Harriet pointed out that 'in his pre-nursery days he kind of lived in a world in which approximately half the kids he knew had lesbian parents'. While this was not the case for all of the families in our study, the fact that primary school parents come to the school frequently, arrange play-dates and so on means that family arrangements are often known from the start and taken for granted by their children's friends.

As children get older, however, and travel to and from school alone, and then move onto secondary education, they have much more control over how their families are portrayed and understood by friends and even teachers. Harriet, noted, for example, that as their son got older 'he's much more responsible for how he presents the family'. This could be a source of distress to parents if it resulted, for example, in changes to how they were named. Harriet and her partner Catherine described how their son had moved from having separate versions of 'mummy' for each of them to calling them both 'mum' outside the house, which they mainly found to be 'mostly fine. But it means you've got a home name and an outside name'. Catherine, however, who is not their child's birth mother, went on to describe a further development of this which had upset her:

> I think something came up recently when it turned out that he was calling me by my name, and I felt a bit sad, because I don't want to be called by my name, it feels as though I am, yeah, it feels that maybe

he's . . . he of course is not putting me, he's just tried to find a way of presenting me to the world in a way that maybe protects him a little bit more, but it made me a little sad.

In families such as this, where both parents have parented the child since birth and both consider themselves full parents, the public erasure of the mother relationship could be experienced as painful, even when the child's perspective and reasons for doing this were understood.

One aspect of the lower parental visibility occasioned by the move from primary to secondary school is that children are no longer obliged to tell everyone about their family situation. Parents sometimes felt that this could cause problems, particularly if it had not occurred to their child that a friend visiting the house might need to know about the family setup in advance. Jane and Paula described an occasion when their son wanted to bring home a Muslim friend and they were concerned that her family might be uncomfortable about it being a LGBTQI+ parented home. Jane explained what happened:

> He's met this girl who—who knows, friendship, fancies her, not sure—and she is Muslim. He's talking away and he's saying, 'I'm going to bring Salma for tea', and she wears a scarf and she's fairly, well, who knows how strict or not she is or whether she's wearing a scarf for her own political statement. Either way, when he said, 'I'm going to bring . . .' I said, 'does Salma know that you have two mums? He looked at me as if I was nuts, he said, 'I don't know.' I said, 'Well, do you think she might need to know before you bring . . . anyone coming into our home needs to feel . . . you don't want to bring somebody in and for them not to feel. . . . We don't want to feel uncomfortable and we don't want anybody else to feel uncomfortable. So he said, 'oh, I'll have to think about that one, I'll have to talk to her'. He, obviously, texted, and then he came back and she said, yeah, 'I said, oh, by the way, I have two mums', and she came back with, 'that's fine, I know someone else with two mums. So,' he said, 'she seems to be OK'.

In this case, Jane and Paula were acting on an (unfounded) assumption that a Muslim child might come from a homophobic family. In other cases, however, parents were aware that their children knew of others in their schools that came from families in which LGBTQI+ parents were not fully accepted. They felt, however, that older children could protect themselves from abuse simply by choosing their friends carefully. As Sylvie put it:

> There are such different groups in the secondary school. So the kids that my kids hang out with pretty much all come from families who

want to be accepting of diversity, and I think both of them have found ways to protect themselves from kids who might have quite different views.

Thus, while their children were also at a school known rapidly to address homophobic bullying, Sylvie felt comfortable that their children would, if necessary, choose their friendships in such a way as to avoid being exposed to bullying or other problematic behaviour.

Even in these circumstances, some children were proactive in taking an 'out and proud' stance within their schools, at least sometimes. Sylvie recounted how their older child wanted to be very explicit about his parentage in front of both teachers and students:

> I remember the first time we went into parents' evening, or it might have been to meet his tutor . . . and him walking across the playground and putting his. . . . Me and my ex were exes at that point. He wanted to put his arm through both our arms and then walked in and said, 'these are my mums' to the teacher.

The same child, in a biology lesson in which IVF was mentioned, told the teacher 'that he was an IVF baby, and no qualms about saying this'. Similarly, Kevin was pleasantly surprised to find that his foster son, who, when he joined them at 14, 'one of his concerns was, what would his friends say about having two dads' within a short time openly referred to Kevin and his husband as 'my dads' at school. Kevin also pointed out, however, that his son was proactive in insisting on good behaviour around himself and his parents:

> He made it quite clear to them, no comments, nothing like that, and they are my dads, kind of thing.

This reflects the approach of many parents, particularly those who, like Kevin, want to be treated as 'friendly people who happen to be gay'. By being out from the start about their parentage, teenagers can work out at an early stage who is safe to hang around with and who is not.

Conclusion

Most of the parents we interviewed were at least partially visible to the school as LGBTQI+. However, they did not always have complete control of how visible they were: those parents who were not part of a co-parenting couple had to come out much more explicitly to people at their children's schools. Being open with the school and other parents about one's LGBTQI+ status was usually unproblematic, and relations with children's teachers, classmates and classmates' parents were generally friendly and straightforward. Being already out to a school community also made it easier for parents to deal immediately and directly with any LGBTQI+ related problems without having to out oneself at that point. For one of our two mothers of trans history who still had children at school, not being out to her son's school was a source of continuous anxiety and made it harder to deal with potential bullying.

While the parents generally felt accepted by teachers and other parents, this did not mean that everything was always wonderful. While fears about bullying almost always turned out to be unfounded, lower level omissions and erasures did occur and upset some parents. Most schools see bullying as the main LGBTQI+ issue that they have to deal with, reflecting, as we saw in Chapter 4, the tendency in school and national policy documents (Department for Education and Employment, 2000; Department for Education and Skills, 2004; Paechter, 2017; The Church of England Education Office, 2017). While the elimination of anti-LGBTQI+ bullying is of course essential, parents feel that schools could go much further in welcoming and including their families. This might be as simple as having explicitly inclusive posters up around the school, so that the acceptance of LGBTQI+ parented families was made explicit to all. Parents also felt that it was important for their children's home lives to be visible within the school curriculum, through: inclusive picture books; acknowledgement on dates such as Mothers' or Fathers' Day that a child might need to do more than one card; and age-appropriate inclusion of information, into sex and relationships education, about non-heterosexual relationships, different means of conception and non-penis-vagina sex.

Schools need to be aware that the LGBTQI+ status of some parents is invisible to them most of the time. In many ways this invisibility would not matter if schools had a more proactive stance with regard to LGBTQI+ inclusivity rather than addressing issues as they come up, for example when such a family is known to join a school community or when a child comes out as gay or trans. Instead, schools need to work on the basis that all children need to know about LGBTQI+ families and to learn that they are part of wider society, even if they do not have direct contact with any at that time. More explicitly inclusive strategies and greater awareness that some LGBTQI+ parents may be relatively invisible would mean that schools were already supporting such families and individuals even before they arrive in the school, and would make it easier to welcome those families from the start.

Schools need to be aware that even though many LGBTQI+ parents are not complaining about their children's experiences, it does not mean that they are entirely happy. Being LGBTQI+ is not parents' only, or, usually, their main concern, so it tends to get pushed down the list of priorities compared to other matters, such as mathematics teaching, friendship problems or appropriate special needs support. That parents complained that even welcoming and supportive schools did not have books in their classrooms that reflected LGBTQI+ family life, or taught sex education in an inclusive way, is a concern that should be addressed. While the parents we interviewed generally felt comfortable and accepted by their children's schools, there is still work to be done to fully include LGBTQI+ parented families in school life.

References

Brown, G. (2012). Homonormativity: A metropolitan concept that denigrates "ordinary" gay lives. *Journal of Homosexuality, 59*, 1065–1072.

Brown, T., Lundgren, A., Stevens, L.-M., & Boadle, J. (2010). Shared parenting and parental involvement in children's schooling following separation and divorce. *Children Australia, 35*(1), 7–13.

The Church of England Education Office. (2017). *Valuing all God's children: Guidance for Church of England schools on challenging homophobic, biphobic and transphobic bullying* (2nd ed.). London: The Church of England Education Office.

Clarke, V., Kitzinger, C., & Potter, J. (2004). "Kids are just cruel anyway": Lesbian and gay parents' talk about homophobic bullying. *British Journal of Social Psychology, 43*(4), 531–550.

Cloughessy, K., Waniganayake, M., & Blatterer, H. (2017). "This is our family. We do not hide who we are." Stigma and disclosure decisions of lesbian parents in Australian early childhood settings. *Journal of GLBT Family Studies*, online advance publication.

Dalton, S. E., & Belby, D. D. (2000). "That's our kind of constellation". Lesbian mothers negotiate institutionalized understandings of gender within the family. *Gender and Society, 14*(1), 36–61.

Department for Education and Employment. (2000). *Sex and relationship education guidance*. London: Department for Education and Employment.

Department for Education and Skills. (2004). *Sex and relationship education—Schools' responsibilities*. London: Department for Education and Skills.

Dunne, G. A. (1997). *"Pioneers behind our own front doors": Towards greater balance in the organization of work in partnerships. Working paper 22, Cambridge Sociological Research Group*. Cambridge.

Hines, S. (2006). Intimate transitions: Transgender practices of partnering and parenting. *Sociology, 40*(2), 353–371.

Holman, E. G., & Oswald, R. F. (2011). Nonmetropolitan GLBTQ parents: When and where does their sexuality matter. *Journal of GLBT Family Studies, 7*(5), 436–456.

Kessler, S. (1998). *Lessons from the intersexed*. New Brunswick: Rutgers University Press.

Kosciw, J., & Diaz, E. M. (2008). *Involved, invisible, ignored: The experiences of lesbian, gay, bisexual and transgender parents and their children in our nation's schools*. New York: Gay, Lesbian and Straight Education Network.

Oakley, M., Farr, R., & Soherer, D. (2017). Same-sex parent socialization: Understanding gay and lesbian parenting practices as cultural socialization. *Journal of GLBT Family Studies, 13*(1), 56–75.

Paechter, C. (2017). Beware the Nursery Gender Police: Why church guidance on homophobic and transphobic bullying falls short. *The Conversation.* Retrieved from https://theconversation.com/beware-the-nursery-gender-police-why-church-guidance-on-homophobic-and-transphobic-bullying-falls-short-8746420/12/17.

Pallotta-Chiarolli. (2010). *Border sexualities, Border families in schools.* Plymouth: Rowman and Littlefield.

Platt, L. F., & Bolland, K. S. (2017). Relationship partners of transgender individuals: A qualitative exploration. *Journal of Social and Personal Relationships, online advance publication.*

Pyne, J., Bauer, G., & Bradley, K. (2015). Transphobia and other stressors impacting trans parents. *Journal of GLBT Family Studies, 11*(2), 107–126.

Ryan-Flood, R. (2009). *Lesbian motherhood: Gender, families and sexual citizenship.* Basingstoke, Hants: Palgrave Macmillan.

Santos, A. C. (2013). Are we there yet? Queer sexual encounters, legal recognition and homonormativity. *Journal of Gender Studies, 22*(1), 54–64.

Sikes, P. (1997). *Parents who teach: Stories from home and from school.* London: Cassell.

Taylor, Y. (2009). *Lesbian and gay parenting: Securing social and educational capital.* Basingstoke, Hants: Palgrave Macmillan.

Weeks, J. (2007). *The world we have won.* London: Routledge.

6 Experiences of Children of LGBTQI+ Parents at School

I am at work when my mobile phone rings. It's my daughter: she is 14 years old. I glance at my watch. She must have walked out of her maths class. I step out of the office into a cold stairwell to answer the call. 'Mum', she whispers, sobbing. My heart plunges into my stomach. This is happening every day, at the moment at least on the days when I can get her to go to school. 'Are you in the toilet again love?' 'Yes. Mum, I can't face them. They're looking at me and laughing and the teachers aren't even noticing'. Things were ok until she told someone that she had a lesbian mum. Now she's being bullied and ostracized. The school won't do anything about it. While the girls' behaviour is deadly effective, it is subtle, and staff don't see it happening. After a year of meetings at which the head teacher gives me platitude after platitude, I give up trying to fix it and move her to another school. But it takes nine months for the local authority to find her a place, and she misses most of Year 10.

Anna

Introduction

Our school-aged children exist in borderlands: they traverse the home-school boundary day after day, strategically selecting the cultural markers they carry with them in each direction (Carlile, 2012). Most of the children of LGBTQI+ parented families could be said to be culturally queer, at least to some degree. This is a concept that 'understands children and young people with LGBTQ parents as part of queer communities, and as having specific experiences and competences that are not necessarily defined by sexual identifications as queer' (Gustavson and Schmitt, 2011: 158; Epstein, 2009). The interviews we discuss below suggest that for some of these children, this means they are especially sensitive to pervasive school heteronormativity. This is particularly inherent in the homophobic, biphobic and transphobic (HBT) language heard in schools which otherwise goes unnoticed, in the same way that white privilege is usually unseen by privileged white people (Logie and Rwigema, 2014). These children have what might be termed borderland subjectivities (Anzaldua, 1987, Carlile, 2012), and as adept as they are at traversing the home-school boundaries day after day, their voices are crucial to the larger task of understanding the experiences of LGBTQI+ parented families and their relationships with schools.

In this chapter we focus on the voices of the children of LGBTQI+ people. In the first part, we address the worries some children have for their parents, and the concurrent desire to be nevertheless visible as the children of LGBTQI+ people. We also address the lengths many children go to, from an early age, to advocate for themselves, their families and their queer community. The chapter then discusses the relationships which the children of LGBTQI+ people have with their peers. This starts with a discussion of the bullying experienced by some. We examine the decision-making process children go through in 'coming out' as the child of LGBTQI+ parents at school within this environment, and then look at the importance of friendships as a source of children's resilience. Related to this, we also address the significance of knowing and spending time with other LGBTQI+ parented families. The final part of the chapter considers the actions of schools more specifically. We begin by looking at groups for LGBTQI+ students and allies (such as the Pride Youth Networks described in Chapter 7) and their value in building a support system. We then address children's experience of school disciplinary responses to HBT bullying and language. We discuss the approach taken by our respondents' schools to including LGBTQI+ people and issues within curricula. We finish this section with a summary of the advice given to schools by the children we interviewed—including on whether teachers should come out, and how the scant LGBTQI+ content which is delivered needs to be more nuanced and inclusive.

This chapter is based on in-depth interviews with 19 children from LGBTQI+ parented families. We found our respondents via convenience sampling and the snowball method, but also through a Rainbow Families camp and our LGBT Parented Families and Schools Facebook group. Two of the children were part of the school-based focus groups undertaken to evaluate the Educate & Celebrate 'LGBT+ Friendly Schools' programme discussed in Chapter 7.

One of our goals in this research was to strive for a diverse set of interviewees. The 19 children we interviewed ranged in age from 6 to 16, and came from 15 families. Typically we would ask how their family came to be. Five described themselves as having an unknown donor father, three with lesbian and two with bisexual mothers. Five were adopted (two by gay men and three by lesbians), one fostered by lesbians, and two had a known donor father. Finally, six were born into straight relationships, after which their parents came out as LGBTQI+: three as women of trans history and four as lesbians. Five of our interviewee children had special educational needs, ranging from dyslexia and depression with anxiety to a chromosomal moderate learning disability and Asperger's Syndrome. As far as we are aware (we didn't ask), ten identified as female, nine as male and one as non-binary/lesbian. One identified as cisgender male and bisexual. Nine of the children lived in one or other of two large cities in England, and nine lived in small rural towns or villages. The jobs their parents worked in tended towards those usually described as 'middle class', but varied somewhat, and included: school lunchtime supervisor; academic; psychologist; teacher; nurse; IT technician; pest control manager; and doctor.

Interviews with the children were conducted in a variety of ways. Some, where the families chose this, were conducted as part of a joint interview with parents, or with parents present. Most took place in people's homes, others during a Rainbow Families camp as we walked together around gardens, campsites and farms, with Anna holding the voice recorder and the child skipping along beside her. Interviews were semi-structured and mainly face to face, but some were conducted over Skype. Several of the children interviewed have parents whose interviews are discussed in the previous chapter. Consequently, when children were not interviewed with their parents, we have attempted to protect the children's anonymity by not saying anything about who their parents are. This includes not using even the parents' pseudonyms or other identifying features when discussing the children's accounts, to make it less easy for parents to identify what their children said. Given our finding that children often tried to protect their parents from knowing about their experiences, and that we had promised them confidentiality, we feel that this sacrifice of detail is necessary to protect the children's privacy.

Where parents and children were interviewed together, and we are able to use both pseudonyms, it is important to note that many of our child respondents called their parents by their first names. For children in same-gender parented households, this may be partly because some parents may differentiate themselves by using names (for example, 'Mummy Jo' and 'Mummy Anna'). This convention also functions to establish parenting roles, particularly of non-biological parents. The children we interviewed whose parents were of trans history both called their parent by their original pre-transition title (for example, 'Dad') alongside their post-transition name and gender (for example, 'Kristy' and 'she'). In any case, because of histories of family rejection, LGBTQI+ parented families are often embedded into a queer culture which values 'chosen families' consisting of friends and ex-partners who eat, holiday and celebrate together (Bergman, 2013), and in which children may frequently hear their parents called by their first names. Finally, the children of LGBTQI+ parents hear about mummies and daddies from nursery school upwards; as we saw in Chapter 5, this can lead some children to move to using first names instead.

We discuss the interview responses under three broad themes: the child and family; peer relationships; and schools, although, mirroring the home/school borderlands, these themes overlap to some extent.

The Child and the Family

Being the Child of LGBTQI+ Parents

In order to disrupt a pathologizing approach, one of the things we asked interviewees about was 'the best thing' or 'what is good' about having an LGBTQI+ parent. Some children tended to refer to the sort of thing they could expect from any parent, regardless of whether they were LGBTQI+. For example, 12-year-old Joe's feelings about the benefits of just having more parents was similar to something any child of separated parents with step-parents might say. His parents had separated when his mother came out as a lesbian, and he recounted the experience of having more parental figures in his life:

> It means that you have two mums but you still also have your dad, it is just like having one more mum really, it is nice because it is a bigger family. . . . Because you see them more and you get used to them and they are part of the family, and you get used to them. It is just one more person to be with.

Kieron, aged eight, who had been adopted two years before the interview, said that 'it's good to have nice parents and I just don't know why'. This may well relate more to having a secure adoptive family than to the fact that he has two fathers. Riley, aged ten, explained that she felt it was better to have two mothers because:

> Well, the good thing is, like, they don't fight as often because I know that sometimes men and women don't always get on. Like, because they have their differences in lots and lots of different ways. They don't always get on like boys don't normally like girls and girls don't normally like boys. They normally have girl friendship groups and boy friendship groups.

It is interesting here that, while Riley expresses a clear belief that there are definite advantages to having two mothers, she does so in strongly gender-stereotyped terms.

For some children, positive feelings about having LGBTQI+ parents seemed to be partly something to do with a sense that they experience elements of queer culture, either through knowing other families like theirs, or because of their involvement in LGBTQI+ events. Kieron, adopted with his brother by a gay male couple, had thought about this, saying:

> because you have two dads and you know that other people have two dads, so, you know people have two dads so, you can trust them.

Isla, Joe's older sister, was also proud to be part of a visibly LGBTQI+ family:

> I wanted to go to Pride in support of my mum because I wanted to show people that I am not ashamed of her. And actually the atmosphere there was amazing! Oh, I can't wait to do it again this year because even people who aren't gay themselves, like me and [someone she met on the march], me and him spent time together at Pride and we are both not gay ourselves but just the atmosphere there, everyone just wants to be there and it's really, really nice.

This involvement in LGBTQI+ cultural activities and demonstrations such as Pride could inculcate political awareness in some of those children of LGBTQI+ parented families who participate in such events. Fairtlough (2008) found that the children of the lesbian and gay parents she interviewed often cited positive effects on their own developing progressive identities. One of her interviewees reported that 'growing up with my mother's openness about her lesbian lifestyle has encouraged me to become an open, honest and broad-minded person' (524). Our findings support this: Isla told us that having a lesbian parent had made her 'very open minded'; and Piero, aged 13, said that having a parent who was a woman of trans history meant he was 'much more . . . open-minded and . . . much more understanding and sort of, I know much more about the world and have sort of quite matured quite a lot for my age'. There was, therefore, a sense amongst some of our respondents that being part of a queer community and a queer culture was one of the benefits of having LGBTQI+ parents, not just because of a sense of belonging, but because it gave them an ethical and political sense of equality and open-mindedness.

The negative aspects of having LGBTQI+ parents described by the children we interviewed were related to discrimination from people outside the family and the community (Knight et al., 2017). This discrimination can sometimes be experienced as bullying. Isla described how

> maybe people might think that having a lesbian mum makes you suddenly lesbian but I don't, yeah I think that's probably just it, people just don't know, people don't talk about it enough.

From her point of view, it was the fact that others may be unfamiliar with the idea of having a lesbian mother which might prompt a negative response. This generous acceptance that negative responses may be largely due to ignorance was mentioned in many of the interviews. This and the experience of bullying are discussed in more detail later in the chapter.

Assumptions underpinning heteronormativity, especially stereotypical expectations surrounding gender roles, could have an impact on children's experiences of having LGBTQI+ parents. Kristy, a woman of trans history, felt that her 11-year-old son could be embarrassed at football practice, especially as he had just joined a new team where Kristy was not previously known:

> It's a bit of an issue because he plays football and the football thing is very macho. It's that sort of crowd of parents. Very footballing guy-type macho-type working class people. All lovely, don't get me wrong, but I think he's a bit embarrassed when we go to watch him because he's just changed to a much better team.

Kristy's reading of the heteronormative atmosphere at football practice draws on her experience of what she identifies as her own socioeconomic class. Similarly, Jon felt that a disadvantage of having lesbian parents meant having to deal with other people's assumptions about what they perceived as a lack of a masculine role model in his family:

> I know some people say like, oh, like, what about having a really good dad figure who plays football with you? And stuff like that. But I think like, mums are really actually good at that . . . playing what would be the traditional dad . . . my mum, she plays football with me but she's terrible. But yes, that's fun.

Jon identifies the heteronormative assumption here, but even at the age of ten, is able to patiently analyze his peers' responses as incorrect in the face of his personal experience. This awareness of heteronormativity could also be described as demonstrating an element of his queer culture (Logie and Rwigena, 2014).

Children's Worry About Their Parents

Some of the children we spoke to worried about their parents. This appeared to be related to experiences of prejudice, either in the street or at school. Children did not want to upset their parents by talking about the HBT bullying or language they had heard at school. Their reticence seemed to be related to a desire to be proud of, rather than ashamed or embarrassed by, their parents. One child was justifiably concerned about their parent being attacked in the street. We can only guess as to the impact these worries might have on children's educational experiences.

Children's concern for their parents sometimes led to them not taking advantage of support for themselves. Piero had been offered counselling and psychological support, but did not want to upset his parents by taking up the offer:

I've wondered about going to the doctors here like, I often get referred to somewhere but I just don't feel like it because it means talking to my mum and stuff, which I don't want to do.

It appears that Piero's worries about himself took second place to his concern for his parents, and this affected other aspects of his life:

When I go out in public places where my parents are, like in big towns or festivals, I don't worry about *me* getting lost, I worry about *them worrying about me* being lost.

(his emphasis)

Piero was very clear about his motivations, telling us that 'I don't want my parents being upset or sort of like fussing over me. I don't really like anyone doing that'.

It is perhaps unsurprising that Piero felt so protective of his parent. He told us about two occasions when she, a woman of trans history, had been verbally assaulted in public:

I was with [her] and she was trying to get into the women's changing rooms at a swimming pool and some guy comes up and starts shouting at her and says she can't go in there and like . . . loads of slurs flying and sort of . . . not very nice! I think he was drunk. If I'm in public, walking with her and I see like a couple of people staring at her or like a kid going . . . and like then they start staring at [her], it's just like . . . it's instant sort of . . . like . . . it's a sort of like, anger! Like, a bit ago, some kids were sort of having a little go at [her] and [she] sort of like called up the community police and said, 'There's some kids causing trouble'. . . . I just sat on a bench and I sort of like . . . I was crying and I just. . . . [She] came over and I was like, 'If those kids do that again, I'll like smash their faces in and knock their teeth out!' [She] doesn't like it when I do that, surprisingly!

It is likely that Piero's experience was more marked than that of some of the other children we interviewed because of the virulent transphobia often experienced by his parent, who was, at the time, very obviously a woman of trans history. The homonormative mainstreaming of lesbian, gay and trans people who fit neatly into the gender binary make other(ed), often bisexual, genderqueer and intersex people even more vulnerable and noticeable.

Piero's desire to protect his parents was, however, by no means unique. Of the families we spoke to, almost all of the parents told us that their children had not told them about bullying or HBT language at school, despite the fact that many of the children reported these negative experiences in their interviews. Those parents who were in the same interviews as their children often gave a surprised facial expression at this, or exchanged concerned glances with each other. In Piero's case, he decided not to speak out about the bullying in order to protect his parent from the risk of being further upset by HBT experiences.

Wanting to Be Visible as Children of LGBTQI+ People: 'I'm Different in a Little Way to Everyone Else'

Despite their worries, the children of LGBTQI+ people across socioeconomic groups and in both urban and rural environments generally wanted their family structures to be known and visible to others, as part of social acceptance (see Chapter 5). This is important for schools to understand: normalizing strategies can undermine visibility, yet having one's particular family culture acknowledged and appreciated can have beneficial effects for learning (Sarmento & Freire, 2012). In any case, there was a sense of pride in being different. When asked about what it was like being the child of LGBTQI+ people, Riley, aged ten, explained 'it's like you feel special . . . [you] just feel special in yourself and that makes you boost your confidence. . . . It feels quite, like, it feels really nice'. Kelly, also aged ten, told us: 'some people do get interested when I tell them about stuff like this. They do get interested. Sometimes they want to know more, sometimes they don't.' Ada, also ten, told us about how she actively wanted her mothers to come along to parents' evenings as visible lesbian parents:

> I think that one of the benefits [of coming to a parents' evening with both mums] is that you find that you're not just in a big group . . . an enormous group of people . . . I mean. . . . I mean that I'm different in a little way because I just . . . I'm just not identical to everyone else. . . . I don't really enjoy being like everyone else.

Where schools work to make LGBTQI+ people and families more commonly included across the curriculum, their children sometimes feel a sort of loss of identity, albeit tempered by a safer environment and fewer HBT experiences. This dissonance between an established queer cultural identity as 'special' and a new experience of becoming normalized can feel like a loss. This is a risk acknowledged by other researchers (Gustavson & Schmitt, 2011).

Advocating for Themselves, Their Families and Their Queer Community

From the youngest children upwards, almost all of our interviewees talked about or gave examples of advocacy and peer education. Ada talked about how she taught her peers about same-gender relationships:

I've had quite a few people . . . pester . . . just asking me over and over again. . . . They ask me, 'why don't you have a dad?' And . . . 'why have you got two mums?' . . . and those sorts of questions. . . . And I just say, 'I don't have a dad . . . I do have a dad but I don't know him because he was a donor dad, he was an anonymous donor dad. . . . And why shouldn't two people of the same gender love each other?' They don't really say anything. They just walk away normally.

Ada also finds herself having to compensate for inadequate school provision for her family situation:

ADA: And on Mother's Day I write two cards. . . . Or I write one card to both mums.
ANNA: And does the . . . teacher remind you to do that or talk about it at all, or do you just do it yourself because that's what you do?
ADA: No, because that's just what I do.

Another of our interviewees, Nick, aged eight, said that he was glad we were interviewing him as he wanted to use this book as a tool for self-advocacy at school:

When it's finished I hope and I'm sure I will from Anna, get a copy of the book and I'll bring it into school and . . . I'll probably . . . read them extracts from the book.

Joe told us that he often had to stand up to the casual use of 'gay' as a derogatory term:

I stand up to [homophobia] straight away. I don't let them affect me at all. . . . If someone says, 'that thing is gay', then I will go up to them and go and say, 'is that a problem with someone being gay?', and they will just mutter 'no' and walk off. I usually ignore them or stand up to them. It doesn't really affect school life much.

Isla, however, explained that she has to choose when and where to 'police' her peers' HBT language:

Derogatory terms [are] used all the time. . . . I don't like it, I don't like it at all because it's not nice and it's, it's derogatory. It's horrible but if people, you can't go round policing every single person in the school and telling them to stop because you are going to end up not having anybody to talk to if you do that. And it's just not, I suppose, I wouldn't say you get used to it but it just becomes so common in schools. . . . If we are in a lesson and I know the people fairly well then I will say 'you shouldn't use that', but I wouldn't actively go out and go up to somebody in the corridor and say 'you don't say that'. But if someone just shouts something then I will turn around and say 'that's rude, you should not be using that language'.

Isla has to decide when she feels safe and whether or not to advocate for herself. Her experience requires a fairly consistent level of vigilance and self-awareness which will not be required by many of her peers from heteronormative families.

Piero also carries out emotional work in order to process the HBT language and comments he hears at school:

If I hear anyone being homophobic or transphobic at school, it's just like if someone like . . . if someone calls someone gay or calls me a gay, I will just be like, 'What's wrong with being gay?' I think they can obviously see the wrong answer isn't going to go well for them. They sort of just go, 'Nothing' and sort of back off.

When asked whether he would tell a teacher about any negative comments about his parent, a woman of trans history, or deal with it himself, Piero told us 'I'd beat the shit out of them, honestly. I'd try at least'. He did not have much faith in the school advocating on his behalf, so was ready to self-advocate whenever it was needed:

At my school . . . the school doesn't really do anything, to be honest. Like, I've told the school about people doing stuff that they shouldn't be and they don't really do anything about it so, usually, you're just better off taking it into your own hands.

Jad, aged 15, a non-binary lesbian who uses the pronoun 'they', described conducting some whole-school education in order to advocate for LGBTQI+ people:

This teacher . . . let me do a presentation about LGBTQI+ stuff and I did this presentation and I asked people if they knew what the whole 'LGBTQI+' stands for and only two people put their hands up in my whole form. That's twenty-eight kids and only two people knew what I was talking about.

Jad expressed frustration at their peers' ignorance, but continued to work away at their HBT language:

When I hear people saying stuff like 'Oh, that's so gay' or 'Are you gay?' . . . like students, or stuff like that, I confront it. I say, 'Is that a bad thing, is that actually a bad thing or are you just saying that?' They say, 'No, no, no, it's not a bad thing'. I've confronted it so much and people know about who I am so, if I confront it then they know that it's wrong and they actually stop. I've actually told people, 'You need to stop this, it's homophobia, you can't say stuff like that'. They say, 'I'm sorry, I didn't mean to, I didn't realize'. They don't actually know that they're being homophobic.

Jad is patient with their peers' lack of knowledge, but at the same time does not let them get away with HBT language. It was clear, however, that all the children found it frustrating to have to do educative work that should have been their schools' responsibility. Without meaningful institutional change, the emotionally taxing 'diversity work' carried out at school by Ada, Nick, Isla, Piero and Jad becomes what Ahmed (2012) calls 'a banging-your-head-on-the-brick-wall-job' (26).

Jad's and Piero's parents are professionally active in the inclusion movement for LGBTQI+ people. Consequently, both young people may well have learned these self-advocacy strategies and activities at home. Jad was also interviewed alongside their parent, so this may have influenced some of what they talked about. However, whilst they are also articulate about LGBTQI+ rights and equality, Nick, Isla, Kelly and Ada's parents could not really be described as activists. Advocacy seems to be a common activity amongst the children we interviewed, whether or not their parents are advocates or activists. Even where a young person is new to having an LGBTQI+ parent, they are ready to respond if necessary. When asked how he would react to HBT language at school, Ethan, aged 15, whose parent had only recently come out as a woman of trans history, distinguished between friendly banter and the aggressive use of HBT comments. He explained that

> if they were joking I would be like, 'come on, don't say that again', I wouldn't really mind. I would find it hard to get offended. But if it was [said] angrily, I would be like, 'please don't say that', or I would say something.

Children of LGBTQI+ people, like other children, are generally proud of their families, and this makes them want to stay visible at school, to some extent. This is despite the fact that they worry for their parents in an atmosphere of HBT language and bullying. The seriousness of what these children experience can vary depending on the family and the school, from microaggressions (Kosciw, Greytak, Diaz, & Bartkiewicz, 2010) and mild HBT comments to aggressive shouting in public places. All the children of LGBTQI+ parents we interviewed were hesitant to tell their parents about their own experiences of homophobia, biphobia and transphobia. However, they often recognize that their experiences and background have helped to make them politically aware and social-justice oriented. They are committed to self-advocacy and to advocating for their families, for queer culture and the LGBTQI+ community.

Friends and Enemies: The Peer Relationships of LGBTQI+ Parented Children

As we saw in the previous section, HBT bullying and hearing HBT language from peers is, whilst not universal, a common experience (Russell, McGuire, Lee, Larriva, & Laub, 2008; Jones & Clarke, 2007). In this environment, one of the most pressing concerns experienced by these children was the decision about whether or not to come out as the children of LGBTQI+ people. Their decision-making processes around coming out illuminated the deep importance of friendships. A clear theme emerges from our conversations with children and young people around the importance of good close friendships to their ability to be resilient in a heteronormative and sometimes HBT context. Spending time with other children of LGBTQI+ people can help with this resilience, even if only to give children a break from the vigilance and emotional work required to survive and thrive in such an environment.

Bullying and Homophobic, Biphobic or Transphobic Language at School

In line with other research (Jones & Clarke, 2007; (Russell, McGuire, Lee, Larriva, & Laub, 2008), all of our interviewees reported hearing homophobic, biphobic and transphobic comments in their schools, most commonly the ubiquitous use of the word 'gay' as an insult. For some children, these experiences are unproblematic. Davide, for example, felt that the word 'gay' was not a specifically homophobic term, but just a general term of abuse used towards everyone; he was unconcerned about it. For others, however, they can create an unpleasant environment. Other HBT incidents which children and young people told us about were more directly aggressive. Incidents might be personally tailored to the victim: for example, when Philippa, at 13, got her hair cut short, she was for a time being teased with the name 'Phil' by other students. Whilst this was about Philippa, not her parents, the heteronormative taunts would have contributed to creating an environment in which coming out as the child of two women might feel unsafe.

Sometimes the children of LGBTQI+ parents join in with HBT language or behaviour, in order to fit in or to avoid telegraphing the fact that they have LGBTQI+ parents. Ted, who is 15, often adopted this strategy. When asked if he joined in with homophobic language, he said,

> I do, not all the time, but sometimes, I do join in. Not every time . . . when I feel it's the right time to join in . . . Because, I would like the

Experiences of Children of LGBTQI+ Parents 121

friends who do it, not to think that there is something wrong with me or I have two mums or anything like that.

Riley, who has two mothers, was bullied by another child who had two fathers from the age of about seven to nine. At 10 years-old she was very aware of the possible reasoning behind this:

> I was getting bullied by someone that had two dads. Which was just unacceptable really. They were bullying me for that I had two mums . . . I think she was bullying me because she had them too and . . . she wanted me to feel bad for having two mums. That's basically what bullying is. . . . They either want to just bully you for the sake of it, or just want to make you feel bad for what you've got but which is actually really good. She would say . . . 'you're different and you can't have friends and you can't have a life and' . . . just mean stuff like really and just being a pain.

Riley knew that her bully had her own two-father family, but this did not stop her from feeling hurt by the bullying. It is also possible that it is the bully's own cultural queerness that allowed her to realize that her LGBTQI+ parentage would be a weak spot for Riley.

Some of the children in stable and relatively affluent family situations had been able to develop a range of constructive strategies and a resilient emotional response. Nick lives with his two mothers, both of whom have professional jobs, but like many of the other children we interviewed, regularly sees his father, also a middle-class professional. He therefore has three engaged parents and plenty of cultural capital. At age nine, he had already developed an articulate answer to negative uses of the word 'gay':

ANNA: So . . . does anyone in your school ever use the word 'gay' as an insult?
NICK: Well . . . I do have kind of arch enemies and they usually insult me with that word. They insult me about having two mums and guess what I do, insult them back about having two . . . erm, I'm like . . . 'huh! Only a mum and a dad?! Inadequate!'. That's what I say, because I've got two mums and a dad. So, I've got three.
ANNA: Yeah. You've got three parents.
NICK: I'm like, 'inadequate!' That's what I say to them.
ANNA: It's a good word.

Nick also felt able to ask for help from a teacher if he was being bullied:

NICK: sometimes I do get a little bit of abuse but when I tell the teacher, erm, it never happens again. I have an arch enemy in my class, two actually . . . and they were like, 'two mums?! That's just weird and

freaky' and I told the teacher and let me tell you, I believe, green form . . . green form, going to the Head Teacher and detention.
ANNA: Okay, so what's a green form?
NICK: A green form is like if you do something really bad, actually basically like it goes to the Head. . . . I think, like the proper big name for it is, erm . . . Notification for Unacceptable Behaviour and then, when the teacher does it out, writes the form out, it goes to the Head and at the end of the year it goes to your mum.

Despite some of the children's opinions (outlined below) that their schools are getting better at dealing with HBT language and bullying, the heteronormative, sometimes HBT environment does impact on the friendships of the children of LGBTQI+ parents. Jon's experience demonstrates how this could partly be to do with a lack of familiarity with different kinds of family:

Well basically like in the early years people sort of like ask, 'how are you alive if like you only have two mums?' And like you have to answer them. It takes quite a long time to get through that. Like still Year 5 and 6 people come up to you who you don't really know and say 'wait, so how are you alive if you only have two mums?' And I have to explain to them.

Nick also reported that 'once or twice I've been asked crazy things like, erm . . . erm, were you born half and half? Half in one [mum] and half in the other!' These experiences illustrate why it is important that schools do not merely respond to HBT bullying, but act to recognize LGBTQI+ parented families and to educate children about different kinds of family. Where schools do not even address bullying, serious emotional and behavioural responses can ensue (Jones & Clarke, 2007).

Piero's experience reflects the work which still remains to be done in some schools, particularly around women of trans history. He told us about how badly his primary school coped with his parent's transition, and how this affected his emotional well-being:

The first [school] was absolutely terrible with like dealing with my trans parent. Like there were a couple of parents who just had a massive problem with her and they . . . would tell their kids not to play with me or not hang out with me. Like, the worst parent, tried to get [my parent] kicked off the PTA. And the head teacher just didn't really do anything to sort of back [her] up or say that the parent was in the wrong because it was early transition and those days it would be like . . . a lot of people would sort of stare and like . . . just a bit of a hard time. I didn't really know what was going on because I was quite little. I was usually upset most days and I'd have panic attacks a lot. A lot of kids would just ignore me. They would sort of treat me as an outsider.

As a young child, Piero had felt completely unsupported by his school. He quickly learned to fight his way out of trouble:

> at primary school, what would happen is, kids would be mean to me and like stuff would happen and I would sort of like not tell anyone, bottle it up, bottle it up and at some point, I just snap! I think the most serious one was, a couple of kids . . . were calling me names and I just sort of snapped and I sprinted after one of them and sort of tripped him over and got him in a headlock, punched him and then he got up and ran again and I did the same and then he ran out of the school gates—because it was home time—sort of like, screaming and a parent happened to sort of grab him and put him in a car and like . . . I sort of cooled down a bit and I was like, 'Oh, my god, what have I just done?'

Piero's response was at the more serious end of the spectrum. However, it is salutary: most of the children we interviewed expressed some form of discomfort at the HBT atmosphere they sometimes experienced at the hands of their peers.

Coming Out at School as the Child of LGBTQI+ Parents

Within the sometimes stressful context described above, most children we interviewed had to make a conscious decision about whether or not to come out as the child of LGBTQI+ parents. Like their parents (Taylor, 2009), they may have to make the 'coming out' decision repeatedly. The heteronormative climate at school impacted deeply on Jad's coming-out experience. They are doubly disadvantaged in that they are coming out both as queer themselves and as the child of LGBTQI+ parents. As a queer person, Jad is already subject to schooling's regulation of student bodies (Paechter, 2004). When they recently came out as non-binary, they received permission to wear the uniform usually reserved for boys, so they have to think about coming out every time they get up in the morning to put on their school uniform. The atmosphere at school is not entirely safe: whilst Jad's school is very strict with bullying, this has not stopped them from hearing their peers making frequent HBT comments: '[They say] oh, 'That's so gay' or 'Are you gay?' Oh, my god, it drives me crazy. They always say it in such a rude or sarcastic way'. Jad explained how this atmosphere has affected their friendships: 'I don't really get along with people in my own year that much. I think in school now I feel like I'm going to be judged all the time because a lot of the time I am, and the people in my year are really judgmental'.

Jad's experience is particularly difficult to negotiate, and they lost friendships through the coming-out process:

JAD: After I came out I did lose a lot of friends. I used to be friends with a lot of people in my year. Actually, when I came out it all went wrong. I had two friends, one called Sasha and one called Charlie. And Sasha was supposed to come over. This made me cry, it was really bad. My mate Sasha was supposed to come over for a sleepover and then we were going to go to Pride in the morning. When we told her parents, her mum was fine with it but her dad was so homophobic that he wouldn't let her talk to me anymore. I wasn't allowed to see her ever, apart from in school. Then we got so distant after that, that we don't really talk anymore.
ANNA: Was that because you were gay?
JAD: Both. Because I was and my parents were. Then, there was this mate Charlie, that I had. We're still kind of mates and I used to go around to hers and she used to come around to mine all the time. When her mum found out. . . . That I was gay and that my parents were gay, her mum met both of my parents. . . . She said 'you're not allowed to talk to them anymore. You're not allowed to see them, to talk to them in school, outside of school, they're not allowed round here, you're not allowed round there'.

Given the risk of such incidents occurring, the children we interviewed had developed a form of vigilance, or a set of techniques for reading the safety of a person or a relationship before coming out as the child of LGBTQI+ parents. Aidan, who has two fathers, says that he tells 'only people I know and people I can trust'. Similarly, Ada takes her time getting to know people before she says anything:

> I prefer to know people, like, their names and . . . I like to get to know people a bit before I say. . . . Because I just don't tell a complete stranger. I just don't walk up to a stranger and if they ask questions then I don't just answer, oh I've got gay parents and. . . . Well . . . because, why should I?

Like Ada, Philippa had devised ways to read people before coming out:

> I've only told a few people that I have two mums, people I can actually trust, others I wouldn't really talk about my family to them. . . . The ones I have known for the longest. . . . I asked what did they think about it. I said, what would they think if I said I had two mums? I listened to what they said and they said they wouldn't mind because they've got friends of their own who has two mums, two dads. So, I told them.

Coming out stories were often related to discussions about parent-teacher meetings, in the UK often held at whole-year-group events called 'Academic Review Days', or more traditionally, 'Parents' Evenings'. These occasions are often critical moments for coming-out experiences, especially in secondary school, where parents are less likely to be seen regularly at the school gate. Like standing on the sidelines at a child's football practice, Parents' Evening can become a critical moment of erasure, recognition, anticipation, planning, protection, passing and representing.

Most parents want to make a good impression at school: close collaboration between parents and teachers can have a beneficial impact on students' academic progress (Sarmento & Freire, 2012). Parents' Evenings may understandably cause apprehension as they are the moment when students experience their parents' responses to their schools' reports on their behaviour and academic progress. Parents, however, also have to confront their own memories of the power imbalance inherent in their childhood relationships with teachers: what Lawrence-Lightfoot (2003) calls 'the ghost in the classroom'. Consequently, Parents' Evenings already carry an emotional weight and a particular significance, becoming a site of negotiation between institution, parent and child. In addition to all of this existing stress, LGBTQ+ parented families are conscious of the fact that Parents' Evenings are a key stage on which the heterosexual matrix (Butler, 1993) is played out within the institution of the school. Ted described what happens when his two mums come to a parent's evening:

> To be honest, I feel all right but, at the same time it feels a bit awkward because all the other parents are not gay and it feels a bit awkward. I like having [my mums] but, it's just that I'm used to just having one parent come in and not both of them all the time . . .
> Whenever my parents come in, I do eventually go up to them and say hi, but I usually hang out with my mates round the school and not try and avoid them, but try . . . not pretend to not know them but, keep out of their way for a bit until their parents have gone home and the boys and girls who know I have two mums, it's just me and them, I'll just go up and I'll stay with them for the meeting. . . . I'm not that sure what [my mates] would think of them and what their reaction would be if I told them or something like that.

Piero and his parent, a woman of trans history, are also cautious around parent-teacher meeting events, perhaps because of the extreme transphobia they experienced at Piero's previous school. If his parent needs to meet with Piero's teachers, they usually arrange for a time after school, or while other students are in lessons so that Piero can feel more in control of whether and when he comes out as the child of a woman of trans history.

While coming out is sometimes precipitated by a parent-teacher meeting or a friend's visit to the family home, sometimes children come out merely because the conversation invites it. In this they are assisted by the self-advocacy and peer-education skills described above. Kelly, aged 11, whose separated mums are bisexual and lesbian, reported,

> I have sometimes been asked, when people have been talking about their dads and then I've been asked about my dad and they don't usually understand how I don't have a dad. . . . I just say that I have a donor dad who donated some sperm to my mum, that's about it. They usually seem like, 'oh, that's a bit different'.

Some children are simply not believed by their peers. When Nick comes out as the child of two mums, his peers sometimes question what he says:

> What I find really annoying is sometimes they say which one is actually your mum and sometimes . . . and I'm like both and they're like 'Both?! No, one's a child-minder'.

Coming out as the child of an LGBTQI+ parent is not always difficult, however. Ethan's parent, Kristy, came out recently as a woman of trans history. Ethan and Kristy discussed this together in their interview:

KRISTY: You've not had any problems with anyone at school regarding me at all?
ETHAN: No. There's no, 'your Dad's transgender', they don't really care. Some people are interested but no one really says anything.
ANNA: Are you out as a child of a trans person?
ETHAN: Yeah, definitely. I never did it in one big go. I just said 'my Dad is transgender' and they're like, 'cool'. They know of it but some people don't know. I told them the other day and they're like, 'interesting'.
ANNA: And that's it?
ETHAN: Yeah, no one says anything. They're like, 'that's really interesting'.

When we asked Ethan if he called Kristy 'Mum' at school, he told us 'I call Kristy my Dad but as she'. This made sense to Kristy, to Ethan and to his friends. Whilst at the time of writing the UK is in an enormous state of transformation regarding LGBTQI+ positive legal and cultural changes, LGBTQI+ parented families are in a process of finding 'ways of being', which can include uncomplicated acceptance, as is the case with Ethan's friends.

It is possible that their better-than-expected coming-out experience is also partly because Ethan and Kristy are established members of a monocultural, rural community which has not been subjected to disjunctures between cultures sometimes experienced by families in more multicultural city areas. People who have brought their faith and culture with them into diverse urban environments are under hegemonic normative pressure to fight hard against what might be perceived as degenerate values in order to retain a sense of respect towards and within their religious or cultural identity. Freire's (1996) conception of horizontal violence may also explain some of this: where oppressed people have no space to develop a meaningful hierarchy, they can jostle for position and strike out against each other. When 'subordinate groups seek to mobilize along boundaries drawn for the purposes of domination' (Solomos, 2001: 202), they may be forced into more rigid heteronormative approach in order to look as 'normal' as possible in an environment which is hostile to people who are not white and/or local. Sometimes this can be expressed as HBT beliefs. As was suggested by some parents (see Chapter 5), the lack of racial or religious identity politics in a more monocultural area may make it easier for a community to accept gender diversity. In addition to where a family is living at the time, coming out as the child of a transgender parent can also be affected by whether the parent wants to be openly trans or not. Because Kristy had stayed in the same village she lived in before her transition, secrecy was not possible, for either her or for Ethan, but it was also the case that hiding her past did not appear to be a priority for her, which left the choice about whether to tell his friends up to Ethan. Where a parent of trans history is strongly committed to being known only in their preferred gender, this can make it impossible for their children to be out about their parentage.

Coming out as the child of LGBTQI+ people at school can be a much easier experience if other adults are 'out' at school. Children can then gauge their peers' response before coming out themselves. At his new school, Piero was in a school pantomime, and realized that one of the sound technicians was a woman of trans history. Piero was heartened by the fact that his friends did not have a negative response to her:

> No one really had a problem with that. Just like most of the time, I'm like, it's not going to really matter, they're friends and it's nothing to not like me about, and I think, the worst that's going to happen, is maybe they'll stop being friends with me. . . . It was just like . . . it made me think, like, sort of . . . maybe people are a bit more sort of like . . . open-minded and like much more sort of accepting.

Having out LGBTQI+ teachers and other school staff can feel similarly supportive.

The Importance of Friendships: Love, Trust and Resilience

Loving, trusting friendships can be enormously important in the coming out process for children of LGBTQI+ parents, and also in their resilience within heteronormative and occasionally hostile school environments. Iris, aged nine, who has a bisexual single parent, thought of her coming-out story as intimately entwined with her closest school friendship. She explained, 'I say I was donor conceived, which means I didn't have a dad when I was born . . . They understand it, especially Cecilia. I've been with her since nursery'. Kelly, who has two mums, experienced plenty of bullying at school, but describes how important her friendships were to her recovery from this experience, and how she saw them as important to her resilience as she progressed into secondary school. After the period of bullying, Kelly explained:

KELLY: I got some more friends from that and then I sort of developed.
ANNA: Do they all know that you've got two mums?
KELLY: Yeah.
ANNA: And they're all fine about it? You said earlier that if someone said something homophobic they'd come and tell you and they're sort of protective?
KELLY: Yeah. They obviously won't tell me the specific words because they knew that would hurt me, but they told me to be aware with who I truly am friends with. If they're saying stuff like that, I don't really want to be friends with them, especially because they know.
ANNA: Are they going up to secondary with you?
KELLY: One of them is, two of them aren't, but I'm still going to stay in touch and we're still going to be friends forever.

Kelly's friends do not merely protect her: they help her decide how to manage her peer relationships within the context of her coming out and being out as the child of two mums.

We also found that safe, close friendships can sometimes be characterized by the children recognizing that each other's parents know and are accepting of each other. Piero does not know anyone else with an LGBTQI+ parent, but acknowledges it might be useful: 'I think it would be interesting to hear of other people's experiences and like how this sort of life has treated them'. Most of the children we interviewed did feel more comfortable with friends and classmates with LGBTQI+ parents. Ada, who has two mums, talked about another child in her class who had two fathers, telling us: 'it's just nice to know that I'm not the only one. . . . Someone's there who gets it'. This classmate and Ada were not particularly close, but seemed to enjoy the mutual understanding derived from their shared experience. This points to one of the benefits of children feeling safe to be out about their families at school: the more that are out, the less frequently children will think they are the only one to be in that situation. Riley also expressed the sense of belonging she gets from knowing there are others (apart from the girl with two fathers who bullied her) like her at school: 'I know some other people in my school that have parents with two daddies and also two parents, two mums. . . . So it's kind of like . . . we have like a big family. . . . It makes me feel that I'm not the only one'. In such situations, openness and security can be self-reinforcing by making schools more welcoming to LGBTQI+ families generally.

Schools: Peer Support, Discipline, Curriculum

Pride Youth Networks

Given the importance of friendly, open-minded peers with similar experiences, we were interested in what our respondents had to say about whether or not their schools facilitated these sorts of relationships. The Educate & Celebrate Pride Youth Networks described in Chapter 7 function to achieve this, but in order to succeed the school needs to take an institutional approach. This became clear after hearing Jad's story about their attempts to set up a Pride Youth Network in their school. Jad's school did not have an institution-wide programme like Educate & Celebrate in place. As a consequence, they found it difficult to establish a Pride Youth Network, reporting that 'the teachers are quite reluctant'. They tried speaking to an out lesbian teacher, but found 'that was a real waste of time. She wasn't bothered, she barely even listened to me'. Jad and a friend then decided to try and organize a Pride event as part of LGBT history month. The teacher was initially enthusiastic: 'she was really nice and she listened to us and said, you need to do this, this, this. I'll email you or get in touch'. But the teacher never did get back in touch. As Jad's parent Gray explained: 'It's the only way the Pride Youth Networks work. It's not so much driving it, it's just being there to fill out the forms and send the bloody emails when they need to'. Jad repeatedly tried and failed to get a Pride Youth Network up and running:

> We went to one teacher, then she sent us to another and another and another. We asked Miss Neill and we got sent to this teacher and she was really nice. She took down notes but she didn't get in touch with us.

As we note in Chapter 7, these ideas usually succeed only where a senior member of staff is committed to making it work. Diversity work in institutions often falls to representatives of a particular community. Without genuine institutional change, this work can in fact lead to a damaging sense of not being heard.

Disciplinary Responses to Bullying

One rather more commonly implemented school strategy was a clear focus on bullying. Despite Jad's problems in getting a Pride Youth network set up, as their parent Gray explained, HBT language and bullying is definitely not tolerated at their school: 'They will deal with it, if you tell them, they will deal with it. They'll ring parents, they won't shirk out of that responsibility, which is really good'. It was this kind of approach which also helped Nick to really feel safe at his primary school. He trusted his head teacher to deal with any bullying. That, despite his need to explain his family and educate his peers, was what made him resilient:

> One of our main rules in our school is my favourite: our Head Teacher really doesn't tolerate abuse to anyone. She is, oh, strict. She doesn't tolerate any abuse whatsoever, so I don't really get abused . . . so I'm just . . . at my school I'm just a normal boy with two mums.

Kelly similarly felt the benefit of a firm approach to the use of HBT language:

> The child would be really badly punished. . . . I know at our school they're really strict about stuff like that. Even if someone calls someone a name, then they'd be in a lot of trouble, they'd be calling home and telling the parents about what happened.

Kelly had also considered this as part of her criteria for choosing a secondary school, explaining: 'I have loads of older friends that go to the school that I'm going to. I've heard from them that the teachers are really nice and really strict about that sort of stuff'. Similarly, Ethan's school recorded all homophobic and racist incidents in a special book:

> If someone said it and a teacher's found out about it so they actually said it to someone to offend an LGBT person, I think they'd get in deep trouble. I don't think many people say it because they know how bad it is and they'd probably not be allowed to go in a lesson and get [put in] isolation. There is a book in my school. There's a homophobic book and there's also a racism book that if you make any comments it's reported. You have to put your name in that book and you don't leave [the book] until you leave school.

Piero, who had previously seen some intense bullying and prejudice towards his parent, felt much happier at his new school, partly because they were very clear about the consequences should such behaviour recur:

> And I got to [my new school] and basically, my parents had talked to the head teacher beforehand and they were like: 'If anything happens, like at all, if we pick up on any bullying, or any sort of hate against [his parent of trans history] or anyone finds out about it,

we will crackdown on somebody' . . . and that child would receive very . . . bad consequences.

Such a strong line was important for Piero's security and peace of mind.

Hardline disciplinary tactics are not always successful. As Joe explained, most of his classmates 'probably wouldn't care if they got told off' about HBT language. It is also important to critique this kind of zero-tolerance disciplinary approach in terms of the way it can set up arbitrary oppositions between groups. Government education departments and head teachers in the UK can sometimes see HBT behaviour as evidence of Black African or Caribbean Christian Evangelist and Muslim children's failures to align with the school's 'values' (Kulz, 2017). This is in line with what Habib (2017) has identified as an unimaginative nationalistic UK government conception of 'British Values' (Department for Education, 2014). This polarizing view fails to understand the pressure towards 'horizontal violence' (Freire, 1996) experienced by non-white and working-class students who are forced to jostle for position within an oppressive system. Eurocentric schooling is built by and for the white hegemony, and does not make life easy for other subjectivities (Kulz, 2017; Pallotta-Chiarolli & Rajkhowa, 2017).

An Inadequate Curricular Response

A particular problem with schools' zero-tolerance behavioural focus on HBT bullying is that making this the sole area for their consideration of LGBTQ+ people can function to pathologize them as victims (Jones and Clarke, 2007. However, whilst some of the schools our respondents attended did manage to implement a partly LGBTQI+ friendly curriculum, it was not a common experience, and usually amounted to a tokenistic one-off assembly, or a book on a shelf somewhere (Taylor, 2009). For example, Nick had noticed that 'there is a book about this girl that has two mums' in the library. He had clearly noted this fact: having a literary representation relating to his own family structure was important to him (McInroy & Craig, 2015). Without a curricular framework, however, the book just lay quietly on a library shelf. Joe reported that in his school 'they have a lot of PSHE [Personal, Social and Health Education] lessons and assemblies and there's posters up'. Demonstrating a patient, educative stance at odds with his sometimes violent HBT experiences, Piero thought there should be more of this: 'I think at schools they should like, maybe start assemblies or lessons on PSHE days . . . about what trans is, what it means, like it's okay to be trans and like explaining it'. Given his very difficult experiences, his reasoning was insightful: 'because usually, when people hate and sort of don't like something, it's usually because they don't understand it, rather than having a major problem with it'.

Russel et al. (2008: 25) suggest that 'strategies considered promising for improving the climate for LGBT youth are also perceived as being effective for promoting safe school climates for children with LGBT parents', and the children's advice for schools was in line with this. Vanderbeck and Johnson (2015) found a limited and rather basic approach to addressing issues of gender identity and sexual orientation in schools which was often circumscribed by a lack of teacher confidence and understanding (see also Chapter 7). Jen, who is 15 and has a bisexual mother, had noticed the limited homonormative range of queer sexualities discussed at school. She suggested that schools should:

> focus a bit more on the trans side as well—and the intersex, I think they should focus on that a bit more. And like the different genders as well like. . . . A gender equality between homosexualities. About how sexuality is a spectrum so it's not, it can be permanent but it can not be permanent so there is no, you kind of don't have to show, you don't have to go I'm bisexual, well actually now, otherwise it can change completely.

Jen demonstrated a sophisticated understanding of fluidity, gender and sexuality and of LGBTQI+ subjectivities.

Should Teachers Come Out at School?

Opinion was divided as to whether teachers should come out as LGBTQI+. Piero's grateful recognition of the trans theatre technician described earlier suggests that teachers who come out can really help LGBTQI+ students and the children of LGBTQI+ parents to decide whether or not it is safe to out themselves. Jad felt, however, that individual teachers should not be pressured to come out. They felt the onus should be more on the institution to create an environment within which coming out is possible. They explained:

> I don't think making people do it is the right way. . . . Making people come out is not the right thing to do. Making a space where they can if they want to come out is. . . . Making the space safe for them to come out if they want to is what they should be doing. They shouldn't be making people do it. They should be making the environment safe.

Coming out as a teacher can present a professional and emotional risk. Jad felt that it was perhaps more powerful when a cisgender straight teacher expressed LGBTQI+ friendly practice:

> It's not even about not coming out, it's about . . . straight cis-gender teachers talking about it. There's one teacher in my school that

teaches me . . . my English teacher, Mr. Ashton and he is the one teacher that I've heard talking about LGBT people, trans people and that's it. That's the only teacher I've heard talking about that stuff. He's a really nice person. . . . He is the one teacher that has spoken about LGBT rights and gay people and trans people.

Out LGBTQI+ teachers and cisgender, straight allies, then, can both help the children of queer culture to survive and thrive at school.

Conclusion

Most of the children of LGBTQI+ parents are immensely proud of their parents, and want to be visible at school, but nevertheless report a range of stresses related to their families: some small, and some more significant. In those schools where comprehensive work to change the culture has not been carried out, students still experience HBT bullying or suffer the lack of representation of their families in curriculum (Stonewall, 2010)). Children also continue to experience HBT bullying and language, but are reluctant to tell their parents.

One way to address this reticence is to create cultural change by making LGBTQI+ people and issues ubiquitous throughout the curriculum. According to the children we interviewed, however, the curricular offer is inadequate in achieving this aim. As Martino and Cumming-Potvin (2011) explain, simply dealing with HBT language does not address the cultural conditions which give rise to such behaviour. Furthermore, as we discussed in Chapter 3, negative media representations also need to be counteracted (McInroy & Craig, 2015). Unable because of their cultural queerness to un-see heteronormativity and HBT responses (Logie & Rwigema, 2014), some of the children we interviewed often put time and emotional energy into advocating on behalf of their families. They generally appreciate their schools' firm disciplinary responses to HBT bullying. However, this limited institutional strategy can be at the expense of a relationship-building approach which acknowledges the vulnerabilities and disadvantages of children subjected to other kinds of prejudice, such as is experienced on the basis of race, religion or poverty (Kulz, 2017). Children who are LGBTQI+ and/or the child of LGBTQI+ parents, as well as being othered because of ethnicity, religion and poverty, are likely to be especially disadvantaged by a focus on bullying and victimization rather than inclusivity (Logie & Rwigema, 2014; Pallotti-Chiarolli & Rajkhowa, 2017).

The children of LGBTQ+ parented families can gain resilience from their friendships, particularly those with other children with similar parenting arrangements. Schools can help with this by supporting Pride Youth Networks or similar groups. However, things which might make any child less resilient can heighten the prejudice experienced by the children of LGBTQ+ parents: for example, Riley's separated mothers; Jad's being adopted; Kelly's experience of bullying; several children's special educational needs. By the same token, children like Nick and Jon benefit from their stable families and their cultural capital. A heteronormative environment and HBT language and bullying can also hurt the cisgender, straight children of cisgender, straight parents. Gender stereotypes limit thinking about what all children might learn, enjoy or be capable of achieving. So where schools choose to create a supportive environment for the children of LGBTQI+ parents, they are improving the environment for all students. If they want to facilitate an encouraging, safe learning environment for all children, including the children of LGBTQI+ parents, schools should enable a safe space in which the full range of family types can be visible; provide representation across the curriculum; and support all students to talk openly about and express their pride in their families.

References

Ahmed, S. (2012). *On being included: Racism and diversity in institutional life.* Durham, NC: Duke University Press.

Anzaldua, G. (1987). Borderlands/La Frontera: *The New Mestiza.* San Francisco: Spinsters/Aunt Lute Book Company.

Bergman, S. B. (2013). *Blood, marriage, wine and glitter.* Vancouver: Arsenal Pulp Press.

Butler, J. (1993). *Bodies that matter: On the discursive limits of "sex".* London: Routledge.

Carlile, A. (2012). *Permanent exclusion from school and institutional prejudice: Creating change through critical bureaucracy.* Rotterdam: Sense Publishers.

Department for Education. (2014). *Promoting fundamental British values through SMSC.* London: HMSO.

Epstein, R. (Ed.) (2009). *Who's your daddy? And other writings on queer parenting.* Toronto: Sumach Press.

Fairtlough, A. (2008). Growing up with a lesbian or gay parent: Young people's perspectives. *Health and Social Care in the Community, 16*(5), 521–528.

Freire, P. (1996). *Pedagogy of the oppressed.* London: Penguin Books.

Gustavson, M., & Schmitt, I. (2011). Culturally queer, silenced in school? Children with LGBTQ parents, and the everyday politics of/in community and school. *Lambda Nordica: Tidskrift för homo/lesbisk/bi/transforskning, 16*(2–3), 159–187.

Habib, S. (2017). *Learning and teaching British values: Policies and perspectives on British identities.* Cham, Switzerland: Palgrave Macmillan.

Jones, R., & Clarke, G. (2007). The school experiences of same-sex attracted students in the 14- to 19-year-old secondary sector in England: Within and beyond the safety and tolerance framework. *Journal of Gay and Lesbian Social Services, 19*(3–4), 119–138.

Knight, K. W., Stephenson, S. E., West, S., Delatycki, M. B., Jones, C. A., Little, M. H., Patton, G. C., Sawyer, S. M., Skinner, S. R., Telfer, M. M., Wake, M., North, K. N., & Oberklaid, F. (2017). The kids are OK: It is discrimination not

same-sex parents that harms children. *Medical Journal of Australia, 207*(9), 374–375.
Kosciw, J. G., Greytak, E. A., Diaz, E. M., & Bartkiewicz, M. J. (2010). *The 2009 national school climate survey: The experiences of lesbian, gay, bisexual, and transgender youth in our nation's schools*. New York: GLSEN.
Kulz, C. (2017). *Factories for learning: Making race, class and inequality in the neoliberal academy*. Manchester: Manchester University Press.
Lawrence-Lightfoot, S. (2003). *The Essential Conversation: What parents and teachers can learn from each other*. The Random House Publishing Group: New York.
Logie, C. H., & Rwigema, M. (2014). "The normative idea of queer is a white person": Understanding perceptions of white privilege among lesbian, bisexual, and queer women of color in Toronto, Canada. *Journal of Lesbian Studies, 18*(2), 174–191.
Martino, W., & Cumming-Potvin, W. (2011). "They didn't have out there gay parents—They just looked like normal regular parents": Investigating teachers' approaches to addressing same-sex parenting and non-normative sexuality in the elementary school classroom. *Curriculum Inquiry, 41*, 480–501.
McInroy, L. B., & Craig, S. L. (2015). Transgender representation in offline and online media: LGBTQ youth perspectives. *Journal of Human Behavior in the Social Environment, 25*(6), 606–617.
Paechter, C. (2004). "Mens Sana in Corpore Sano": Cartesian dualism and the marginalization of sex education. *Discourse: Studies in the Cultural Politics of Education, 25*(3), 309–320.
Pallotta-Chiarolli, M., & Rajkhowa, A. (2017). Systemic invisibilities, institutional culpabilities and multicultural-multifaith LGBTIQ resistances. *Journal of Intercultural Studies, 38*(4), 429–442.
Russell, S. T., McGuire, J. K., Lee, S., Larriva, J. C., & Laub, C. (2008). Adolescent perceptions of school safety for students with lesbian, gay, bisexual, and transgender parents. *Journal of LGBT Youth, 5*(4), 11–27.
Sarmento, T., & Freire, I. (2012). Making school happen: Children-parent-teacher collaboration as a practice of citizenship. *Education Sciences, 2*(2), 105–120.
Solomos, J. (2001). Race, multiculturalism and difference. In Stevenson, N. (Ed.), *Culture and citizenship* (pp. 198–211). London: Sage.
Stonewall. (2010). *Different families: The experiences of children with lesbian and gay parents*. London: Stonewall.
Taylor, Y. (2009). *Lesbian and gay parenting: Securing social and educational capital*. Basingstoke: Palgrave Macmillan.
Vanderbeck, R. M., & Johnson, P. (2015). Religion, homosexuality and the contested legal framework governing sex education in England. *Journal of Social Welfare and Family Law, 37*(2), 161–179.

7 'Usualizing' LGBTQI+ People and Issues in Schools

The Educate & Celebrate Approach to Creating School Change

I had to leave the first school I taught at when a parent governor made a complaint to the head teacher about there being an out lesbian on the staff. The head teacher asked me to leave but suggested I stay one more year before leaving as it was rather late to find a replacement. I resigned on the spot.

Three years later, I have a job supporting young people at risk of permanent exclusion from school. I visit their families, meet with their social workers, and help them transition into new schools for a fresh start. One late summer afternoon I walk into the tall glass foyer of a large London comprehensive. Squinting into the dust motes dancing in the burnished afternoon sunlight, I realize that the whole space is hung with enormous rainbow flags. The walls are covered with rainbow posters about famous LGBT sportspeople, scientists, performers, authors and politicians. It is LGBT History Month, and the school is celebrating it in style. I burst into tears: this is the first time I have ever seen a rainbow flag or a poster of an LGBT person in a UK school.

Anna

In this chapter we draw on an evaluation of interventions by 'Educate & Celebrate', a charity based in London but working throughout the UK and beyond. The charity works to 'usualize'[1] LGBTQI+ people and their lives across school curricula, policy, community and environment. We will outline Educate & Celebrate's approach to making schools 'LGBTQI+ friendly'; describe the context and process within which data on its efficacy and impact was collected; and summarize the findings of this element of our research. Our analysis of Educate & Celebrate was carried out on three levels. First, we address pragmatic and technical issues related to bullying, curriculum, policy and visibility. Second, we have sought to discover the perceptions of the children and teachers involved in the programme and to describe some of their personal experiences of it. Finally, we investigate whether Educate & Celebrate enhanced or subverted homonormative approaches to LGBTQI+ issues in schools. We therefore looked at whether the focus was limited to monogamous lesbian and gay people, and to transgender people who fit within a binary model of gender—or whether terms such as 'bisexual' or 'non-binary' were also included within the curriculum, policy and celebratory elements of the programme. In this vein, we also looked at whether Educate & Celebrate disrupted the patterns of middle-class and ethnic advantage identified by previous researchers (Ryan-Flood, 2009; Taylor, 2009), who suggest that it is easier for middle-class white LGBTQI+ parented families to access schools where their families are able to feel safe and included.

What Is Educate & Celebrate?

The Educate & Celebrate programme is mainly focused on a training-based intervention for schools, staffed by a small group of dedicated trainers and specialists. Most share a history of work as school teachers in English cities. Their roles in the project include: teacher educator; children's book specialist; and youth voice worker. Expert trainers offer input to the programme on policy, curriculum and transgender issues (Educate & Celebrate, 2017).

The Educate & Celebrate approach was developed following eight years of fine-tuning, first in the founder/CEO's original school, where she was a music teacher, and then in other schools and local authorities, including a large tranche of work conducted in schools across a city in the English Midlands and a local authority area in the North of England. The period during which we were collecting data on Educate & Celebrate interventions represented a significant scaling-up of the project, covering 30 primary and 30 secondary schools in regions across all corners of England.

The Educate & Celebrate model involves certain key elements designed to go beyond challenging prejudice: 'training'; 'environment'; 'policy'; 'curriculum'; and 'celebration and community'. The programme's focus on these key elements seeks to 'usualize' LGBTQI+ people and their lives in a sustainable way, and at all levels of the school. Examples of related activities are provided in Table 7.1.

The Educate & Celebrate project was one of several funded by the Department for Education (DfE) and the Government Equalities Office (GEO), aiming to reduce homophobic, biphobic and transphobic (HBT) bullying. The funding application included a requirement for each organization to develop an external evaluation procedure. The data in this chapter is drawn from the evaluation work which fulfilled that function. The original evaluation addressed three aims: to inform Educate & Celebrate as to its successes and areas for development; to report back to the DfE and GEO on how successfully the organization had delivered the work it was funded to deliver; and to feed into a wider evaluation of the whole HBT project across several organizations, carried out by the national social research charity NatCen (2016). Whilst the original

138 *'Usualizing' LGBTQI+ People and Issues*

Table 7.1 Educate & Celebrate activities

Element	Examples of related activities
Training	Whole-school training sessions, including management, teaching, support, administration and maintenance staff
	Cluster-based training sessions, drawing school staff from a range of local schools
Environment	Welcome notices in school foyers, explaining that the school celebrates diversity according to all the characteristics in the Equality Act 2010[i]
	Posters and displays around the school
Policy	Audit and updating of school policies to ensure inclusion on the basis of gender identity and sexual orientation, including those relating to bullying, uniform, behaviour and equalities
Curriculum	Curriculum reviews
	The embedding and 'usualizing' of LGBTQI+ people and issues throughout updated schemes of learning
	The provision of collections of books with LGBTQI+ inclusive subjects, themes and images, for early years, primary and secondary phases
	Sample lesson plans and ideas, available on the Educate & Celebrate website
Celebration and community	Community celebrations including 'Rainbow Bake-offs' in which LGBTQI+ themed cakes were baked, and musical performances
	Pride Youth Networks: school-based youth groups for young people who are LGBT or who are allies (similar to Gay-Straight Alliances in the US). The groups socialize, discuss issues, go on trips, support each other and campaign on LGBT and gender equality issues

i The Equality Act 2010 protects people from discrimination on the basis of eight 'protected characteristics', which include gender reassignment (though only across a binary) and sexual orientation. Schools are also subject to the Public Sector Equality Duties (Equality and Human Rights Commission, 2017), which require that they actively promote equality. They are inspected in relation to both of these.

evaluation looked across a wider range of impacts, this chapter will focus on issues related to LGBTQI+ parented families. We draw on around 40 hours of recorded and transcribed focus groups and interviews at 13 of the schools involved in the Educate & Celebrate programme. We also include information about displays, exhibitions, book collections and similar material, from notes taken during guided tours of each school's wall displays and library collections.

Before the project started, in June 2015, we visited 12 of the 60 participation schools, to find out about how students and teachers thought and talked about LGBTQI+ people and issues before they had experienced the Educate & Celebrate programme. The schools visited included six primary schools and six secondary schools including one for students with moderate learning difficulties (MLD), and were spread across England, including urban and rural locations. During each of our visits we held a recorded focus group discussion of about 60 minutes with between two and 15 students (usually five or six), and a 60-minute recorded interview with a staff member, usually the Educate & Celebrate Coordinator (known as the 'ECCO'). School environments were also noted, including images and welcome messages in school foyers, posters in classrooms and displays of work in the corridors.

The evaluation plan included visits to the sample schools at the end of the project, to find out about the changes which had occurred. Due to staff turnover, we were able to visit eight of the original schools, and three replacement schools. The end-of-project visits involved follow-up focus group discussions with students, and 60-minute interviews with seven ECCOs, a local authority Equality and Inclusion Officer, one head teacher, two deputy head teachers, and two learning mentors. As well as observing school foyers and welcome messages, the follow-up visits also involved three school tours to look at library book and wall displays, and at art-work and writing students done by students as part of the project.

Before each visit at both the start and end of the project, ECCOs were asked to select around five students for a focus group. This was the most common number of students in each focus group but teachers sometimes selected up to 15 students; sometimes there were only two in a group. We asked ECCOs to use their own judgement in selecting these students, so some of them were already in Pride Youth Networks (that is, they were themselves LGBTQI+ or allies). In other schools, staff selected those they perceived as particularly articulate students; and in others, ECCOs sought to provide a broad cross-section of age, ability and ethnicity in the focus group members. The student groups selected by ECCOs in the second round of visits were, in most of the schools, substantially different: they were those who had been particularly involved in the project and who were eager to tell us about their experiences. Often (but not always) these groups included students who, during the project, had come out as LGBT or Q, become very interested in continuing the equalities work started in the school, or both.

In total, around 80 students and 16 staff members participated in the recorded discussions across the focus groups and interviews. The students in the focus groups ranged from Year 2 (aged 6–7) to Year 13 (aged 17–18). The second round was undertaken in April 2016, by which time some students had left, and others were involved in examinations. However, there was a significant cross-over in the membership of the focus groups and they usually contained at least three of the original students. In mixed-gender secondary schools, the majority of students in the focus groups tended to identify as female, usually with one or two identifying as male. In primary schools the focus groups generally consisted of a relatively even gender split. In terms of ethnicity, faith and cultural background, some of the schools were monocultural. In those which were more mixed, the focus groups represented the full range of backgrounds, including many combinations of Somali, Pakistani, Bengali, Ghanaian, White British, Polish and Nigerian; atheist, Evangelical Christian, Catholic, Muslim, Sikh, Hindu and Jewish. We asked teachers to choose whether they would prefer to stay with the children for the focus group discussions. Teachers participated in most of the Primary School focus groups, and occasionally in some of the Secondary School groups. Sometimes they participated in the discussion, and occasionally they just sat in the room, either observing or carrying out their own work.

The questions to both focus groups and staff members were generally open and designed to generate discussion. This was intended both to give scope for a wide range of responses and to be sensitive to the emotional well-being of all participants. The potential for respondents to discuss their own gender identity and sexual orientation was inherent in the subject matter: these issues can raise concerns related to acceptance or rejection by friends, families and employers. Further, the problematic history of school-related policy around LGBTQI+ issues (Jones & Clarke, 2007) has generated a level of anxiety amongst some school staff. This strategy invited respondents to volunteer only that information which they felt comfortable volunteering. In order to find out about general attitudes towards gender and to break the ice, it was usually helpful to begin by asking students to say a bit about their school uniform, and then whether anything related to LGBTQI+ people or their lives ever came up at school. In the one-to-one interviews with teaching staff, the first question sought to discover how they had become involved with the project. The discussions were semi-structured, allowing participants to raise issues as they felt comfortable. Prompting questions were used to elicit specific information where it had not already emerged in the discussions.

School Contexts

The breadth of schools visited for the evaluation meant that we were able to compare discourses across a wide variety of school contexts in both rural and urban areas of the country. These included schools where the whole student population had a Pakistani Muslim heritage; those in which all students were White British working-class and first-language English speakers; and schools in diverse areas where up to 24 languages were spoken in any one classroom. Some schools were already well versed in addressing specific equalities issues other than those related to LGBTQI+ people. These included racist attitudes deriving from locally popular White supremacy movements such as the British National Party; pressures on Muslim communities deriving from global conflicts which have led to racist attacks in some areas; and resourcing issues related to the need to educate students from many parts of the world with a wide range of linguistic competencies. Most of the schools visited were also working hard to address the effects of poverty and deprivation and lack of local employment.

The schools we visited need to be understood as existing within a specific 'policyscape' (Ball, 2001: 46). As we discussed in Chapter 4, some LGBTQI+ people's rights are protected in law, albeit within the constraints of a homonormative discourse. However, they are still subject to both direct and institutional prejudice deriving from a school culture currently in a state of emergence from the preceding, less inclusive policy context, in which teaching about LGBTQI+ relationships, particularly in the context of family life, was discouraged (Jones & Clarke, 2007; DePalma, 2010; Walker & Bates, 2016).

Educate & Celebrate and Its Effects

In this section we discuss the findings of the evaluation. We begin with an overview of the thoughts and ideas students and teachers expressed before the project had started in the schools, starting with HBT bullying and language; moving on to curriculum and policy; and then discussing visibility and the school environment.

Before Educate & Celebrate: The Baseline

HBT Bullying and Language

HBT bullying and language was prevalent in both primary and secondary schools before the Educate & Celebrate programme was carried out. One Year 5 student explained:

> When I'm like . . . hanging around my friends or I'm just playing randomly, some people, they'll just start calling people 'gay'; and they mostly call me 'gay'- I don't know why, they're just like 'oh you're so gay', and I'm thinking, 'I'm not sure why you're calling me gay because I'm not trying to be gay or anything'.
>
> Male student, aged 10, Hotel Primary School baseline focus group

This experience was common. At Mikey Secondary School, a female student in Year 10 reported that 'a lot of people use the word faggot, I've heard that a lot and people have a go at . . . particularly people who are openly bisexual'. Whilst these comments relate to other students as opposed to their parents, they could nevertheless lead to a hostile environment which might have an impact on students with LGBTQI+ parents. As Russell, McGuire, Lee, Larriva, & Laub, 2008) explain in their study of adolescent perceptions of school safety among the children of LGBTQI+ parents:

> same-sex sexuality and LGBT issues are a major contemporary issue around which harassment is often based. . . . Thus, LGBT adolescents or adolescents with LGBT parents are expected to experience peer rejection due to their personal or family difference.
>
> (14)

As we saw in Chapter 6, HBT language in a school can sometimes (but not always) be enough to convince children that it is unsafe to out themselves as the children of LGBTQI+ parents.

Curriculum

Prior to having conducted specific work to address the issue, school staff seemed to focus on a minimal and narrow curricular approach to dealing with sexuality, gender and relationships, and to lack the confidence and knowledge to expand their repertoire (Vanderbeck & Johnson, 2015). This limited the relationships and sex education discussed in class to a range which failed to be inclusive of either the family set-ups or the ways in which the children of LGBTQI+ parents are conceived. As we saw in Chapter 6, the children of LGBTQI+ people can sometimes end up educating their teachers and peers about the alternative conception methods by which they themselves were made. Within the Educate & Celebrate schools, at the initial baseline focus-group stage, students and teachers reported a focus on heterosexual and technical aspects of sex education, confined to assemblies, Personal, Social, Health and Citizenship Education (PHSCE), and science lessons. For example, students in Years 9 and 10 at Mikey Secondary Academy told us that 'we only used to talk about friendships and healthy relationships but not . . . never anything other than heterosexual relationships'. They also discussed their experience of the curriculum in science:

STUDENT 1: Like in science, we only learn about straight sexual contact, we don't learn about . . .
STUDENT 2: Sex education.
STUDENT 3: We don't learn about, you know, like lesbians or anything like that, we learn about how straight sexual activity occurs.

The teacher interviewed at William Secondary School also recognized this problem. She predicted some resistance from staff around embedding LGBTQI+ people and issues across the curriculum, suggesting that this was despite the fact that there was rich potential to do so:

from a humanities perspective, English perspective, the performing and creative arts. It's just such a wealth of material there and nobody seems to mention it.

She was slightly frustrated, explaining that:

I can't believe you can teach in a Science lesson, and still not find yourself moving into questions of you know, just exploring the topic basically. So I think that's going to be the greatest challenge here.

Research by Sauntson and Simpson (2011) on sexuality discourses in the UK Secondary English Curriculum corroborates this. Teachers they interviewed

saw the curriculum as having potential for exploring issues around sexuality and, importantly, for normalizing homosexuality and challenging homophobia, but reported that this potential was not being realized through curriculum delivery.

(966)

Part of the reason for this, they felt, was that

the language used in the curriculum did not explicitly mention sexuality while simultaneously highlighting other forms of social identity such as race, ethnicity, and gender.

(966)

This meant that teachers were more likely to 'do diversity' in their curriculum with a focus on other topics such as ethnicity. Other reasons for reticence towards embedding LGBTQI+ people and issues given in our data included fear of saying the wrong thing and fear of upsetting parents, especially those with a faith background, and these too are reflected across previous research findings (Warwick, Aggleton, & Douglas, 2001; Sauntson & Simpson, 2011; Malins, 2016). This is fundamental for the children of LGBTQI+ parents: if information about human sexual reproduction is exclusively heterosexual, then the very genesis of a whole group of students could be omitted from what is presented as 'truth' in textbooks and classrooms.

Policy

School policies are moving towards more inclusive language due to the changes required by the Equality Act 2010 (UK Government, 2010), but, as we saw in Chapter 4, tend not to mention LGBTQI+ parented families.

144   *'Usualizing' LGBTQI+ People and Issues*

The Educate & Celebrate schools visited at the beginning of the project, in May and June 2015, were generally already working on updating their inclusion, equalities and behaviour policies in order to comply with the Equality Act 2010. Nevertheless, LGBTQI+ parented families were mentioned very rarely and their rights and freedoms tended to be protected by implication rather than specifically. For example, the William Secondary School ECCO explained that the treatment of LGBTQI+ people and issues would be governed under their

> Equal Opportunities Policy, which effectively was rewritten when the Equality Act came in. . . . And it would be in the Behaviour Policy . . . But I think we'd struggle to find the term actually specified with the parenting side.

Registration forms at the schools visited still usually required 'mother's name' and 'father's name'. LGBTQI+ parents, then, were invisible at the documentary level of the school.

Kosciejew (2015) describes 'the central role of documentation in the creation, stabilization, materialization, and emergence of information' (114). Policy documents also need a level of co-construction if school staff are to take them seriously (Ahmed, 2012), and some of the Educate & Celebrate schools did involve quite junior teachers who became the driving forces behind inclusive policy changes. However, those senior managers normally tasked with leading policy writing and updating are gatekeepers to whether LGBTQI+ parents and LGBTQI+ parented families are tabled for potential inclusion in the first place. If they are not sufficiently aware to recognize that inclusion in these documents is important, it is unlikely to happen.

Schools' Lack of Awareness of LGBTQI+ Parents and the School Environment

Despite the fact that recognition of their unique family model can have a positive effect on a child's learning (Feiler, Greenhough, Winter, Salway, & Scanlan, 2006), LGBTQI+ parents were not visible in the schools visited at the beginning of the programme. Generally, the environment in the schools visited did not construct parents as potentially LGBTQI+. In fact until the question was asked, staff had usually not considered the issue. At William Secondary School, for example, the ECCO expressed her feeling that this was an unfortunate omission:

> I am concerned because I don't think we ever refer to the parents as so far as LGBT. . . . I'm not even sure in the rewritten admissions

pack, whether there are any questions that would allow people to answer in that sort of way. Presumably that should be addressed?

Other ECCOs did not feel that it was appropriate to name any of the protected characteristics in the Equality Act 2010 in their foyer welcome notices, arguing that if they mentioned any they would have to include them all, and that there were too many to do so. At Eastchurch MLD Secondary School, the deputy head teacher was asked in her interview about whether there was any visible signage welcoming people of diverse backgrounds. She explained that there was not:

> (w)ell there's nothing specific there but it is not something that we have ever drawn attention to . . . we don't draw attention otherwise we would have a big long list with . . . all the needs and the things that some of our parents have, so that's why.

It is important to acknowledge here that a visible commitment to equalities work does not necessarily result in a changed experience (Ahmed, 2012). Where a school does explicitly mention sexual orientation or gender identity as part of the protected characteristics within a publicly visible Equality Act 2010 statement, this can in fact serve to lull the organization into a false sense of security that they are actually doing something useful. Unfortunately, this can amount to a tokenistic approach, as described by the ECCO at Mikey Secondary Academy before the Educate & Celebrate programme had started:

> I think the website says that they adhere to . . . we adhere to the Equality Act 2010, that we don't discriminate. I think walking around, there's no evidence of that. There is no evidence to support that and in which case I can't actually answer that without saying I don't know why you'd send your child here, if that was the case. . . . Which is actually a really sad thing to admit but it's kind of true.

In such cases, promises in policy documents and on websites did not seem to be translated into action.

In addition to invisibility within official school documentation, LGBTQI+ parented families themselves were also invisible to teachers. We asked the William Secondary School ECCO before the beginning of the programme whether she was aware of any LGBTQI+ parented families at the school. She replied:

> I'm not. And as the girls [interviewed in the focus group] were answering that question, I was racking my brains to think whether I knew in any other year groups. And I think there might be one in

the sixth form . . . that's been spoken about. But I was thinking, actually it's probably something that we should know as a statistic.

Her concern that the existence of LGBTQI+ parented families in the school is 'probably something that we should know' was a common refrain running through the data relating to this theme of invisibility.

Successive UK governments have promoted to schools the idea that home-school liaison is important for students' academic success (Feiler et al., 2006). Having one's family make-up recognized and accepted is an important element of a student's potential sense of belonging in a school. Furthermore, those who study this phenomenon acknowledge that there is a frequent and problematic erasure of attention to systemic inequalities (Feiler et al., 2006; Crozier & Davies, 2007). For example, schools and policies treat all parents as if they are equally able and available to help their children with homework. In the case of LGBTQI+ parented families this is exacerbated by a lack of available data. Although, as we saw in Chapter 2, there are some UK statistics recording the number of children in same-sex couple parented families, this does not take into account those families with one LGBTQI+ parent, or those with polyamorous or LGBTQI+ parenting groups. This lack of comprehensive data further hides the existence of LGBTQI+ parented families in particular schools, by not priming schools to expect them.

After Educate & Celebrate: The Impact

It can be seen, then, that before the Educate & Celebrate programme students experienced HBT bullying; a lack of awareness of LGBTQI+ people and their lives across the curriculum; and invisibility of LGBTQI+ parented families throughout policy and school environments. We will now discuss what we found when we returned to the research schools after the programme had been completed.

HBT Bullying: Feeling Safer

Following the Educate & Celebrate programme, HBT bullying was perceived as less prevalent. However, children's reluctance to betray their social group by reporting bullying behaviour undermined progress. We found that schools had tended to tighten up their discipline policies so that the official response to HBT language was now the same as the response to racist language. Students and staff felt much more empowered to respond, and teachers reported that the Educate & Celebrate training, LGBTQI+ friendly wall displays, changed policies and inclusive curriculum had all supported them to respond to HBT language with confidence. This upgrading of responses to HBT language meant that it was overtly taken seriously by schools. For example, the Hotel Primary

School ECCO described the changes in her school in response to the use of the word 'gay' as an insult:

ECCO: we have incident reports based on that and it is taken extremely seriously here, you know there's meetings, there's parent phone calls, there's the child sat down. Sometimes you might find the child . . . [has] heard older people maybe saying it and they literally don't know what it is.
ANNA: Has that changed since you've been doing Educate & Celebrate?
ECCO: Definitely changed. I don't think it's used as much and I believe but I haven't had to fill out one incident report. . . . I think it's the fact that we've introduced it and made them face up to what's going on that they now realise what the word is all about and how it's applied to people. . . . It's different now because they've got a better understanding of what's going . . . and then we do treat anything like that very seriously.

However, the changes were not universal. One of the main barriers to resolving HBT bullying is the pressure against 'snitching', or telling teachers and other adults about bad behaviour, even amongst LGBTQI+ students and allies who are members of Pride Youth Networks.

Students' expectations of group loyalty have previously been found to act as a restraining pressure to keep problems within the group and not seek adult involvement (Paechter & Clark, 2016). Reluctance to snitch is a recognized response to all kinds of bullying in schools, including that related to sexuality or sexual violence, and is consequently a significant barrier to intervention (Weiss, 2013; Woldoff & Weiss, 2010; Whitman & Davies, 2007). Delta Secondary School students discussed the tensions, anxieties and contradictions involved, in a post-programme focus group:

ANNA: So, if someone is being bullied, who would you tell, what would you do?
STUDENT 1: It's the whole, being a snitch situation, it's like, this secret code, that if you go and you turn your back against your, like, group of people, like, even if you're not that close, it's like, he's a snitch, he's a snake, you can't do that. . . . I'd want to get involved, because I want to be like, that is wrong, stop picking on other people, it shouldn't happen, you're here to learn, just stop. But I also don't want to get involved, because then it's gonna be like, oh you're a snake, and you don't want to go to the teacher, because it's like, oh no.
ANNA: So that's a problem, across the board, for any bullying.
STUDENT 2: It's any kind of bullying.
STUDENT 1: It's like honour, or like, being reliable, or trustworthy. Somehow, that's worth more than actually telling the truth, sometimes.

Like, I get if you're copying out homework, you're not gonna just go up to the teacher. But if somebody is being really horrible to someone, just because they're part of your group, doesn't mean, you know, you should not tell anybody that they're being horrible. Obviously, that's stupid, but . . .

STUDENT 3: Yeah, especially when you're younger. It's all, trying to fit in, and suddenly, you're just outcast. If you, like, speak up about something, you would just be thrown away.

This problem was ubiquitous across the schools visited, and the problem is exacerbated by the fact that, as we discussed in Chapter 6, children of LGBTQI+ parents tend not to tell their parents if they hear HBT language or are bullied, mainly because they do not want to upset them.

A Systematic Review of the Curriculum: Effectively Usualizing LGBTQI+ People and Issues in Secular and Faith Schools and Communities

The majority of the schools investigated after the Educate & Celebrate programme had successfully embedded references to LGBTQI+ people and issues across the curriculum; others were in the process of achieving that. This required an explicit focus on the issue. Saunston and Simpson (2011), in their study of the existing English curriculum, suggest that, while there is room for teachers to address LGBTQI+ people and issues, this is by no means expected and may in fact be quite easily avoided. For example, one of the teachers they interviewed 'noted that while the work of the current UK poet laureate (Carol Ann Duffy), who is openly lesbian, is included on the English curriculum and GCSE examination syllabi, her more overtly lesbian poems are notably excluded' (Sauntson & Simpson, 2011: 964). It was consequently important for the Educate & Celebrate schools to take overt, focused action to address this absence. Teachers' anxiety about raising a controversial issue turned out to be relatively unfounded: in the Educate & Celebrate schools where embedding was successful, these inclusions were so ubiquitous that students often failed to remember mention of LGBTQI+ people in class, and their teachers would hasten to show us evidence in the teacher interview following the focus group.

The use of library book packs proved to be an effective and appreciated element of the Educate & Celebrate programme. Walker and Bates (2016) explain that there are inconsistent levels of knowledge about LGBTQI+ people and issues amongst school librarians across England, and that problems arise from this. They cite multiple studies which suggest that 'the display of LGBTQI+ materials and positive portrayal of LGBTQI+ issues can have encouraging impacts on the physical and mental well-being of LGBTQI+ young people', adding that these resources are also important for people who regularly work with adolescents . . . for children who have LGBTQI+ friends and/or family members . . . and indeed for everybody in order to raise awareness and to widen people's views on LGBTQI+ identities and issues.

(270–271)

The Educate & Celebrate library book packages provided each school with a wide range of books appropriate for each age group, and seemed to have been helpful for schools. They were discussed by several of the teachers interviewed. At Foxtrot Secondary School, the books had been placed within the 'Accelerated Reader' collection. This flags up the books as available and helped with the idea, often mentioned by teachers and children, of the children having broadened horizons. Schools were also careful not to segregate the books in a separate section, but to embed them fully. The ECCO at Eastchurch MLD Secondary School explained how the library books underpinned their new English curriculum:

> English has gone really well so we have had the books in the library but again we have been conscious not to put them in an LGBT section, they have just been incorporated. The most popular one is *And Tango Makes Three*. Ali [an Educate & Celebrate trainer] was in the other day and she was chatting to a group of the kids that have read the book, they just happened to be in the library, and they could tell Ali all about it and, you know, the fact that there is two mummies and that's okay and different types of family, so the books have been the main driver for the English lessons in the library. . . . A lot of our curriculum in English is based around, we use books as a base very much as a primary school would really.

The curriculum reviews carried out by schools such as this one seemed to be a good way to consolidate the Educate & Celebrate training right across the staff, including in faith schools and schools serving faith communities.

The LGBTQI+ parents we interviewed (see Chapter 5) occasionally expressed fears (mostly unfounded) about potential homophobia on the part of religious parents of other children in their children's classes. It has also been our experience as teacher educators that the issue of teaching about LGBTQI+ people and issues in faith schools and faith communities is something that worries beginning teachers. This has not been helped by governmental approaches to curriculum development. Vanderbeck and Johnson (2015) argue that, in England, a conservative form of

> religious considerations and interests continue to be influential in maintaining an educational landscape in which young people face

disparities in their access to teaching and discussion about issues pertaining to homosexuality and same-sex relationships.

(161)

They explain how, when developing official curricula,

> the Government repeatedly rejected arguments made by some campaigners for including some teaching about homosexuality in different sections of the statutory curriculum. For example, the Government rejected the view of several respondents that some discussion of homosexuality be incorporated into the science programme of study. This was partially justified with recourse to the concerns of religious groups about the loss of the right of parental withdrawal should this topic (or other aspects of sex education) become statutory.

(166)

It is interesting that these concerns about upsetting parents do not extend to those who are LGBTQI+. However, the Educate & Celebrate programme has demonstrated the potential for faith communities to take this work in their stride. For example, the ECCO at Romeo Secondary Academy, where 100% of the students and many of the staff are from a Pakistani Muslim heritage, explained how her school had embedded LGBTQI+ people and issues successfully across many subjects within the curriculum:

> It's gone quite well with the music part of things. . . . We've got it in poetry, some of the poetry that we've had in English. . . . We've done it in RE when they're looking at matters of . . . marriage and family life. There's lots of things. And then History has looked at it as well. I know Science had British Science Week and we looked at some of the different scientists as well.

This teacher had developed a clear approach to talking to religious parents about the concerns they sometimes raised. These parents were told about the protected characteristics in the Equality Act 2010 and that the approach to and need for teaching about LGBTQI+ issues and people was exactly the same as that underpinning teaching about Islam and Muslim people. Pat, the ECCO at Indigo Primary School, which has a large proportion of African Evangelical Christian parents, took a similar approach, telling us that even quite angry parents asking questions about the curriculum at the school gate could be mollified by this kind of explanation.

In her interview, Jones, the ECCO at Mikey Secondary Academy, part of a Christian group of schools, explained that she thought the systematic process of looking though the curriculum and mapping LGBTQI+ people and issues into the plans worked well. She noted that

> it really was very simple and just to sort of give people ideas and say, because we'd already sort of thought that we needed to revamp the key stage three curriculum so I said while we're doing that why don't we just try, just look at a little bit of inclusion.

Jones gave some examples of what they had done, arguing that ideas about different family forms had become so embedded that children would not necessarily notice their inclusion:

> I know maths have kind of done it so that they look at sort of topics within so if they're doing like area or data or whatever its been how about we look at building a house for this family, it's [for] two women and two children so let's do it like that. I would imagine, I'm hoping that it's kind of gone over their heads a little bit which you would kind of hope eventually that it would become blind that it has kind of gone over their heads. I know that's the same with technology as well that they were designing houses and they had different scenarios of the types of families and the types of people who would be living in these homes and what they would design for that particular family compared to other people. . . . But I am hoping it kind of just went over their heads in some ways because that would be better . . . it would be normalised, it would be the norm.

In parallel with reassurances ECCOs often offer to religious parents who raise concerns about the Educate & Celebrate work, a focus on looking at the curriculum in terms of LGBTQI+ people also meant that staff became aware of other inclusion issues. Jones explained that this included

> just little things like when I would do day to day lesson plans I realised that a lot of my images and a lot of my imagery was probably very white which I suppose was quite, you know I was just thinking about myself, I was probably thinking about the cohort of students that I have they're usually majority white, but actually realising I probably need to change that up a bit, I need to be more inclusive and I need to think a bit differently about it.

We discuss this effect on wider inclusivity later in this chapter.

Policy

As we noted in Chapter 4, the needs and concerns of LGBTQI+ parents and their children are often invisible within school policies, so it is useful to look at the impact of a concerted effort to update school policies, especially in relation to the risk of policy being merely tokenistic (Ahmed, 2012). Policies in the Educate & Celebrate schools sometimes took a little longer to change than curriculum, partly because, as many teachers told us, they had to pass the documentation through the governors for agreement (Department for Education, 2014: #2579). It also depended, to some extent, on the seniority of the ECCO as to how quickly and easily policy could be rewritten and accepted. Jones at Mikey Secondary Academy suggested that this could be a status issue, saying, 'I'm just head of RE: that's it, that's me'. She explained that she managed to eventually get a policy changed 'with difficulty; yes I think because I felt that I was kind of interfering at a level that perhaps wasn't mine, it was difficult'. School uniform and staff dress code policies were a fruitful area of focus as they tended to bring key questions about identity and concrete expressions of inclusion to the fore. Jones explained:

> I looked at the school uniforms [policy] for the students and there was actually nothing in there about gender anything, you could wear whatever you wanted provided it was the school uniform, regardless of gender but for staff there was this whole thing about how women had to wear blouses and skirts, men had to wear blazers and ties. So I took it to my line lead, so just one above me and I said 'that's ridiculous', I said, 'you're basically saying that I have to come into work in a dress or a skirt and I said I don't feel comfortable coming into work in a dress or a skirt', I said, 'I don't feel comfortable doing that'.

This suggests that school uniform and similar policies constrain staff as well as students.

Another area around which policy change was easier to justify to senior staff was the behaviour policy, particularly as it related to differences between disciplinary responses to perceived racist and homophobic language. Working with Educate & Celebrate in some cases exposed inconsistencies between the treatment of different forms of bullying. For example, Jones told us:

> I remember having a conversation with one of our senior leaders about policies ... and I said, 'look, we need to have a policy around what we do, and I don't know what we do when homophobic language is used ... because there doesn't seem to be a clear system about it' ... and he said to me 'well if it was a racist remark they would be excluded'. I went, 'okay, so what would it be if it was a homophobic remark?' And he said, 'they would have isolation.' And I said, 'why? ... Either they've both got to be excluded or they both have isolation but they can't be different'. Then it was kind of, 'yes, you're right!' And a new policy developed out of it when we

realised how ridiculous it was that there was two totally different things.

Whilst policy can be read as a discourse (Maguire, Hoskins, Ball, & Braun, 2011; Taylor, 2004), policy changes can also become tokenistic substitutes for action (Ahmed, 2012). A change in policy is only, therefore, really powerful when it is followed by action. Jones recounted resistance to the new behaviour policy from staff and students, but her eventual victory illustrates both the anxiety involved in institutional change (James & Connolly, 2000) and the potential for it to be effective, when senior management stand strong on the issue. Jones recounts how the school population responded to the change in the behaviour policy to deal with homophobic language:

> when we put that into force, the kids' reaction at first, when we sort of said 'if you say 'that's so gay', if you use 'faggot', anything like that, you're going into isolation, that's it'. It was kind of a shock for them, and I don't know whether it was shocking for them because all of a sudden it was being taken seriously, as seriously as if they'd said 'nigger' – or whether it was because they just hadn't ever considered it before and it was just a shift in their attitude. In December you know, the senior leaders were coming back to me and saying, 'it's ridiculous, we can't have this many kids in isolation!' I said, 'but I know it's really annoying now but it'll be so much better in January when they just don't do it anymore!' And I started to hear less and less and less of it in the corridors, in my lessons, it just wasn't a terminology that was just used to describe anyone anymore.

Eventually the homophobic language at Mikey Secondary Academy became almost inaudible to teachers, although as the children whose interviews we discussed in Chapter 6 suggest, it may not have disappeared but just moved out of the earshot of staff. However, in classrooms and near teachers, students were able to challenge their peers. As Jones explained:

> (a)lthough there were kids who kind of made fun and go 'you should be put in isolation for that!' – It was almost kind of in their heads they were clocking it, going, 'that language is unacceptable', it's not tolerated so we just don't use it.

Drawing parallels between homophobia and other forms of discrimination could also support additional challenges to inequality. Foxtrot Secondary School students had independently started a programme of anti-racist education alongside their LGBTQI+ education programme, and had written a story book about it for primary schools in the area.

The school is in an area where (according to the staff) many adults are supporters of the right-wing racist British National Party, but the students saw an opportunity in the softening of attitudes towards LGBTQI+ people which could help to deal with the prevalent racism in the community. Similarly, at Bravo Primary Academy, the children were reading *King and King* (de Haan & Nijland, 2000). The story involves a young prince who interviews hundreds of princesses only to realize at the end that he is in love with his manservant, whom he then marries. The class teacher explained that the children had then led a long discussion on socioeconomic differences, asking whether rich and poor people should be allowed to get married and what sort of family arguments could get in the way of these sorts of relationships. Teachers also stressed their general commitment to equality. For example, the Hotel Primary School Learning Mentor explains her approach:

> I enjoy teaching and, what I do with these children is I make sure that they don't hate anybody because I said there's, I'm really, I think it's probably because I see what's going on in the world, I just see so much destruction in the world and I just say to them we can't do that here we have to love and respect each other here because look outside these gates. You know it starts here and we need to do as much as we can here in order for the children to be able to have better lives, you know I just want them to respect and love each other.

These findings were consistent across the schools we visited, most of which were serving children in working-class areas. This suggests that it is not only middle-class LGBTQI+ parented families (Taylor, 2009) who have access to schools where equalities interventions have been successful.

An Increased Awareness of LGBTQI+ Parents and a More Inclusive Environment

A lack of visibility can lead to the silencing of the specific needs of LGBTQI+ parented families, underpinning a context of pervasive heteronormativity that circumscribes options for parents and children by perceived gender, and impacting on access to appropriate health education (Horn et al., 2010). This is also recognized as disruptive to children's learning (Feiler et al., 2006). Before the Educate & Celebrate programme started, there was a clear problem with the visibility of LGBTQI+ parented families in the schools, as was also found in the wider policy analysis we discussed in Chapter 4. The programme did change this situation, with some schools, such as Eastchurch MLD Secondary School, recognizing the existence of a family with two female parents in their school population where this had not previously been acknowledged.

Other schools focused on community celebrations. For example, Foxtrot Secondary School generated an LGBT-themed 'Creative Day' and took part in an area-wide rainbow-themed singing competition culminating in an enormous community celebration. The ECCO explained that 'some of the students created an LGBT song and they were our competition winners . . . and then we changed displays around school and things . . . the Creative Day brought a lot of it together'. For this school, celebration helped them to embed the Educate & Celebrate approach. This was partly because it involved people in activities rather than discussions or policy writing. The ECCO suggested that 'the bit that worked best for us was . . . the celebration part. That allowed us to get everybody involved and it wasn't just a paper chase with the policies'. The community involvement in celebrations had a profound impact in this school and the others involved in the event. The Foxtrot ECCO described her experience of:

> seeing primary school students stand up in Year 4 and saying, . . . 'some people have two mams and some people have two dads, and that's okay because we were all born equal'. This tiny little boy saying that was just lovely for me.

Another teacher noted that their community celebration and the lead-up to it allowed the explicit inclusion of one particular LGBTQI+ parented child:

> We've got one young lady in school who has two mams. . . . I had a bit of a chat with her because she won the competition, she wrote the song. I had a bit of a chat with her about whether she'd struggled and how she got on and she said when she was very young, she struggled because there was a little bit of, you know, I don't think it was bullying, I think it was just lack of understanding but she said since she's come here here's nothing and it is fine and it is accepted . . . and when [she] did the assembly she stood up and said, 'oh I've got two mams', in front of a hundred and odd students and just stood up and said 'I've got two mams'. . . . That was really brave. To her it was just nothing. That's what we are trying to go down that avenue where we can just say and that's fine, that's okay. So that is why we've been doing all of this, certainly from my point of view just to make the kids realise that it is okay.

Similarly, LGBTQI+ parents at Mikey Secondary Academy were also reported to feel more visible in their school as a result of the changes made. As the ECCO explained:

> feedback that I have had from students is that parents have said that the visibility wasn't there when they were young and they're glad

that it is there, they're pleased that it's there because it just didn't exist. Certainly when some of the parents do come to parents' evening they notice the board that's out in the humanities area with all the LGBT stuff on it and they comment on it and they say how great it is to actually see the visibility in the school. So I think certainly some of the students have come back and they say they feel better, they feel safer and I think that's because the parents are seeing it if that makes sense, so they feel it as well.

Despite these benefits, keeping LGBTQI+ people and issues visible could take some sustained effort on the part of the ECCOs. The ECCO at Romeo Secondary Academy told us how she had to remain vigilant as staff rapidly forgot to include LGBTQI+ families:

For example, at assemblies I will look at the assembly PowerPoint and I'll be like, 'right, add that in there because you haven't put it in', and the member of staff just puts it in. So that's what we did with the recent one about family and love, so I made her put in, you know, same sex families and she did. She just added it. She goes, 'oh, I forgot'. Some people just need that prompting and we put it back in and they were fine.

The Educate & Celebrate programme went some way towards increasing the visibility of LGBTQI+ people and their lives. As we saw in Chapter 6, this is important for the children of LGBTQI+ parents, particularly in terms of their sense of identity and belonging.

Homonormativity, Heteronormativity and Neoliberalism

We referred in Chapter 2 to Wittig's (1989/1992) understanding of the heteronormative assumptions of civil life and to Butler's (1990) heterosexual matrix. We also described how these concepts inform Duggan's (2002) concerns over the pressures of homonormativity to force lesbian, gay and transgender people into a non-radical, non-fluid and gender-binary mirroring of heterosexual life. In this way, Duggan argues, LGBTQI+ parented families are made acceptable through their suitability for participation as consumers in a neoliberal economy. Given the long history of these processes, and the fact that media representations tend also to be homonormative (see Chapter 3), they are particularly insidious. This led us to ask whether Educate & Celebrate works to challenge homonormativity, or whether it also excludes non-normative LGBTQI+ individuals and groups. Specifically, we wanted to work out whether schools focused only on lesbian, gay and non-fluid transgender people, or whether bisexual, gender-fluid, queer, openly intersex and polyamorous parents were also included.

Secondary school students in the focus groups often reported that hetero- and homonormative discourses and body-gender correspondence were still prevalent. However, the Educate & Celebrate intervention did at least give the students some of the language they needed to challenge their peers. One Delta Secondary School student, for example, talked about a discussion she had had with a friend about another student who was transitioning:

> I was having this chat with my friend, because there's a transgender boy in the year below us. And I was having a chat, and I was just like totally, they had like a wall of acceptance, and what they believed was what they believed. And I was trying to tell them, like, but no, it's what they think, and how they feel themselves. And they were just like, 'no, he has a vagina—he has a vagina, it's a she—okay'.

This resistance on the part of her friend suggests, nevertheless, that gender was not universally understood by students in this school as being independent of bodily form.

The understanding of some school staff of the complexity of heteronormative and homonormative discourse also still has some way to go. For example, one deputy head teacher appeared to be open to a student coming out as gay but still retained the traditional belief that boys need a father figure at home:

> Well there is one student in Post 16 that we suspect probably is thinking along sort of homosexual lines but hasn't actually said anything but his behaviour suggests that there is a possibility and he just doesn't . . . he is quite angry at the moment and lives with his mum, hasn't got a male role model at home so, you know, but we wouldn't sit him down and have a conversation with him and say 'have you thought about this?'

It was also unclear whether the 'behaviour' referred to included stereotyped ideas about how a gay teenager might behave.

Nevertheless, the Educate & Celebrate training does appear to have the potential to challenge homonormative assumptions of static LGBTQI+ identity. This is partly because it provides teachers and students with alternative discourses for talking about gender and sexual orientation. An ECCO from Hotel Primary School, for example, described her experience of learning a whole new vocabulary:

> When I came on the course I saw all of these words. I was like, 'this is new to me!'. . . . And it was good when we had a vocabulary discussion and it was like, 'okay right yes, yes heard that, heard that, no idea what that is' . . . God there were tons of them; most of them, the

158   *'Usualizing' LGBTQI+ People and Issues*

> ones I'd heard I knew what they were so things that I hadn't heard [included] 'intersex'. . . . The differences between, just a clarification on differences between 'transgender', 'transsexual', how to speak to somebody if they are, so, [asking] 'what do you want to be called?' 'Trans' covers everything, apparently. 'Pansexual'- that was a new one, yes and 'genderfluid', I've forgotten what that meant now.

The training has also had a clear impact on the work of those staff involved who were not ECCOs, suggesting a broader reach than just those teachers who were directly involved. A Learning Mentor at Hotel Primary School described, for example, how she now challenges the embodiment of heteronormative constructions of gender:

> In our literacy lessons . . . we as much as we can get the children to dress up and boys absolutely love dressing up. One of the things I have changed about the way the boys perceive women, as soon as the boy puts a wig on and a handbag he walks across the floor wiggling like there's no tomorrow, I don't know where they get that perception but they wiggle right across the floor. [I say] 'actually do I walk across the room like that? 'How do you know? Why do women have to walk across wiggling?'

The Learning Mentor explained how she would show the boys how she walks across the room and ask them to identify how different that is to their exaggerated 'wiggling'. She also talked about how she was careful to avoid gender-normativity when selecting children for parts in a school play:

> I'll never go 'I need a girl' . . . it's like 'I need somebody to play the part of X' and if it's a girl and there's a boy who's fantastic, 'you're fantastic at acting can you come up here?!' And they put the wig on and the dress and bumf done. We never go 'I need a boy/ I need a girl', they get given the parts based on their ability rather than their gender, so.

That the Educate & Celebrate programme has the potential to challenge hegemonic discourses about gender and sexual orientation was evident in the way that some of the teachers, other staff and students interviewed at the end of the programme could recognize homonormativity in the media and critique it. For example, Jones, the Mikey Secondary Academy ECCO, questioned American sitcom representations of gay fathers, using an approach very much in line with Littler's (2013) analysis of acceptable diversity in a neoliberal context:

> I don't like the way that America portrays their gay characters particularly and I get that, particularly for Fox, there's . . . we can accept

gayness so long as they are extreme stereotypes. So that you can almost make fun of them in a way and so the very camp, flamboyancy is not . . . it really aggravates me because I do think that actually that's not, that is not true and it's not representative of every couple anywhere and it's just kind of, it's used because that makes people feel safe, I think. That makes Americans feel safe almost.

By the end of the programme, even 6-year-olds were able to make this analysis. At Hotel Primary School, the children were reading 'The Three Little Pigs' with their teacher, who reported that one child asked why the three little pigs were always male, adding that there could be 'one boy, one girl and one transgender'.

The more flexible discourse introduced by Educate & Celebrate also allowed young people in some circumstances to feel more able to express their non-normative gender identities. At William Secondary School, where querying the girls' traditional kilts in their uniform policy had caused a small uproar amongst the governors, a student described a fashion show they had held as part of their LGBT community celebration events:

STUDENT 1: They did a whole segment on diversity and this included doing signs for LGBT and gender and lots of other subjects, and you'd walk around with signs and we coloured in shirts as well.
STUDENT 2: There was this one boy who came out in a dress and it wasn't really stuck to one gender.
STUDENT 3: It was received quite well.
STUDENT 4: Nobody really reacted. It was just a fashion show and it was really fun.

This suggests a significant change in attitudes regarding who can wear what in this school, blurring gender binaries.

Conclusion

Interventions such as Educate & Celebrate do appear to have the potential to improve things in schools for the children of LGBTQI+ parents. Through a comprehensive institution-transforming programme of training, curriculum review and policy updating, the system develops sustainable change, not just in the school but often in the community it serves. Most of the schools visited at the end of the programme had succeeded in reviewing curriculum and embedding LGBTQI+ people and issues in a range of subjects. This does not merely help LGBTQI+ people: it has the potential to dilute pervasive heteronormativity, and to offer positive outcomes for anyone who does not fit a binary gender stereotype.

The Educate & Celebrate programme demonstrates that it is possible to have an impact in diverse environments: the middle-class homogeneity of Delta Secondary School; the diverse small-town deprivation of Bravo Primary School students; the all-Muslim Romeo Secondary School; the right-wing white heartland of Mikey Secondary Academy; and the rural setting of Eastchurch MLD Secondary School.

It is clear, however, from the most recent Stonewall Report (Bradlow, Bartram, Guasp, & Jadva, 2017) that where schools have not undertaken some form of systemic change programme, problems still abound. Part of this is to do with the historical silencing of teachers. Teachers lack confidence in addressing LGBTQI+ issues: often Anna arrived at a school for a focus group to find that the teacher had been waiting for her arrival in order to avoid being the first person to say the words 'lesbian' and 'gay' to the students. This stifling coyness meant that where LGBTQI+ people were mentioned, it was in very narrow, medicalized contexts. Even where they are delivered comprehensively, programmes of this nature are not a panacea: it is very difficult to address the tendency of children to keep some of their experiences to themselves. In part this is due to a reluctance to report problematic behaviour to teachers; the children of LGBTQI+ people are also reluctant to upset their parents. As we saw in Chapter 4, school policies exacerbate this: LGBTQI+ parents are unlikely to feature in even updated school policies and documentation.

Teachers do, however, recognize that there can be a positive impact on children's learning where their unique family situations are recognized. Building on the tangible areas of staff dress code and student uniform rules, schools were able to rethink and update their policies and procedures in ways which were more than tokenistic. Behaviour policies, in particular, were quickly changed once staff realized that there were inequitably different approaches to racist and HBT language. The successful formula employed by Educate & Celebrate is the combination of long-term planning through policy and curriculum change, alongside more immediate, community and environment-enhancing activities such as Rainbow Bake-offs and community performances. This combination seems to be essential to the fuller engagement of the wider school community and therefore greater embedding of change.

Note

1 'Usualizing' is a term used by Educate & Celebrate as an alternative to 'normalizing'. 'Usualizing' is perceived as less pathologizing, but also denotes ubiquity.

References

Ahmed, S. (2012). Whiteness and the General Will: Diversity work as willful work. *philoSOPHIA*. 2155–0891. *1*(2): 1–20.

Ball, S. (2001). Labour, learning and the economy: A "policy sociology" perspective. In Fielding, M. (Ed.), *Taking education really seriously: Four years hard labour* (pp. 45–46). London: RoutledgeFalmer.

'Usualizing' LGBTQI+ People and Issues   161

Bradlow, J., Bartram, F., Guasp, A., & Jadva, V. (2017). *School report: The experiences of lesbian, gay, bi and trans young people in Britain's schools in 2017.* London: Stonewall and University of Cambridge.

Butler, J. (1990). *Gender trouble: Feminism and the subversion of identity.* London: Routledge.

Crozier, G., & Davies, J. (2007, June 2007). Hard to reach parents or hard to reach schools? A discussion of home—school relations, with particular reference to Bangladeshi and Pakistani parents. *British Educational Research Journal, 33*(3), 295–313.

de Haan, L., & Nijland, S. (2000). *King and king.* Berkeley: Tricycle Press.

DePalma, R. (2010, Fall). The no outsiders project: In search of queer primary pedagogies. *Transformations, 21*(2), Winter 2011.

Duggan, L. (2002). The new homonormativity: The sexual politics of neoliberalism. In R. Castronovo & D. D. Nelson (Eds.), *Materialising democracy: Towards a revitalised cultural politics* (pp. 175–194). Durham and London: Duke University Press.

Educate & Celebrate. (2017). Retrieved November 28, 2017, from www.educateandcelebrate.org/award/

Equality and Human Rights Commission. (2017). *Public sector equality duties.* Retrieved from April 1, 2018, from www.equalityhumanrights.com/en/advice-and-guidance/public-sector-equality-duty.

Feiler, A., Greenhough, P., Winter, J., Salway, L., & Scanlan, M. (2006). Getting engaged: Possibilities and problems for home—School knowledge exchange. *Educational Review, 58*(4), 451–469.

Horn, S., Konkol, P., McInerney, K., Meiners, E. R., North, C., Nuñez, I., Quinn, T., & Sullivan, S. (2010). Visibility matters: Policy work as activism in teacher education. *Issues in Teacher Education, 19*(2).

James, C., & Connolly, U. (2000). *Effective change in schools.* London: Routledge.

Jones, R., & Clarke, G. (2007). The school experiences of same-sex attracted students in the 14- to 19-year-old secondary sector in England: Within and beyond the safety and tolerance framework. *Journal of Gay & Lesbian Social Services, 19*(3–4), 119–138.

Kosciejew, M. (2015). Disciplinary documentation in Apartheid South Africa. *Journal of Documentation.* 0022–0418, 71(1), 96–115.

Littler, J. (2013). Meritocracy as plutocracy: The marketising of "equality" within neoliberalism. *New Formations: A Journal of Culture/Theory/Politics, 80*, 52–72.

Maguire, M., Hoskins, K., Ball, S., & Braun, A. (2011). Policy discourses in school texts. *Discourse, 32*(4), 597–609.

Malins, P. (2016). How inclusive is "inclusive education" in the Ontario elementary classroom?: Teachers talk about addressing diverse gender and sexual identities. *Teaching and Teacher Education, 54*, 128–138.

NatCen. (2016). Evaluation of an anti-homophobic, biphobic & transphobic bullying programme. Retrieved August 18, 2017, from http://natcen.ac.uk/our-research/research/evaluation-of-anti-hbt-bullying-programme/.

Paechter, C., & Clark, S. (2016). Being "nice" or being "normal": Girls resisting discourses of "coolness". *Discourse: Studies in the Cultural Politics of Education, 37*(3), 457–471.

Russell, S. T., McGuire, J. K., Lee, S., Larriva, J. C., & Laub, C. (2008). Adolescent perceptions of school safety for transgender parents. *Journal of LGBT Youth, 5*(4), 11–27.

Ryan-Flood, R. (2009). *Lesbian motherhood: Gender, families and sexual citizenship*. Basingstoke, Hants: Palgrave Macmillan.
Sauntson, H., & Simpson, K. (2011). Investigating sexuality discourses in the U.K. Secondary English curriculum. *Journal of Homosexuality*, 58(6–7), 953–973.
Stonewall Report. (2017). Retrieved August 24, 2017, from www.stonewall.org.uk/school-report-2017.
Taylor, S. (2004). Researching educational policy and change in "new times" using critical discourse analysis. *Journal of Education Policy*, 19(4), 433–451.
Taylor, Y. (2009). *Lesbian and gay parenting: Securing social and educational capital*. Basingstoke, Hants: Palgrave Macmillan.
UK Government. (2010). *Equality Act*.
Vanderbeck, R. M., & Johnson, P. (2015). Homosexuality, religion and the contested legal framework governing sex education in England. *Journal of Social Welfare and Family Law*, 37(2), 161–179.
Walker, J., & Bates, J. (2016). UK Developments in LGBTQI+ provision in secondary school library services since the abolition of Section 28. *Journal of Librarianship and Information Science*, 48(3), 269–283.
Warwick, I., Aggleton, P., & Douglas, N. (2001). Playing it safe: Addressing the emotional and physical health of lesbian and gay pupils in the U.K. *Journal of Adolescence*, 0140–1971, 24(1), 129–140.
Weiss, K. (2013). "You just don't report that kind of stuff": Investigating teens' ambivalence toward peer-perpetrated, unwanted sexual incidents. *Violence and Victims*, 28(2), 288–302.
Whitman, J. L., & Davis, R. C. (2007). *Snitches get stitches: Youth, gangs and witness intimidation in Massachusetts*. Washington, DC: National Center for Victims of Crime.
Wittig, M. (1989/1992). On the social contract. In M. Wittig (Ed.), *The straight mind and other essays* (pp. 33–45). Boston, MA: Beacon Press.
Woldoff, R. A., & Weiss, K. G. (2010). "Stop snitchin": Exploring definitions of the snitch and implications for urban, black communities. *Journal of Criminal Justice and Popular Culture*, 17, 184–223.

8 Conclusion
Ways Forward for LGBTQI+ Parented Families and Schools

I am at our two-year-old's nursery 'Parent's Evening', sitting on a tiny chair in a room filled with colourful wooden toys and displays of painted autumn leaves, glittery hand prints, and pictures of animals. Across the low desk from me is his keyworker, Charlie, a cheerful young woman full of warmth who tells me with real feeling that she loves playing with our child and watching him grow and develop. She asks me if there is anything specific we would like her to do with our child in the next term. I tell her that we really appreciate her work with him and that he is very happy at the nursery, and talks about her at home, often—but that they could perhaps offer a bit more in terms of books and texts which more closely reflect his family. She looks at me, perplexed but smiling: I realise that she is wholly willing, and only needs the institutional support, materials and training to deliver it.

Anna

As we complete this book, ideas about gender, sexuality and identity are changing at an unprecedented pace. In the affluent North and West, LGBTQI+ people are more visible than ever before, and are increasingly incorporated into wider society. While much of the mainstream media has an ambivalent approach to LGBTQI+ people, celebrating the relationships and identities of the rich and famous while ignoring or taking a more negative stance towards those whose lives are more ordinary, it remains the case that LGBTQI+ people feature more frequently, and in greater variety, in news stories than was previously the case. Schools can no longer (if they ever could) assume that children will only know about LGBTQI+ people if they actually meet them: young people's interest in and consumption of stories about LGBTQI+ celebrities and others was evident from our research. This greater media saturation is also allowing children and young people to be aware of a wide range of examples of how people understand their gender and sexuality, and to want to know more about what that means for LGBTQI+ people in the media and in ordinary life.

At the same time, the homonormative incorporation of many LGBTQI+ people into mainstream society means that they are more likely to be visible in person to children and young people. This is especially true of those people who have embraced the 'ordinariness' (Weeks, 2007) of homonormative family life. With the legalization of gay marriage and increased access to IVF, sperm donation, surrogacy, adoption and fostering, LGBTQI+ parents and their families are everywhere, including schools. This means that every school needs to consider the best ways of including and recognizing LGBTQI+ parented families in all their varied forms. It is not sufficient for a school to have an equality policy that meets its statutory duties but to otherwise do nothing until they notice such a family in their midst. Not all LGBTQI+ parented families are visible to school communities, and the needs of those who are invisible are equally important.

Our research shows that in their relations with LGBTQI+ parented families, school interventions can be described as falling into two categories: addressing discrimination (for example, bullying or HBT language) and fostering representation. With a few exceptions, the schools we visited or heard about from LGBTQI+ parents, carers and their children implemented reasonably confident and robust approaches to bullying. Policies relating to behaviour were usually comprehensive and met the requirements of the Equality Act 2010 (UK Government, 2010); consequences of those bullying incidents which had come to the attention of teaching staff were clear and tended to be consistently implemented. As a result, most of the children we interviewed felt that their schools' responses to HBT bullying were effective. Many of them spoke of feeling safe and protected in their schools and by their head teachers. There are remaining problems, however, mostly relating to a continued use of HBT language which has largely 'gone underground', into playgrounds and toilets out of earshot of staff. These are exacerbated by students' unofficial code of silence and reluctance to tell teachers about other children's behaviour. Nevertheless, it seems that where both primary and secondary schools know about incidents of bullying and are therefore able to respond, they usually take their role seriously.

However, schools' success in intervening when they are aware of bullying masks a continued lack of visibility and representation (Gustavson & Schmitt, 2011), mentioned by many of our respondents. School discourses around LGBTQI+ people tend to focus on HBT language and actions and the need to address bullying and eliminate unlawful discrimination. However, the implementation of interventions which support representation and the more positive, proactive public sector equality duty (Equality and Human Rights Commission, 2017) to 'foster good relations' between people with different or no protected characteristics are much rarer. As Kulz (2017) and Pallotta-Chiarolli and Rajkhowa (2017) have pointed out, the sorts of disciplinary interventions implemented in response to allegations of bullying can be divisive in many ways, often impacting inequitably on children who are not members of the dominant white community. School interventions which work to familiarize children and young people with LGBTQI+ issues and to celebrate diverse LGBTQI+ people going about their daily lives are much more constructive, and yet much less common. As we have discussed, for LGBTQI+ parents, representation often means a quietly but firmly accepted visibility; for their children it can involve an aspect of pride and a celebration of their individuality. Further, a lack of visibility can have negative impacts associated with children's diminished sense of belonging at school (Gustavson & Schmitt, 2011). As Sarmento and Freire (2012) point out, children whose families are recognized at schools have a better learning experience.

Conscious tweaks to established school practice can make a huge difference in the level of representation and belonging experienced in schools by LGBTQI+ parented families. School interventions can support, enhance and relieve children's own efforts in advocating for their families. Children who are used to hearing and talking about families like theirs at school may feel more inclined to let their parents and teachers know when they have experienced an incident of homophobia, biphobia or transphobia. Representation is both important to these families (McInroy & Craig, 2015), and relatively simple to implement. For example, most teachers make extensive use of posters and exhibitions of work: including diverse people in wall displays is something schools are often already familiar with when it comes to other characteristics, such as ethnicity and gender. Schools could also work to welcome LGBTQI+ people both onto the staff and within the school's wider community of students, parents, carers, governors and neighbours. Representation can take place through the various forms of text used in schools: books, websites, test papers, worksheets, curriculum, policies and teaching materials are all places where schools talk about people already, and so are fertile spaces for the depiction of diverse people, including of LGBTQI+ parented families. This fine-tuning of customary school activities can work to provide an environment where good relations between diverse students and families can be fostered and where all school staff, parents, carers and children have the potential to feel a sense of belonging and recognition.

While small changes like these can make a lot of positive difference, it is also important to be aware that negative things that a school thinks are relatively unimportant may be a much bigger deal for LGBTQI+ parented families. For example, several of the parents we interviewed complained about the standard forms schools use to record information about parents and carers. These frequently assume that every child has two known, opposite-sex parents, with spaces for 'mother's name' and 'father's name'. This is simply not the case for many children, and not just those whose parents are LGBTQI+. For same-gender co-parenting couples, such forms serve to exclude one parent altogether, and this situation is exacerbated if a child has more than two parents actively involved in their parenting. Some parents told us that their children's schools had replaced a gendered form with one that asked for 'first parent' and 'second parent'. This was felt to be excluding by co-parents who wanted to be seen as entirely equal in their parenting roles, an issue that is particularly sensitive when one parent is the birth mother. It would be better for all families if schools could simply have a form that allowed for a list of all parents the child has, without any obvious priority.

A second area which matters to parents much more than schools appear to think is the celebration of Mother's Day and Father's Day. Parents and children told us that children were not always supported to make a card for each parent, or to address one card to both their parents using the appropriate names. While schools do seem to be taking on board that some children will not have a mother or father to make cards for, and provide alternatives appropriately, the existence and significance of more than one same-gender parent does not seem to be treated with equal sensitivity. Where schools mark these celebratory days, they should do so equally for mothers and fathers: making Mothers' Day more important sends an exclusionary signal to children whose only parents are male.

The use of the generic 'mummy' and 'daddy' is also something schools take for granted but which some parents find very distressing. For a child with only one mother, 'your mummy' has an obvious, singular referent, even if the person in question is called by a different name. For a child who has two mothers, however, 'Mummy' may differentiate one of these mothers from the other, and refer only to her. Using the generic 'mummy' may therefore be confusing for the child, who is used to that term being used specifically for one person and one person only. Addressing a Mothers' Day or Christmas card to 'mummy', while taken for granted in a heterosexual context, may be experienced as insensitive in an LGBTQI+ one. The use of the generic 'your mummy' when talking to a child may also make the mother not called 'Mummy' feel excluded or invisible, and imply that the school does not recognize her equal parenting role. Schools need to be sensitive to this, and staff should endeavour to remember the names all children actually use for their parents. At the same time, however, it is important for parents to remember that teachers do not intend to exclude them in this way, and that the use of the generic 'mummy' has arisen in a context in which the child is at the centre and all adults are known, discussed and thought about in terms of their relation to that child, rather than as individuals.

Schools have become a lot more inclusive in recent years, and it is now much easier for LGBTQI+ parented families to become accepted members of the broader school community. Although still often invisible in policies and documentation, LGBTQI+ parents are generally welcomed and accepted by their children's schools, and their children protected from HBT bullying most of the time. More work needs to be done to include more diverse family forms and practices into school policies, curriculum and daily practices, to make their commitments to equality visible, and to ensure that all families are represented in displays, teaching materials and everyday examples. Schools should also be mindful that some LGBTQI+ parented families are more visible than others, and to take this into account in their work, so that the invisible are not also excluded. The world of gender is changing, and schools need to work harder to keep up, if they are to ensure that everyone feels part of their communities. Nevertheless, the evidence of our research shows that, for most LGBTQI+ parented families, schools have the potential to be safe and friendly places, where children and young people can be out and proud about their parents.

References

Equality and Human Rights Commission. (2017, February 20). Public sector equality duty. Retrieved from www.equalityhumanrights.com/en/advice-and-guidance/public-sector-equality-duty

Gustavson, M., & Schmitt, I. (2011). Culturally queer, silenced in school? Children with LGBTQ parents, and the everyday politics of/in community and school. *Lambda Nordica: Tidskrift för homo/lesbisk/bi/transforskning*, 16(2–3), 159–187.

Kulz, C. (2017). *Factories for learning: Making race, class and inequality in the neoliberal academy*. Manchester: Manchester University Press.

McInroy, L. B., & Craig, S. L. (2015). Transgender representation in offline and online media: LGBTQ youth perspectives. *Journal of Human Behavior in the Social Environment*, 25(6), 606–617.

Pallotta-Chiarolli, M., & Rajkhowa, A. (2017). Systemic invisibilities, institutional culpabilities and multicultural-multifaith LGBTIQ resistances. *Journal of Intercultural Studies*, 38(4), 429–442.

Sarmento, T., & Freire, I. (2012). Making school happen: Children-parent-teacher collaboration as a practice of citizenship. *Education Sciences*, 2(2), 105–120

UK Government. (2010). *Equality Act*.

Weeks, J. (2007). *The world we have won*. London: Routledge.

Index

Academic Review Days 125
adoption 17, 22, 90, 99, 164
allies 16, 110, 133, 139, 147

Beatie, Thomas 7, 36, 51
biphobia 50, 119–120, 165
bisexuality 19, 44–45
bisexual people 2, 7, 19, 29, 38, 43, 66, 69, 74, 110, 115, 126, 128, 132, 141; media representations of 43–45; men 42, 43, 44; *see also* parents
'bodily capital' 39–40
body 23, 25–26, 49, 51, 157; effacement of 26–27; masculine 23; non-homonormative 28
borderland subjectivity 109–110
British National Party 140, 154
'British Values' 131
bullying 7–8, 20, 29, 31, 37, 56, 57, 58, 62, 66–67, 70, 83, 85, 86–87, 89–90, 93, 105, 106, 109, 110, 113, 115–116, 121, 123, 128, 129–130, 134, 136, 147–148, 152, 155, 164–165; anti- 60, 66, 89–90, 92, 93, 106; homophobic 66–67, 89–90, 105; homophobic, biphobic and transphobic (HBT) 110, 114, 119–121, 122, 130–131, 133–134, 137, 141, 146–148, 164, 167; potential 106; protective strategy 90–91; reluctance to report 146–148, 160, 164; transphobic 90
Butler, J. 13–15, 21, 156

children: adopted 75, 77, 84, 91, 93, 99, 110, 112, 133–134; birth 75; bisexual 111; cisgender 111, 134; fostered 75, 76, 77, 83, 84, 87–88, 93, 100, 102, 105, 110; gay 83, 106; LGBTQI+ 132, 133, 142, 148; non-binary/lesbian 111; protectiveness of 114–116; queer 123; of queer culture 133; resilience of 91, 110, 120–121, 127–128, 130, 133; straight 134; trans 106; *see also* students
Church of England 62, 89
cisnormativity 78
civil partnership 58, 62; same-sex 61
civil rights 17
Collins, Joan 44
coming out 25, 27, 28, 36, 45, 49, 67, 75–76, 82, 85, 86–87, 90, 93, 98, 100, 105–106, 110, 119, 123–124, 139, 157; as children of LGBTQI+ people/parents 8, 110, 120, 123–128, 132, 167; of teachers 110, 127, 129, 132, 136
couple(s) 17, 23, 74–75, 82, 84, 159; binary 75; co-parenting 105, 165–166; female 74; gay 16, 18, 19, 24, 25, 28, 30, 99, 112; gay male 25, 30, 112; heteronormative 24; heterosexual 31, 78–79, 83, 100; homonormative 20; intersex 75; lesbian 16, 17, 18, 19, 21–22, 24, 25, 28, 37, 44, 75, 82, 96, 99; LGBTQI+ 15; male 24, 25, 30, 112; monogamous 18, 19; non-binary 75; non-heterosexual 31; polyamorous 74; same-gender 165–166; same-sex 13, 18, 65, 91, 146; straight 27, 30
Cox, Laverne 2
cross-dressing 86
culturally queer 109
cultural queerness 121, 133

curriculum 8, 27, 28, 30, 62, 67–68, 86, 88, 93, 106, 116, 131, 133–134, 136–137, 141–143, 146, 148–152, 159–160, 165, 167; English 143, 148–150; History 150; maths 151; music 150; Science 142, 150

'daddy': as generic term 166
Department for Education (DfE) 38, 137
disability 37–38, 58, 61, 62, 84; learning 91, 110; London 2012 Paralympics 38
diversity 15, 18, 38–39, 49, 51, 61, 68, 70, 88, 91, 105, 119, 143, 158–159; family 18, 91; gender 51, 127; policy 62; school 93; 'work' 119, 129
donor insemination 19, 75
Duffy, Carol Ann 148

Educate & Celebrate 'LGBT+ Friendly Schools' programme 3, 4, 8, 110, 129, 136–160, 160n1; library book packages 148–149
England 3, 6, 37, 55, 56, 59, 74, 111, 137, 139, 148, 149; Eastern 58; Midlands 137; North 137; West Midlands 58
Equality Act (2010) 2, 37–38, 58, 67, 143–145, 150, 164
Equality and Human Rights Commission 65
ethnicity 4, 38, 61, 133, 139, 143, 165
Europe 18, 74
European Union 18
evangelical Christians 140, 150

family 19, 27, 56, 64, 73, 121, 144, 151, 160; alternative 1, 28; bisexual 19, 37, 57, 69; blended 4; definition 18–19; gay 2, 16, 57, 68, 69, 121; heteronormative 6, 8, 15, 18–19, 21, 27, 29, 76, 118; heterosexual 17; heterosexually parented 66, 75; homonormative 2, 6, 13, 18–20, 27, 28, 30–31, 48–49, 164; lesbian 16, 57, 68, 69, 149, 154; LGBTQI+ parented 5, 35, 42, 51, 55–58, 61, 63–64, 67–70, 73, 80, 81, 85, 86, 88, 93, 99, 100, 103–104, 106–107, 109–111, 113, 125, 129, 137–138, 143–146, 151, 154, 156, 164–167; middle-class 137, 154; monogamous 29; multiple-parented 37; non-heteronormative 28; non-homonormative 28; non-normative 20, 51, 103; normative 17; nuclear 18, 48, 76; opposite-sex couple 19; polyamorous 29, 146; queer 18, 37, 48, 57; queerly mixed 19; same-gender parented 111; same-sex couple 13, 19, 66, 146, 156; single-parented 68, 146; straight 31; transgender 57; white 137; working-class 30; see also family forms; parents
father(s) 13, 21–22, 24, 44–46, 79–80, 94, 101–102, 112, 121, 124, 128, 144, 157, 165, 166; biological 24, 25, 37; donor 110, 117, 126, 128; gay 22, 24, 46, 95, 110, 158; gay male 1, 22; heterosexual 22; step- 48; straight 22, 95; trans/transgender 7, 36, 103
fatherhood 6, 12, 21, 22, 24; biological 25
Fathers' Day 4, 95–96, 106, 166
femininity 21, 24
Finland 86
fluidity 132
fostering 17, 81, 100, 164
friendships 105, 110, 120, 122–124, 127–128, 133, 142

'gay' as a term of abuse 5, 66, 91–93, 117–121, 123, 141, 147, 153
gay culture 16, 17, 24; see also queer culture
gay people 6, 16, 38, 49, 66, 69, 90, 100, 102, 113, 115, 124, 137, 156, 157, 160; man (men) 1, 16, 17, 22, 24, 27, 28, 30, 41, 43, 45–46, 110; media representations of 43–45; see also children; father(s); parents; students
gender 4–6, 13–15, 20, 22, 27, 37, 47, 51, 62, 68, 76, 78, 82, 117, 132, 140, 142, 143, 152, 157–159, 163, 165, 167; binary 5, 6, 15, 39, 102, 115, 156, 159; binary model of 37, 137; cis- 4, 15, 16, 23, 28, 48, 74, 111, 132–134, 137; diversity 51, 127; equality 18, 132; exploration 103; expression 68, 89; -fluid 158;

Index

heteronormative model of 37; identity 37, 41, 68, 103, 132, 140, 145, 159; intersex 74; non-binary 5, 28, 74, 137; non-conforming 68, 77, 103; non-normative 159; normativity 158; norms 24; perceived 154, 157; performances 13; presentation 102–103; -queer 19, 28, 74, 76, 78, 115; roles 114; stable 13, 15; stereotypes 134, 159; traditional ideologies of 21, 22; *see also* identity; gender reassignment; gender transition surgery; transition (gender)
gender reassignment 37, 58, 61–63, 86
Gender Recognition Act (2004) 2
gender transition surgery 39–41, 47, 78
global/affluent North 15, 163
global/affluent West 15, 163
Government Equalities Office (GEO) 137
grandparent care 56, 65, 68, 95
Gypsy 62

HBT environment 122, 123, 127
HBT experiences 116, 131; *see also* biphobia; bullying; homophobia; language; transphobia
heteronormativity 4, 12, 15–17, 19, 23, 25–27, 30, 48, 51, 68, 69, 96–97, 100, 109, 114, 123, 120–121, 127, 128, 133–134, 154, 156–159; cisgender 48; of parenthood 17
heterosexism 66
heterosexuality 13–15, 18, 20–23, 25–27, 64; "heterosexual contract" 13–14; invisibility of 20, 27
heterosexual matrix 6, 12, 13–15, 18, 21, 26, 125, 156
Hirst, Keegan 45
'homonationalism' 38
homonormativity 2, 6, 12–13, 15–17, 19–20, 23, 26, 27, 30, 31, 48, 84, 132, 136, 141, 156–158, 164; media representations of 156, 158–159
homophobia 4, 50, 62, 66–67, 80, 82, 87, 89, 90, 91, 93, 104, 117–120, 124, 130, 143, 149, 153, 165; anti- 67; *see also* bullying; language
homophobic language *see* language
homosexuality 44, 61–62, 143, 150, 157; UK legalization of 44

horizontal violence 127, 131
hypervisibility 12, 25

identity 4, 5, 15, 24, 25, 47, 74, 84, 85, 113, 152, 156, 163; binary 15; bisexual 45, 132, 137; butch 23; cis 5; cis-gender 132–133; development 39–40; female 139; gay 79; gender 13, 15, 37, 41, 68, 103, 132, 140, 145, 159; genderqueer 23; intersex 6, 7, 79; LGBTQI+ 89, 99–101, 105–106, 149, 157; loss of 116; male 139; non-binary 5, 123; outsider 18; performative 15; politics 84, 127; queer 5–6, 76, 79, 109, 123; queer cultural 116; self- 18; self-branding 39–41; sexual 62; social 143; straight 132–133; transgender 36; work 39
inclusivity/inclusion 2, 3, 5, 8n1, 12, 51, 61–62, 64–65, 68–69, 106–107, 110, 133, 141–142, 144, 146, 151, 152, 166; of language 143
intersex people 2, 6, 7, 74–75, 78–79, 97, 115, 132, 156, 158
invisibility 6, 7, 12–13, 19–20, 25, 27, 28–30, 55, 63–64, 66–69, 73, 75–76, 144–146, 151, 164, 166–167; of family structure 97, 106; of one parent 97, 166; precarious 86–87; relative 75, 81, 106; social 19; temporary 97; unwanted 78–81; visible 81–86
Ireland 7, 20, 24, 35, 42, 45–46
Islam 150
IVF 39–40, 75, 105, 164

Jenner, Bruce/Caitlyn 2, 36, 40–41, 47–48
John, Elton 36

Kardashian, Kim 36, 40, 48
Kardashian family 40

language: 'faggot' 141, 153; homophobic, biphobic and transphobic (HBT) 66–67, 92–93, 109, 110, 114, 115, 117–122, 123, 128, 130–131, 133–134, 141–142, 146–148, 152–153, 160, 164; inclusive 143; 'nigger' 153; racist 146, 152, 160; *see also* 'gay' as a term of abuse

lesbian(s) 1, 4, 16, 20, 30, 35, 42, 43, 49, 57, 73–75, 77, 79, 81, 82, 83, 90, 98, 99, 110, 112, 142; non-binary 118; *see also* children; mothers; parents; students
LGBT history month 129, 136
LGBTQI+: definition 5–6
LGBTQI+ equality 119
LGBTQI+ issues 35, 50, 56, 58, 62, 63, 65, 84, 88, 106, 110, 136–160, 165; homonormative approaches to 136
LGBTQI+ people 1–3, 6–8, 15, 17, 36, 39, 50, 62, 66, 110, 116, 118–120, 127, 130–133, 136–160, 163–165
LGBTQI+ policies 93; *see also* school policy
LGBTQI+ rights 24, 37–39, 119, 133, 141
liberalism: economic 39; social 39
London 3, 7, 38, 44, 58, 63, 74, 76, 83–84, 99, 101, 136; South-East 58

Madonna 43
mainstreaming: homonormative 115
marriage 16, 24, 27, 31, 45, 58, 61–62, 65, 69, 150; equal 17; gay 15, 46, 164; heterosexual 25, 27; rights 37; same-sex 17, 38, 46, 49, 61, 65
Marriage (Same-Sex Couples) Act (2013) 2, 37
masculinity 24–25
Massow, Ivan 43–44
media representations 3, 6–7, 35–51; of celebrities 36, 39–41, 43–45, 48, 163; 1987 HIV/AIDS awareness campaign 36; homonormative 156, 158–159; of immigration 38; of lesbian mothers 42–43; of LGBTQI+ parented families 35–51; of LGBTQI+ parents 41–42, 50–51; of LGBTQI+ persons 133, 163; of people living with disability 38; reality television 39–40; of working-class people 38
microaggression 7, 30, 119
misgendering 98
monogamy 15–16, 19–20, 29, 39, 136–137
Morgan, Nicky 38
mother(s) 1, 4, 13, 21, 23, 24–25, 35, 42–44, 55, 73, 75, 80, 86–87, 90–91, 96, 102, 104, 106, 112, 116, 121, 133, 166; biological 22, 37, 42–43; birth 23, 25, 80, 94, 103, 166; bisexual 110, 132; co- 23; lesbian 1, 22–23, 25, 35, 42, 47, 48, 73, 75, 110, 112, 113; media representations of 42–43
motherhood 6, 12, 21–24; biological 22, 23, 25; lesbian 22
Mothers' Day 4, 95–96, 106, 117, 166
'mummy': as generic term 96–97, 103, 166
Muslims 38, 83, 100, 104, 131, 140, 150, 160

neoliberalism 18–19, 39, 158; neoliberal economy 7, 156; neoliberal state 25
normalization 17, 39, 86, 116, 143, 151, 160n1; hyper- 30; *see also* 'usualizing'

OFSTED (Office for Standards in Education, Children's Services and Skills) 37
'ordinariness strategy' 17, 83
othering 133

pansexual 158
parenthood 25, 77; heteronormative 17, 25; LGBTQI+ 48
parenting 1, 6, 12–31, 36–37, 65, 74–75, 83, 94, 96, 100, 133, 144, 166; co- 22, 24, 28, 30, 75, 94, 96, 105, 165–166; gay 12, 22; heteronormative 20, 24; heterosexual 28; homonormative 20; image of 22; lesbian 20, 75; LGBTQI+ 4, 21, 41, 74, 87, 146; non-heteronormative 25; normative heterosexual 28; rights 17; roles 111, 166; shared 24; single 18, 65, 68, 74, 75
parents 64–66, 77, 93, 96, 110; binary 37; biological 6; birth 75, 101; bisexual 7, 29, 66, 126, 128, 132, 156; celebrity 48–49; cisgender 4, 74–75; co- 22, 23, 24, 25, 27, 74–75, 134, 166; divorced 73, 79; foster 81, 85, 87, 99; gay 2, 7, 12, 20, 27, 37, 39, 43, 45, 46, 47, 69, 81, 83, 95, 100, 102,

105, 113, 121, 124, 128–129, 155; gender of 68; gender-fluid 156; genderqueer 74; gender status of 90; heterosexual 4, 20, 21, 74, 83, 101; homonormative 27; intersex 66, 74, 78, 97, 156; lesbian 2, 4, 5, 7, 12, 20, 24, 27, 35, 37, 39, 47, 69, 74, 82–83, 85, 88, 90, 92, 93, 95, 96, 98, 99, 103, 109, 112–114, 116, 121–122, 124–126, 128–130, 149, 155; LGBT 67–68; LGBTQI+ 38, 39–40, 41–42, 46, 48–51, 56–58, 63, 64, 66–67, 69, 74, 76, 80, 82, 84–89, 95, 97, 99, 102–106, 109–114, 119–121, 123, 126–128, 132–134, 141–144, 148–151, 154, 156, 159–160, 164–166; middle-class 29, 30; middle-class LGBTQI+ 19–20; multisexual 19; non-binary 74; non-biological 6, 48, 111; non-resident 80–81, 94; opposite-sex 165; polyamorous 2, 19, 29, 74, 91, 156; queer 2, 66, 156; same-gendered 20, 166; same-sex 37, 62, 65; separated 101, 112, 126, 133; sexual orientation of 67–68, 79, 82, 90; single 13, 19, 27, 30, 65, 75, 79, 95, 98, 100, 101, 128; step- 112; straight 27, 95, 134; transgender 6, 7, 30, 37, 39, 47, 48, 66, 74–75, 86, 90, 122, 126–127, 130; woman of trans history 118, 119, 125, 126; working-class 21, 29; working-class LGBTQI+ 19–20
parents' evenings 27, 55, 66, 74, 77, 79–81, 83, 87, 94, 105, 116, 125, 156, 163
partnership 15, 25, 66; civil 58, 61, 62; gay 13; heterosexual 17, 22, 25, 28; homonormative 23; homosexual 24; lesbian 13, 22; polyamorous 24, 28; same-gender 82; same-sex 28, 61, 66; *see also* civil partnership
paternal rights 25
Personal, Social, Health and Citizenship Education (PSHCE) 131, 142
politics 2, 36; identity 84; racial 127; religious identity 127; sexuality 84
polyamory 2, 19, 24, 28, 29, 74, 91, 146, 156
prejudice 19, 56, 61, 89, 103, 114, 130, 133, 137, 141; anti- 35; institutional 4

Pride 81, 113, 124, 129
Pride Youth Networks 110, 129–130, 133, 139, 147
protected characteristics 37, 56, 58–62, 64, 66, 145, 150, 164

queer culture 111–114, 120, 133

race 21, 37–38, 58, 61–62, 133, 143
racism 4, 130, 133, 140, 146, 152–154, 160; anti- 153; *see also* language
Rainbow Families camp 5, 74, 110, 111
relationship(s) 2, 17–19, 23–24, 29, 39, 44–45, 47, 56, 59–62, 64–65, 77, 83, 91, 142, 154, 163; binary 39; biological 22; -building 133; church-state 24; committed 27; heterosexual 15, 18, 67, 74–75, 100, 142; homonormative 27, 31, 65; intimate 18, 65; LGB 64; LGBTQI+ 17, 67, 141; monogamous 15, 39, 43; mother-child 104; non-heterosexual 106; normative 23; with other children 100–103; with other parents 97–100; parental school gate 97–100; parent-child 23, 28; parenting 37; peer 7, 110, 111, 120–129; polyamorous 19; same-gender 116–117; same-sex 43, 62, 64, 150; with schools 1, 7, 12, 17, 24, 28, 73, 76, 87, 93–97, 110; stable 31, 65, 69; straight 110; with teachers 125
relationship and sex education *see* sex and relationship education
reproductive rights 17
rights: gay 39, 44; lesbian 39; trangender 39; *see also* LGBTQI+ rights

Sackville-West, Vita 45
safe space 134, 167
school choice 87–93
school environment 128, 139, 141, 144, 146
school policy(ies) 7–8, 28, 55–70, 141, 143–146, 151–154, 160, 166–167; behaviour 58, 144, 152–153, 160, 164; education 37, 62; equality 55–70, 70n1, 144, 164; inclusion 143, 144, 151–152; school uniforms 152, 160; sex and relationships education 59, 61, 64
self-actualization 39–41, 49

Index 173

self-advocacy 116–120, 126, 165
sex and relationship education 26–27, 58, 59, 61, 64–66, 77, 106–107, 142, 150; *see also* Personal, Social, Health and Citizenship Education (PHSCE)
sex education *see* sex and relationship education
sexism 4
sexual activity: and homosexuality 62; non-penis-vagina 77, 106; straight 142
sexuality 13, 17, 20, 25–26, 30, 47, 62, 66, 67, 84, 132, 142–143, 147, 163; body and 26; gay 20, 27; history of 20; homonormative 27, 132; lesbian 20, 27; non-procreative 25; politics 84; queer 132; same-sex 142; schools and 26; teaching of 26; *see also* bisexuality; heterosexuality; homosexuality
sexual orientation 4, 19, 27, 28, 37, 41, 58, 61, 64, 66–68, 73, 74, 76, 79, 82, 84, 85, 90, 103, 132, 140, 145, 157–158; gay 19; lesbian 19; straight 132–133
sexual reproduction: hetero- 143
social contract 14, 21, 31
socioeconomic differences 41–42, 51, 61, 116, 154; class 38, 114
students: gay 12; lesbian 12; LGBTQI+ 56, 64–67, 110, 132, 139, 147, 165; non-white 131; trans 38, 157; working-class 131
surrogacy 19, 36, 39–40, 43–44, 46–47, 164
Sweden 20, 24, 25, 78

teachers: lesbian 129; LGBTQI+ 127, 133; out 127, 129; trans 64
terrorism 38; 'Prevent' guidelines 38
tokenism 30, 131, 134, 145, 152, 153, 160
trans/transgender people 2, 17, 19, 35, 38, 47–50, 63, 66, 90, 115, 131, 132–133, 137, 156, 158, 159; definition 5; issues 137; media representations of 47–48; non-fluid 156; trans man/men 5, 7, 18, 27, 74–75, 78, 86, 90, 101; violence against 2; *see also* gender reassignment; gender transition surgery; transition (gender); woman/women of trans history
transition (gender) 27–28, 39–41, 75–76, 84, 86–87, 97–98, 101, 111, 122–123, 127, 136, 157; *see also* gender reassignment; gender transition surgery
Trans Media Watch 35, 47
transphobia 38, 50, 86–87, 97, 115, 118–120, 125, 165; *see also* bullying; language
transsexual 47, 48, 51, 158
Traveller 4, 62

United Kingdom 2, 7, 13, 35–39, 41–42, 44, 58, 61, 69, 125, 126, 131, 136, 146; government of 2, 37–38, 66, 146; media in 36–39, 41–42; poet laureate of 148; politics in 36–39; *see also* England; Wales
United States 7, 29, 36, 39, 69
'usualizing' 136–160, 160n1

Vanity Fair 36, 40
victimhood/victimization 60, 66–68, 70, 93, 131, 133
violence 2, 8; sexual 147; *see also* horizontal violence
visibility 1, 7, 12–13, 25, 27–31, 35, 55, 63, 66, 73, 75–78, 81, 86, 103–104, 105, 116, 133, 136, 141, 154–156, 164–165, 167; active 76–78, 83; institutional 19; unwilling 75
visibility/invisibility strategies 29–30, 73, 75–87

Wales 6, 37, 56, 59, 74
Wilson, Jaqueline 1; *The Illustrated Mum* 1
Wittig, Monique 13–15, 156
woman/women of trans history 5, 7, 28, 74–76, 84, 86–87, 90, 97, 98, 106, 110, 111, 113–115, 118, 119, 122, 125–127; definition 5